JAZZMAN CHRONICLES

VOLUMES I - X

BY JACK RANDOM

CROW DOG PRESS
TURLOCK CA USA

Jazzman Chronicles
Volumes I – X

By Jack Random

Published by
Crow Dog Press
1241 Windsor Court
Turlock CA 95380

Copyright 2015 Ray Miller

Cover artwork by Rita DeKelaita

Publisher's Cataloging-in-Publication

Random, Jack.
    Jazzman chronicles. Volumes I - X/ by Jack Random.
    p. cm.
    LCCN 2003100136
    ISBN 978-0692514061

    1. United States -- Civilization. 2. United States — Politics and government. 3. Political participation – United States. I. Title.

E169.1.R36 2015   306.2'0973
                                        QBI33-1137

JAZZMAN CHRONICLES

VOLUMES I – X

Commentaries on American Politics
2000-2014

AUTHOR'S NOTE

The *Jazzman Chronicles* began as an idea in a political novel that imagined transforming the American government by breaking the stranglehold of the two-party system. The original concept was to issue a series of pamphlets toward that end in the tradition of Tom Paine's *American Crisis.* By the time volume one of the chronicles was ready for print the entire political landscape had changed.

Having suffered the terrorist attack of September 11, 2001, our elected government led by President George W. Bush was pushing relentlessly for military retaliation on two fronts, the long war and the wrong war: Afghanistan and Iraq.

Everything had changed. Suddenly, the only cause that seemed to matter and the only cause that could engage the people, our elected officials and the media was war and peace.

The second volume of the Chronicles (The War Chronicles) was devoted entirely to stopping the Bush war machine and the global war on terror. The year was 2004 and the president was standing for re-election. That critical election became a mandate on the Bush Doctrine and the ongoing wars in Afghanistan and Iraq.

History will record that Bush returned to office in yet another hotly contested, highly questionable election against yet another Democrat who seemed afraid to take a stand. In many ways the elections of 2000 and 2004 confirmed my original thesis: that the most critical barrier to an effective, representative government is a major party system dominated by the same money interests.

Unfortunately, as a result of that election, war would remain the dominant issue for another four long and massively destructive years. In truth, both wars were profoundly wrong and both continue to this day.

We have moved on. The economic implosion the Bush administration delivered in its final days sent a shock wave across the globe and forced us to take a fresh look at income inequality, trade policy and the enormous power of the elite. The wars remain a shadow in our daily lives but other concerns have emerged to demand attention: civil liberties, civil rights, racial discrimination, police brutality and the most pressing issue of our time: global climate change.

Partly because of the cost and partly because I could not reach a significant audience through the avenues that the print media affords, the Chronicles became a phenomenon of the worldwide web.

Early Chronicles were published online at such sites as *CounterPunch*, *Dissident Voice*, *Pacific Free Press*, *Global Free Press*, *Albion Monitor* and *Peace Earth & Justice News*. I will forever be grateful to the late Howard Zinn for his words of encouragement and the late Patrick Cockburn for his unspoken support.

While the Chronicles date from 2001 to 2014, I have organized volumes three to ten according to topic with reference to what was happening at the time. Each volume is organized chronologically. Taken together they form a portrait of the nation in the early 21st century from a decidedly progressive point of view. It is an incomplete portrayal, somewhat abstract and at times distorted, but it is also an honest depiction whose goal is always to improve the nation, its people and its political system. It is meant to alter hearts and minds.

I do not know what direction my writings will take. As I write this introduction we are nearing the end of the

Obama administration. I remain convinced that the next step in the evolution of American democracy should be the emergence of an independent or third party to challenge the two-party system. At present, given the unprecedented infusion of corporate money in electoral politics, that prospect remains more remote than ever.

There is hope. There is always hope. The nation has made great progress more often than not despite its political leadership.

Those of us who have witnessed or engaged in the march of progress know it is a long-term struggle and our message is clear: Never give up; never give in. In the fullness of time we will prevail.

Jazz.

CONTENTS

JAZZMAN CHRONICLES

VOLUME I

CORE PRINCIPLES

If you've come to help me, no thank you.
But if your liberation is bound up with mine,
then come, let us work together.

Aboriginal Saying

Meta Mendel-Reyes
Reclaiming Democracy

CONTENTS

PREFACE

A WINDOW OF OPPORTUNITY

Prior to September 11, 2001, a rare wave in the current of political and social consciousness was arriving on the shores of America. Immoral and pointless drug laws were being challenged with success. The notion of the infallibility of American justice crumbled with successive revelations that dozens if not hundreds of innocent people had been condemned to death by a flawed and corrupt system. The case against American foreign policy, its increasing isolation from the world on the Kyoto Accords, the Palestinian crisis, and the International Court of Justice, was finally being heard. With tens of thousands of Gulf War veterans suffering a crippling disease the government had yet to recognize, even that war had come into question.

Meantime, the anti globalization movement had come to America, capturing the attention of the masses with hundreds of thousands of protestors on the streets of Seattle. The people had rallied to the cry of Senator John McCain for campaign finance reform and, with the spectacle of democracy derailed in Florida, were more sensitive than ever to the corruption of the political process. The contrived west coast energy crisis and the chain of corporate scandals further paved the way for radical, wholesale change on the political horizon.

Given a decade of prosperity, Americans had no

enemies, no desire or need for war. It was a time to set our own affairs in order. It was a time to reflect. It was a time to right long neglected wrongs within our own country.

It was a brilliant, shining window of opportunity. It was a moment of hope. It was a time when the promise of freedom, justice and prosperity for all seemed within our grasp.

All that has changed. Now all our efforts must be gathered to stop a war that will – if left unchecked – engulf much of the world and condemn future generations as well as ourselves to violence and terror without end.

But as we fight *against* this beast of war we should not forget that we are fighting *for* a world where war is unnecessary. If we recognize the value of all human life, if we recognize the fundamental rights to life, liberty and the pursuit of happiness, if we recognize that all peoples in all nations are entitled to these rights, we can build a better world.

These Chronicles are about hope. These Chronicles are about the changes that must inevitably occur if we are to survive as a species on a very small planet. Adapted from the novel Cry of The Fathers by the same author, the Jazzman Chronicles are about beginning that process of change at home.

Jazz.

CRY OF THE FATHERS

"If I could not go to heaven but with a party, I would not go there at all."

Thomas Jefferson

Examine the history of politics in America. It is a history fraught with corruption and fraud. From Boss Tweed and Tammany Hall to Big Dick Daley and the Chicago machine; from the Teapot Dome to the contrived energy crisis; from the railroad, steel and oil monopolies to Enron, Halliburton, El Paso Gas and Anderson Accounting; from the Gulf of Tonkin to Iran-Contra; from the Watergate Hotel to the great Florida election fraud; six political assassinations in a hundred years; McCarthyism and the excesses of J. Edgar Hoover.

The election of 1800 is known by some as a reaffirmation of democracy in America, by others as the birth of the two-party system. Two hundred years of subsequent history have witnessed the enfranchisement of the poor, minorities and women, yet the form and shape of government remains unaltered.

In less than thirty years since the emergence of party dominance, we went from Jefferson, Madison and Monroe to the likes of Tyler, Harrison, Fillmore and Pierce. For every Lincoln and Roosevelt, there is a Rutherford Hayes and Quincy Adams. For every

Woodrow Wilson and Kennedy, there is a Truman and Ford. We charged our patriotic historians with the difficult task (more suited to Hollywood) of resurrecting the characters of Lyndon Johnson, Dick Nixon, Gerald Ford and Ronald Reagan. We are living in the age of information. The truth will out though it may take a hundred years.

What has gone wrong with a system that leaves us with the choice of a Zachary Tyler or a Franklin Pierce, an Albert Gore or a George W. Bush? We are a nation born to greatness. Our educational institutions, for all the criticisms heaped upon them, have produced some of the finest minds the world has known. Why have they so rarely found their way to the White House or the halls of Congress?

Where has our political system gone wrong?

We have lost faith. The system has evolved into two parties controlled by the same interests. It is a system that seeks out the corruptible and renders integrity a disqualification. The system has settled in its current mode. It is content with mediocrity. It embraces mediocrity. The mediocre are more easily manipulated and controlled.

It is time for change. But change will not come in the form of a white knight. We have had white knights before. They are vilified, abused, tarred and feathered. They are often assassinated. Even if they succeed in some small measure, their tenures are brief. The system overwhelms and prevails.

It requires more than the one for meaningful change; it requires the many. As Senator Clinton once said, it takes a village. It takes a community. It takes a society of like-minded individuals united in purpose and cause. Tom Paine once said, "It is not in numbers but in unity that our strength lies." The American nation is an extended family in crisis – broken, dysfunctional, divided. It has no unifying cause or purpose and the reasons are many. They extend back to our very roots.

What kind of a family tree begins without a mother? We do not believe the misogynist propaganda that behind every man stands a woman. Whatever influence she possessed was superseded by her daily duties. In the case of the founding fathers, she supervised a work force of servants or slaves and, in her spare time, raised a family.

There were no women amongst our founders. There were no blacks, no minorities, and no natives to the soil we claimed as our own. It was a founding that cried hypocrisy and declared by omission the superiority of white male Europeans. It was a founding that guaranteed disunity, division, and civil war.

Yet the founders had ideals.

Was this what they intended?

Those who have studied the question know it depends on which of the founding fathers are addressed. Even the most progressive among them were generally racist and gave little thought to the representation of women. John Adams was a devout aristocrat whose mistrust of democracy was almost unrivaled, yet he was elected president. To him and his supporters (Hamilton, Arnold, Morris et al), direct democracy was indistinguishable from anarchy and anarchy was hell on earth.

If not for the first true Republicans (Paine, Jefferson, Franklin, Monroe, Sam Adams) it is unlikely that the democratic experiment would have been launched on this continent. Time and again they reminded their aristocratic brethren that it was the rabble, not the elite, who fought against the British. It was their bodies that lie buried in hallowed ground. It was their blood that paid the price of American liberty. It was the cause of democracy that roused their passions and spurred them to sacrifice. They would not have looked kindly upon a new American king.

So the founders were not united by philosophy or principle. They were united by necessity. The constitution they adopted was a compromise – an attempt to balance the principles of democracy against the interests of a privileged class.

Yet the founders had ideals.

Though unwilling to free his own slaves, Jefferson recognized that slavery was an abomination – a crime against humanity. Paine and Franklin foresaw the suffrage of women as inevitable. But there was only one enemy that attracted the wrath of virtually all our founding fathers and that was the emergence of political parties.

Just as Eisenhower warned against the military industrial complex, Jefferson warned us to beware the influence of political parties. Two hundred years later, it is long past time to heed that warning. We have seen the dirty underside of the American political system. We have seen principle and morality shuffled aside in the naked pursuit of power. We have seen influence and corruption boldly flaunted before our eyes. We have witnessed the poison of party politics invade every branch of government. We have viewed politicians embrace in the sinking mire and claim victory for democracy and praise the constitutional foresight of the founders. We have watched a media absorbed by the propaganda machine, spinning stories instead of reporting facts. We have seen what both your houses have wrought and it sickens us.

Let us finally hear the cry of the fathers for, despite their short sightedness, despite their flaws and limitations, despite all they did not or could not do, they saw clearly the nature of this beast. It is a monster so vast, so vile, so omnipotent, that we hardly know where to begin opposing it, yet oppose it we must. It is not a beast that will die of its own volition. It is a self-perpetuating machine, fueled by money, and so entrenched in the system that the people mistake it for the system itself. It is a machine that attracts people of power and influence and corrupts them absolutely. With every election its power is reinforced and the likelihood of its defeat is weakened.

It is not too late. We are still a young nation. It is possible to reclaim the principles of democracy and the sovereignty of the people. For though it is powerful, the party system neglects the vast majority of the electorate. It survives through propaganda, by convincing the people that it represents not them but their interests best.

In the year of the great disenfranchisement, we have seen the truth. Now we must convince the people that there is another choice. It begins, just as it did for our founding fathers, with a declaration of independence.

It begins with a pledge: We will not support the machine. We will not join the major parties. We will not contribute to its causes. We will not vote for its candidates.

Let us hear the cry of the fathers. Let us heed the call of humanity. Let the cry go forth until it is joined by a thousand voices, then a hundred thousand more. Let it gather the strength of unity until it becomes a tidal wave sweeping over the land. Let it begin here and now. Let it begin with us.

The path will not be easy. Many have gone before us and failed. We will face hardships and some of us may fall. But we may have this comfort and consolation:

Never has there been a greater cause: Democracy in America.

Jazz.

DECLARATION OF WAR

"There have been differences of opinion...from the first establishment of governments...and on the same question which now divides our country: whether the power of the people or that of the aristoi (sic) should prevail."

Thomas Jefferson

The American nation has been cheated out of self-government by a system that allows itself to be bought and sold to the highest bidder. There is no democracy where the only candidates are those who have already signed the party loyalty oath.

Who feeds you baby?
Who pays your bills?
Who butters your bread?

Tax relief is a false issue. You pay what you have to pay and you pay for it with taxes. Take your medicine. Social security? Take your medicine. Schools for the poor? Take your medicine. Military might? Take your medicine. The cynics are right: There is no free ride. Everything must be paid for. Everything has a price. To the victors go the spoils and to the payer goes the deed.

Outside of revolution and nationalization, taxation is the only means society has for transferring wealth from the rich to the poor. Given the expanding divide between the ultra-wealthy and the middle class, I suggest closing all loopholes for the top ten percent and distributing the revenues to the remaining ninety percent. Such a proposal is impossible in a system where the ultra-wealthy finance the political machine.

Who owns America?

Who pays the greatest price? Who guards the greatest profit margin? Who possesses the greatest resources? Who has the most to lose? What happens if we cut them off? Will we crumble like the mindless rabble they consider us to be? Will we destroy the institutions that keep this nation afloat? Will we sink into blind anarchy – a one eyed dog chasing its tail?

What are we so afraid of?
Ghosts in the darkness?
Shadows of night?
Eyes that see beyond the smoke and mirrors?

We know who you are. We have seen your faces. Your names are synonymous with American wealth: Rockefeller, Morgan, Kennedy, Gates. You and your ancestors have siphoned your riches off the top of the nation's economy for decades – even centuries. You have controlled the beast through which all the money passed. You have controlled the ebb and flow of profit and deficit, prosperity and recession, war and peace. You have controlled the distribution of wealth and with that power you have controlled the government. You only needed a political system that was fueled by money for you controlled the money. You claimed the prize. You got the best of all worlds: the trappings of democracy without the volatility, the instability, and the risk that true democracy entails.

It is a system that crowns you champions despite yourselves. It is a system that overlooks the blood on your hands, the greed in your hearts, the vacuum of your souls. It is a system that embraces you as heroes rather than reviling you as the villains you truly are. You proclaim your philanthropy to the world while concealing the strings behind corrupt politicians. Everyone loves to hate politicians.

Try as we may we cannot defeat you in the war that is the world economy. You are too entrenched. The web of your influence reaches into every corner, every crevice, and every crack of every branch of the financial, political and intelligence communities. Too many of our brethren spirits have been swept into your lair. We will not blindly follow.

Until now the people have had no one to turn to when they wished to turn their backs on you. Until now they have had to choose between the conscience and the dream – between their values and their ambitions. What they chose did not matter to you. They could either join or be crushed. They could either share in your wealth or wealth could be denied them.

Could anyone blame those who sold their souls? What choice did they really have? They woke up one day to discover that they were surrounded by the enemy: friends, associates, administrators, strategists, middlemen, contractors, partnerships, consultants, wives, lovers, everyone.

We wish to provide another choice: an alternative economy. We ask only a free market on an even playing field. Already we have had enough success to frighten you. We are in the information age now. We are in an age that makes all things possible. While you were guarding the oil wells of Saudi Arabia, we gained access to the information highway. We have freed the open market from your manipulations and the world has prospered. But you have retained control of government and the people still suffer by your corrupt influence.

Now is the time to take the next step. Now is the time to reclaim democracy. Now is the time for the major party system to fall.

Every decision should be taken with absolute resolve. Every decision should be made in seven breaths – seven breaths, seven chakras, seven sacred directions. Once taken, there can be no turning back. We are declaring war against a system that has reigned supreme for over two centuries. We are declaring war against a machine that has never been defeated on the battlefield. We are declaring war against a beast that is capable of any crime and will not hesitate to press any advantage. We are declaring war against the machine but the machine must be the last to know. Let them believe we are the fringe. Let them believe there are but few of us.

One. A cold winter on the northern Pacific. White water crash on the stones of antiquity. *Two.* Kingfishers on a grey horizon. Heaven heaves a silent hush. *Three.* The great waters roar in the deep caves and weathered canyons of an ancient coast, its winds whistling through rocks and trees. *Four.* The shore must always give way to the sea and in this there is hope. *Five.* A thick grey mist blankets the old growth forest, conjuring an image of the birth of continents, a brave new world in waiting. *Six.* Two centuries too long. The vision of the forefathers preempted by party politics. Democracy is an endangered species. *Seven.* Last chance. There can be no more doubt.

Question: How can we make a difference in a world gone awry, heaving and spiraling out of control?

Answer: One step at a time.

Take the pledge.

Jazz.

"All those histories centered on the Founding Fathers and the Presidents weigh oppressively on the capacity of the ordinary citizen to act. They teach us that the supreme act of citizenship is to choose between two white males of inoffensive personality and orthodox opinions."

Howard Zinn

TRUE HISTORY

"History is more or less bunk." Henry Ford

Those who do not know the path they have traveled cannot know where it leads. Those who have been fitted with blinders and led to believe they are on one path when in fact they are on another will continue to wander aimlessly, like a blind woman without a guide, until they reach the only truth they will likely ever know: Everything we have been taught or told is a lie.

Educational reform must begin with true history. Children need only be taught to read and inspired to think. For reading opens all doors to knowledge and thinking guides the way.

For the entire history of our nation, while we may have taught children to read we have also been dedicated to removing the primary reason for doing so. We have declared war on a child's natural curiosity. We have taught that there is nothing to be valued more than loyalty and faith. We have handed our children the mythology of a great nation. We have called it the truth. We have taught our children to be good soldiers – never to question and never to doubt. While pretending to embrace the character and qualities of leadership, we have in fact taught them never to lead, always to follow, never to walk the paths untrodden, never to stray from the party line. Those who walk alone, we are taught, are shunned or worse, stoned by a mindless mob. Even our leaders are followers.

The greatness of our country and the greatest hope is that there are those who have broken free from the bindings of indoctrination and declared themselves free. These individuals have discovered the greater truth that where one falsehood lies it is often accompanied by many others. The have uncovered the lies of manifest destiny and equal opportunity. The have uncovered the lies of blind justice and the moral imperative to war. They have uncovered the lies of American sovereignty, American democracy, American superiority, and they have discovered the underlying truth: We are a nation born of great ideals yet we have failed to live up to them.

It must begin with a reckoning. It must begin with true history. It is not, as the declaimers insist, "revisionist" history for one does not revise lies. Lies can only be corrected.

Let the children know the truth. Let them know that we, as a nation, have committed crimes against our planet and our species. We have fought wars without righteous cause. We have opposed freedom and supported despots. We have poisoned rivers and skies so that the richest among us might become richer. We have denied justice to those with darker skins and lesser means than those of our white European founders. We have enslaved our fellow beings. We have killed the rightful inhabitants of the land we walk upon. We have slaughtered the buffalo, made saints of sinners and sinners of saints.

Let us tell our children the earth remembers what we have done and we must also remember. Give the children the truth and then, let them tell us what must be done to set it right.

Jazz.

"Our laws are the output of a system which clothes rascals in robes and honesty in rags. It is no longer a government of the people, by the people and for the people but a government of Wall Street, by Wall Street and for Wall Street."

Mary Ellen Lease

THE COST OF FREE SPEECH

"Who shall rule the country? The people or those who hide behind the breastwork of corporations?" Theodore Roosevelt

They all saluted when Senator John McCain ran the flag of campaign finance reform up the media flagpole. The Democrats enjoyed the scrambling of their Republican colleagues. McCain was one of their own, a member of the party that stood most to lose, yet he defined it as the most critical issue in American politics. When it seemed possible that his modest proposal, prohibiting "soft" money from corporations and unions, might actually reach the Senate floor, the Democrats fell awkwardly silent and the Republicans took the podium.

First, they argued that soft money is protected by the constitutional guarantee of freedom of speech. Even the venerable George Will has spent his credibility on this tired line of reasoning. The argument holds that since it costs a great deal to deliver any message in our media rich society, money is an essential component of free speech itself. By similar reasoning, the Skinheads of Topeka are denied free speech because they do not have the resources for television programming. Should society be compelled to provide them money to protect their first amendment rights?

"No!" comes the answer: they are not in the political

process. But if they were, would we be obliged to provide them money? Would we ensure their message is heard? "No!" you answer: only the major candidates should be ensured.

So the argument turns on the revelation that it defends only the speech of major party candidates and that speech is anything but free. So the brave defenders of first amendment rights are suddenly cast in the familiar role of the oppressor, denying freedom of speech to anyone but their own.

So the Grand Old Party trots out a second argument, which is little more than a retooling of the "my party, your party" foolishness uttered by our president in his campaign against McCain. The argument then was that campaign finance reform favored Democrats over Republicans. To a large extent this was true because the big money has long favored Republicans over Democrats. But this was not a winning line. It was not the image of a party free from the corrupting influence of corporate America. It was not the image they wished to project to the American public.

So they next persuaded their Democratic ally, Senator John Breau, to test a new line: Campaign finance reform is "unfair to the major parties." That a United States Senator could deliver such a message with a straight face is a tribute to his political talent. Never in the history of electoral politics has a system been so stacked in favor of major parties. Is the electorate so naïve as to think that *they* represent *us*? Do the major parties in fact represent any virtue other than aristocracy and elitism? Do they provide some service that needs protection?

It is a scandal that an independent candidate has virtually no chance in a national election. Must we also have our intelligence insulted by the defenders of major party sovereignty? Not only is the two party system unessential to democracy, it is in fact her greatest danger and sworn enemy. The advent of the party system was a phenomenon much lamented by the fathers of our country. Do not expect us now to pay for your privilege. Do not expect us now to safeguard your corruption.

There is such bittersweet irony in the fact that the Enron scandal allowed for the passage of campaign finance reform. It is to date the only good that has come of that sordid affair. It is interesting to note that when Enron was caught defrauding its stockholders, bankrupting its employees, stripping them of their retirement funds, and undermining much of the American economy, the government chose to go after the accountant. It is analogous to prosecuting the consular for the crimes of the Don.

More than a dozen high-ranking members of the Bush administration were employees of Enron. Where was the Democratic outrage? Guilty by degrees, they accepted the same dirty money – albeit less than their Republican counterparts. When the spotlight began to shine on Enron's infiltration of both major parties, McCain-Feingold's modest proposal suddenly became palatable. It is hardly enough.

To those of us who believe in the power of the people, which is after all the foundation of our government, anything that detracts from major party dominance is to be embraced whole-heartedly. It is the essence of democracy and the foundation of the republic. Watch closely those who argue against campaign finance reform. Peel back the layers of deception. This is class warfare. This is the very rich against the rest of us. It is the same challenge the people have always confronted in the defense of democracy.

Shame on the likes of John Breau and George Will. They have chosen to defend their interests rather than their principles. Or are they true aristocrats after all? The ugly truth is Democrats and Republicans alike will always fight against measures that attack their monopoly on political power. They will always fight to keep the door of independence firmly locked. When the possibility of third party viability presents itself even remotely, they will unite to secure the source of their power. They are all blue bloods behind closed doors.

But they do not own us and cannot buy our loyalty or our votes. They may have fooled our elders but ours is a new day with new and greater possibilities. As long as the web is free they cannot silence the dissident voice. As long as the individual mind is beyond their reach, they cannot contain ideas.

Let the word go forth: Freedom is Independence. Let us renew our spirit and strengthen our resolve. Seeds have been planted. There is something in the air. The two-party system must fall.

Jazz.

You have weighed the stars in the balance,
And grasped the skies in a span:
Take, if you must have an answer,
The word of a common man.

G.K. Chesterton

CREDULITY OF THE MASSES

There are those who do not believe in the virtue of the common man. There are those who hold the masses responsible for a legacy of oppressive government and amoral leadership. These often thoughtful individuals condemn the "mindless rabble" and tar them with blame for believing what they have been led to believe, for electing a president who could scarcely remember his name, for allowing law makers to court riches at their own expense, for falling victim time after time to the shill game of tax relief, for believing in the mythology of an America that stands strong for justice, equality and freedom.

Gently must we be reminded that when we condemn the masses we render ourselves impotent. When we separate ourselves from the common people we surrender all hope for change. If we embrace democracy, as we must do (for there are neither reasonable nor idealistic alternatives), then we must acknowledge our own humanity. We are the people. We are the masses. It is both futile and hypocritical to believe that we are not. If we the people have been guilty of credulity then let us seek remedy, not blame.

Let us begin with the understanding that we have had to overcome centuries of dogma and indoctrination. Let us envision the mass mind as the mind of a child for in the great expanse of human history that is exactly what she is. We have thrown off kings and despots. We have overthrown feudal lords. We have struck down aristocracies. We have thwarted slavery and finally stood up for the rights of woman. We have slowed the wholesale destruction of our planet and compelled the lords of avarice and greed to take notice: There is a limit to our credulity.

Let us acknowledge that our child has learned much in such a very short time. There is of course so much more to learn and to accomplish. We are racing a clock that is counting the seconds to annihilation at our own hands. We must do more. But we must also accept that we have advanced. The child that is our mass mind is growing up. We must have faith that we will continue to grow in the leaps and bounds of a child that is well nurtured. We cannot nurture a child who is disowned, disavowed and ridiculed.

The child that is our collective self is growing up. She will no longer be so easily fooled. But what she does with her maturity is dependent on the choices she is given. When a child is offered a stone or a rock it is difficult to make a determined choice. When a system offers a Gore and a Bush, a Texas oilman and a Tennessee wrangler, for the highest office in the land, it is a child's dilemma. It arrests growth.

There is no greater barrier to the development of our nation and our selves than the clinging pragmatism and dogmatic belief that Democrats represent change and the workingman. If this superstition was ever founded in truth it ceased to be with the assassination of a president. There is no greater credulity on earth than this: To believe that the lesser of two evils is the greater good.

For eight years we waited for a Democratic president to act on the environment. He did so only in his waning days and then only as a political ploy to embarrass his successor. For eight years we waited for an educational initiative, rehabilitation of drug users, alternatives to imprisonment, repeal of victimless crimes, meaningful gun control, shelters for the homeless, women's rights initiatives, national health care, Indian rights and sovereignty, an end to capital punishment, campaign finance reform, renewal of the civil rights movement, on and on. For eight years we waited for a presidential pardon that would free Leonard Peltier and all political prisoners. For eight years we waited for the dreamer to awaken. We were left waiting and wondering why we ever cared. If he was the great liberal hope, then hope is dead and buried or liberal is not enough.

Still we must believe. We must keep hope alive. But no longer can we afford to invest our faith in a system that has betrayed us time and time again. Our child is growing up. The dream of her parents still lives within her but it has evolved. It has matured. She does not believe in Republican gods. Nor does she believe in Democratic gods or gods of lesser evil. She will turn away from those who have abused her faith. She will find new choices, new heroes and heroines, new gods and goddesses within herself. She will not be belittled or chastised for asserting her will. She will choose her own destiny.

It is useful to believe in a sense of destiny. It is useful to believe that an alignment of stars and planets can lead to possibilities that never before existed. This kind of credulity we can embrace. It is the credulity of a dreamer. It is the vision of a child. It is the American spirit at its best. It is the dream of the founders devoid of their omissions and hypocrisies. It is the promise of a new day and the hope of all human kind.

Jazz.

FREE MARKET FAILURES

From each according to his abilities,
to each according to his needs.

Karl Marx

I've worked myself up from nothing
to a state of extreme poverty.

Groucho Marx

One of the great lessons of the twentieth century was
the failure of socialism in a free market global economy.
One of the great lessons of the twenty first century will
be to recognize the limitations of a free market economy.

The generation that survived forty years of Cold War
will never forget the fall of the Berlin Wall. It is
permanently etched in our collective consciousness along
with the assassinations of our most gifted leaders. The
wall was more than a symbol. It was constructed of
concrete, razor wire, brick and mortar, and divided the
world into them and us.

The fall of the wall marked an end to the oppressive
governments of the Red Empire. It was an end to
Communism as a world power. It was also a triumph of
free market economy over state socialism as a viable
economic system. It was not, however, as some might
assume, an end to the socialist ideal.

On the scale of the global economy, the guiding principles of capitalism and socialism (the needs of the one versus the needs of the whole) exist on a continuum that encompasses both schools of thought. Nations that still embrace the socialist ideal are compelled to embrace elements of capitalism while even the most devoted capitalist nations on earth invariably incorporate elements of socialism. The New Deal of Franklin Roosevelt is a clear example of acceptable socialism within the framework of a democratic government and free economy. Social security, national health care, environmental protection and Head Start are further examples of socialistic initiatives embraced by a capitalist culture.

The collapse of state socialism should be viewed as a pragmatic failure, not a moral or idealistic one. It was a battle of economic, not political, systems.

So while we hasten to bury the socialist ideal alongside the communist beast, recent events should serve to remind us that there are failures of the free market as well. In the absence of government regulation, airlines cannot be counted on to maintain schedules or safety standards. In the absence of regulation, energy companies will betray the public interest in favor of profit every time.

The conspiring companies in the fraudulent west coast energy crisis (Enron, El Paso Gas, Halliburton, Reliant Energy, et al) deliberately fixed and manipulated prices, undercut the California economy, triggered an enduring recession, and derailed internet commerce, while hiding obscene profits and creating shortages to their own advantage. The year 2000 witnessed the largest redistribution of wealth in modern American history. It is not the first time companies have hoarded and controlled essential commodities. It is in fact the standard pattern of fortune building in American economics.

JAZZMAN CHRONICLES

The west coast energy crisis is but one in a series of manipulated crises designed to boost the revenues of a corrupt and blatantly greedy industry, an industry whose only charity is the sponsorship of politicians like George Bush. It was no accident of fate that this crisis was aimed at California, a state known for its environmental initiatives, a state led by an ambitious Democratic governor, and one that voted overwhelmingly for Albert Gore in the millennial election. It was no mistake that the crisis was timed for the inauguration. It was no coincidence that the new president immediately pronounced it California's problem and graciously offered to set aside federal environmental law to expand drilling, exploration and plant production. It was not by chance that the deregulated utilities severed their production from their delivery systems after transferring billions to their parent companies in an attempt to cover outrageous fortunes while requesting unconscionable rate increases. It was no coincidence that the corporations in question posted peak profits during the period of rolling blackouts.

But lest we take refuge in the Democrats to oppose the party of greed and avarice, check the contributor's list. Take note that environmental regulations have been turned back while secret deals behind closed doors have sanctioned profiteering and protected the interests of offending parties. Observe the congressional white wash. Once again, it is not a matter of good versus evil; it is only a matter of degree.

When the free market sees an opportunity for profit it will seize it on every occasion. The only factor that holds the free marketers in check is the threat of government intervention. That threat is absent when both parties of government depend on those same corporations for their very sustenance.

The lesson to be learned is that the free market cannot

be trusted with so critical and fundamental an industry as energy. The people have suffered the economics of greed long enough. Wherever essential commodities are concerned (energy, food, water, transportation, medical care), the government must stand ready to impose regulation at a moment's notice. Continued practices such as the Texas energy consortium has shown should result in the nationalization of the utilities. Energy is not something to be trifled with. It is not an opportunity for greedy capitalists to abuse and exploit the system. It is the foundation of an economy upon which hundreds of millions of Americans depend.

The politicians of this country are quick to scoff at allegations of conspiracy. Perhaps that is because they have perpetuated so many. They have a vested interest in the profits of corporate greed. Let us respond appropriately. Let us begin by reasserting government control over the energy industry. Let us recall all politicians who stand with corporate greed over the interest of the electorate, be they Republican or Democrat, conservative or moderate. On this issue there is no middle ground: Either you stand with the people or you stand against us. If you stand with the lords of avarice, they will line your palms with riches. If you stand with the people, you gain only the allegiance of your conscience and the knowledge that this time (for once) you have done the right thing.

It is long past time to throw off the politics of pragmatism. It is time to discard old school politicians. When the same money interests own and control both the media and the political process, it is imperative that the people finally see through the charade.

In a display of impudence beyond belief, at a time when the mythical surplus of the late nineties was fading more rapidly than the integrity of Supreme Court justice, our president delivered a check for some three hundred dollars in income tax rebates to virtually every voter in the country. He asked us, with a wink and a good-old-boy grin, not to consider it a payment for your vote. While he and his party collected billions from Texas fat cats in a blatant display of profit sharing, he offered three hundred dollars, a wink and a grin.

What is an appropriate response to the lowest brand of political pandering? Accept the gratuity and deliver it to your favorite third party or independent candidate along with a message:

Our votes are not for sale.

Jazz.

STAYING THE MOTION

"You can stand me up at the gates of hell but I won't back down." Tom Petty

We have had some small setbacks in the election of 2002. If you believe the pundits of mainstream media, the left has been crushed. If you believe the partisans of the right, the American people have delivered a powerful mandate of support for our president, his wars, and corporate tax relief as a response to corporate corruption.

There was no such mandate. Anyone who did not foresee a Republican takeover of Congress in the wake September 11th is either hopelessly naïve or not paying attention. The biggest surprise of the election was neither the absolute capitulation of the Democrats on the most critical issues of our generation (war and corporate corruption) nor the rightwing takeover; it was the narrow margin of victory. That the party of war and patriotism could not manage a landslide in an atmosphere of fear and loathing is a tribute to the resilience and reemergence of a true opposition.

Beneath their smug grins and behind the drumbeats of war, they have taken note. Behind closed doors in the corridors of power they watched in amazement when hundreds of thousands of loyal Americans took to the streets to protest their war mongering. They remember well the massive protests of the Vietnam era and they are preparing to do battle. Armed with the Patriot Act (never was a document more cynically mislabeled), they are setting their sites on every dissident, dissenter and activist in the country. Greens, Libertarians and independents beware: They will target us for retribution.

Remember what Johnson and Nixon did to the peace movement. Remember Kent State and Jackson State. Remember Chicago and Miami. Remember what Reagan did to the student activists of the Free Speech movement in Berkeley, California. Remember McCarthy and the Red scare. Do not pretend that these totalitarian measures ended with the death of J. Edgar Hoover.

If the power lords are threatened, they will employ everything at their disposal to disarm that threat. They will make false accusations. They will tap our phones and monitor our web activities. They will keep track of our credit card accounts. They will know what books we read, what magazines we subscribe to, what organizations we belong to, and what meetings we attend. If we continue to rise against them, they will threaten and do harm.

Be prepared for all contingencies. The game is on and the price of dissent is persecution.

It is now more important than ever that those of us who have rallied to this cause must remain vigilant or, like the participatory democracy experiments of the past, we will not as a cause survive. We will become a cultural oddity, an aberration, a distraction, and an amusement for future nostalgias. Mainstream historians will paint us as caricatures of dissent, like the hippies and the beats. For their sake, as well as our own, we must position ourselves to *become* the new historians. We must position ourselves as talking heads and media consultants. We must gain representation on the airwaves. We must establish a presence on the Internet.

We must become more than a cause for a cause presumes an effect and once the effect is achieved the cause will rest. We cannot rest. Or if we must we must rest in motion. What we have begun must become a self-perpetuating force. What was a cause must evolve into a movement that is never still. If we stop we die. We must become a fusion of culture and politics so that our political actions are a part of our lives. We must all of us possess a revolutionary state of mind.

What is a revolutionary state of mind? It is a mind that sees the purpose behind television programming, print headlines and editorials, commercialism and media talking heads. It is a mind that recognizes politics in virtually every social event and every issue. It is a mind that answers every question and makes every statement for the movement and the cause.

When a reactionary statement from any source is made in public, the revolutionary mind considers it an invitation to respond in kind. Let the public hear both sides of an issue. Offer an objective choice.

When pollsters ask questions the revolutionary mind realizes that polls are not taken so that the polled can influence public policy. Polls are taken so that politicians can manipulate and control the people. Polls are taken for the purpose of pandering. Lie to them. Lie to them every time. Lie to them with sporadic consistency. Keep them guessing. Let the politicians pander to a public that does not exist. Let them stop using polls to tell them what they think. Ask them to consult their values and consciences for a change.

The revolutionary state of mind votes. We vote every time. No election is too small or too hopeless. Our voices must be heard. Let the people know what you think. Do not pretend that voting is itself a virtue. Do not enable those who do not support the cause or the candidate. Know your allies and enable them. Know your adversaries and encourage them to remain at home.

JAZZMAN CHRONICLES

The revolutionary state of mind welcomes government rebates and tax refunds and channels them into the cause. Encourage artists to take a stand. Make your contributions contingent on political alliance. We have inherited a culture of passive oppression. We must transform it into political activism.

Take your message to the streets. Take it to the university square. That is the proper place for democratic action. The university is the garden of dissent and protest. It is the fertile soil of free thought. Plant the seeds of freedom, justice and democracy. Attend meetings. Put up posters. Support your local activists. Recognize that everything, from the products you buy to the movies you attend, is a political statement.

Democratic action is our right and it is our heritage as Americans. It is what our forefathers did though they did not go far enough. It is what the best and brightest among them intended for us to do. It is our duty and solemn oath.

Stay the cause. Stay the motion.

Jazz.

VIETNAM REMEMBERED

"We are not about to send American boys five or six thousand miles away from home to do what Asian boys ought to be doing for themselves."

Lyndon Baines Johnson

On the occasion of our president's Veterans Day remembrance of Vietnam with a jaunty walk past the Memorial, in rebuttal to those whose great lament is that our soldiers were not welcomed home as heroes, it is time that those of us who were and remain opposed to that war offered our own retrospective. We remember Vietnam, as we remember those who fell at Kent State and Jackson State, and, in tribute to their memory, we will not allow contemporary distortions to go unchallenged.

There is a revisionist movement whose aim is to rewrite history for the purposes of propaganda. These revisionists are not radical extremists or even liberal loyalists. They are instead mainstream historians. Their works are taught in virtually every public school and every government funded college and university in the land.

They begin with the pilgrims who were in fact vicious white supremacists and religious zealots escaping a country they considered too lenient, too promiscuous, too permissive, and yet intolerant of their own particular sect.

They declared the inhabitants of the new world savages and paved the way for five hundred years of genocide.

Omitted from their story of the great explorers is the torture, rape, plunder and murder of indigenous peoples in pursuit of gold and other riches. Omitted from their story of the Spanish missionaries is the enslavement of their savage fold. Omitted from the narrative of Westward Expansion and Manifest Destiny are the broken treaties, massacres, and the concerted attempt to exterminate both the buffalo and the people who depended on them to survive.

Now there is a new revisionism. It regards the late sixties and the Vietnam War. It tells a story of promiscuity and drug abuse. It apologizes for a generation lost, whose only salvation was eventually coming home to become useful and moderate citizens. It tells the story of the Vietnam veterans who returned to our shores only to be shunned and scorned. It paints them as heroes, forgotten heroes, who did their duty, fulfilled their obligation to society, and were never repaid with the gratitude of a nation.

Let us be clear: We sympathize with those who were compelled to serve in an unjust, immoral war, just as we sympathize with those who served in the Gulf War. We sympathize with those who suffered and died. That they did so is the lasting shame of this nation. But they are no more heroes than the Indian killers in Custer's Seventh Calvary. They went to a foreign land and killed men, women and children with abandon. Ask the decorated Senator Bob Kerrey if he believes they were heroes. There was no cause of freedom. There was no cause of justice. We were fighting against a people who had been fighting for more than a century against foreign invaders. Was it easier to kill them because they were Asian? Was it easier to spray their country with bombs and chemical defoliants because they did not share our image of a bearded white god on a golden cross?

Let us be clear: The tragedy of Vietnam is not that we lost the war. Had we managed to secure a paper victory it would have been our worst nightmare. For once you take a country five thousand miles away from home you are then obliged to hold it. Do we really believe that those who fought against the British, French and American invaders for a hundred years – and sacrificed four million lives to that cause – would ever have bowed down to our military might?

Let us be clear: The heroes of the Vietnam era are those who refused to go, who went to jail or risked going to jail, those who were killed on the streets and on our college campuses, those who refused to believe that the killing of Asians was the will of the American people, and those who remember still what the late sixties movement was about. In a word, it was about democracy. It was about reclaiming democracy from a corrupt and war mongering political establishment. It was about stopping the military industrial complex. It was about fighting against an American aristocracy of wealth, greed, racism and ruthlessness. It still is.

Jazz.

THE PRINCIPLES OF FOREIGN POLICY

"When the world's only superpower, which has essentially a monopoly of force, announces openly: We will use force and violence as we choose and if you don't like it get out of the way, there's a reason why that should frighten people."

Noam Chomsky

The founding fathers could not have envisioned a future in which America was the dominant force of the world. The founding fathers could not have envisioned a world in which nuclear, biological and chemical weapons would threaten the continued existence of the human race. The founding fathers could not have envisioned global technologies, global economies, global communications or the inevitability of star wars. The founding fathers could not have envisioned a future in which the United States of America was poised to become both the world's banker and police force.

We can only surmise that the founders would have intended for the world what they attempted to guarantee (albeit selectively) for the citizens of this country: A world of freedom, justice, equality and prosperity. Regretfully, that is not the path we as a nation have chosen.

In the decades following World War II American foreign policy has been one of interference and intervention in nations on every continent in every corner of the globe. Our military and intelligence forces have plotted the assassinations of foreign leaders (Castro, Khadafy, Hussein, Peron), obstructed democratic elections (Indonesia, Nicaragua, El Salvador, Venezuela), armed terrorist organizations (the Contras, the Mujahadeen, Al Qaeda), subverted lawful governments (Argentina, El Salvador, Venezuela), supported military coups and ruthless dictators (Suharto, Pol Pot, the Shah of Iran, Saddam Hussein), imposed crippling sanctions on innocent civilians (Iran, Iraq, Cuba), turned a blind eye to genocide by American supported governments (East Timor), and prosecuted wars lacking moral justification (Vietnam, the Gulf War).

It does not matter whether Republicans or Democrats are in the White House. America's foreign policy has been a continuous line of domination, abuse and control. In the process, after the fall of the Soviet Union, we have become one of the most feared powers in the history of the modern world. Time and again we have demonstrated our awesome military might while showing little restraint in applying it. By much of the world we are perceived as a loose canon with the power and will to destroy any nation at any time.

Our solution to the problem of civilian casualties is to control the media and deny all reports to the contrary. Thus, in the Gulf War the American public was shown Pentagon issued video of precision bombs hitting their targets with unwavering accuracy. Later, we learned that forty percent of our bombs missed their targets but no one counted the civilian dead – just as no one has counted in Afghanistan. We have learned that the sanctions against Iraq, which we alone continue to prosecute, have resulted in over a million civilian deaths – half of them children. It begs the question: How much is enough?

Increasingly, we stand alone in the world. Our Arab

allies in the Gulf War were betrayed when we refused to withdraw our forces as promised when the war was ended. We alone refused to sign the Kyoto Accords, a modest, nonbinding agreement in principle to a global approach to reducing greenhouse gas. With only Israel at our side, we refused to attend the International Conference on Racism because Zionism was to be a topic of discussion. We alone refused to honor the World Court and we choose to follow international law only when it suits our purposes.

Yet a new development in the post Cold War era is the increasing emphasis on global economics through the American dominated World Trade Organization (WTO) and the International Monetary Fund (IMF). The formula is familiar to those who have studied the demise of the American family farmer. The IMF (like the bankers who served the farmers) offers generous loans to developing nations with a promise of sweet prosperity. Inevitably the promise turns out to be long term while the debt is immediate. The debtor nation (like the farmer before him) is trapped in an endless cycle of borrowing just to pay off the accelerating interest on its mounting debt. The catch is: In order to qualify for more loans, the nation must comply with standards dictated by the WTO. Debtor nations are compelled to lift trade barriers and dedicate more and more of their limited resources to exports, which only exacerbates the debt, leading to more loans, perpetuating an endless cycle of desperation. The collapse of their economies, along with the deterioration of social services, is all but inevitable.

The cycle of desperation is not restricted to the so-called third world countries. We now know that Argentina, once the fifth strongest economy in the world, was only the first to fall in a morbid recreation of a new domino theory.

Where will it end? When the nations of the world

default on their loans, do we really believe they will stand idly by while international corporations assume possession of their resources? Will they be content to become nations in servitude to corporate powers? We need not be experts in international affairs to surmise that they will not. It cannot end well.

It is time for global change. It is time to become what American principles and values insist that we must become. It is time to be what our leaders have always claimed that we were: a beacon of justice, human rights and democracy. It is time to fulfill the promise of our forefathers. Our destiny cannot and must not be to dominate the world but, rather, to improve the lot of human kind.

It is for this purpose that we propose the following principles of foreign policy.

I.   The United States will not engage in interventions that support non-democratic governments or governments that violate the inalienable rights of its citizens.

II. Our nation will take appropriate action to prevent, inhibit or halt genocide.

III. We will not act as the police force of the world.

IV. We will take appropriate measures, including debt forgiveness, to reduce and eliminate third world debt. Concomitantly, we will no longer sponsor or support the IMF/WTO perpetual loan scandal. IMF loans must be based on humanitarian concerns and should not be tied to trade policies or internal economic policies.

V.   The United States will not sacrifice human lives for economic gain.

VI. We will practice a policy of restraint in civil wars and civil conflicts.

VII. We will actively engage in negotiations to

resolve conflicts in the world's trouble spots (Israel-Palestine, Northern Ireland, India-Pakistan, et cetera).

VIII. We will support the United Nations and the World Court as the appropriate venue for resolving international disputes.

IX. We will recognize our responsibility in regard to the global problems of hunger, poverty, disease, human rights and environmental protection.

X. The intelligence agencies of the United States will be restricted to their original mandates: The gathering and analysis of information.

These are, of course, but general principles. There will always be situations and circumstances that pose unique, complex and difficult problems. Yet adherence to these principles would fundamentally alter the course of international politics and global economics. The most immediate effect would be an end to the most insidious elements of the war on terrorism and to cease our aggression against Iraq. The nations of the world would breathe easier and the peoples of the world would share a vision of a brighter, more prosperous and safer future. The United States of America would finally begin to fulfill the promise of her founders.

Jazz.

VOLUME II

THE WAR CHRONICLES

CONTENTS

CONTENTS

PREFACE

WAR & PEACE

"In the hearts of people today there is a deep longing for peace. When the true spirit of peace is thoroughly dominant, it becomes an inner experience with unlimited possibilities. Only when this really happens - when the spirit of peace awakens and takes possession of men's hearts - can humanity be saved from perishing."

Albert Schweitzer

It is the nature of war that it outweighs all other concerns. While I believe that the long-term solution to the systemic problems we face as a nation depends on numerous reforms – most critically the defeat of the major party system – everything must now yield to the antiwar movement.

In the next election (2004) we confront the possibility that the Bush Doctrine of preemptive strike and perpetual superiority will face no political constraint. Imagine what might have happened if this president had not faced a second election. A reinstatement of the draft becomes a distinct possibility. Expansion of the war on terrorism becomes a certainty. The unthinkable first use of tactical nuclear weapons becomes a viable military option.

There are many reasons to oppose this president – corruption, incompetence, intolerance, indifference to the poor, the environment and the oppressed. None of these compares to the prospect of four more years of an expanding "war on terror". Study your history: What this president sets in place will not be reversed by succeeding administrations – be they Republican or Democrat. The strategies of intervention and subversion, under the name of the Cold War, were passed on from generation to generation, from president to president, and the likelihood that it will be different with this war is a dismal proposition. It must be stopped now.

The election is about war. There is no other issue. It is not about the economy. It is not about unemployment. It is not about Medicare or Social Security. It is not about democracy or civil liberties. It is not about gay rights, abortion rights, judicial nominees, affirmative action or racial equality. It is not about fair trade. While all these issues are important, they pale by comparison to the policies of war.

The coming election is about young men and women dying on foreign lands. It is about war without end. It is about a philosophy of dominance that promises decades of war. It is about old men and women, who will never see the battlefield, sending young men and women to their last days on earth. Until the soldiers have come home and the Bush Doctrine is forever buried in the desert sands of Arabia, there is no other issue.

These Chronicles have no other ambition but to stop a war machine led by a president obsessed with the dream of glory. There is no more glory in Iraq than there was in Vietnam. These Chronicles are about pounding home the truth and etching it in the American psyche before it is lost to the government propaganda machine. These Chronicles are about changing the course of history.

Jazz.

THE GREAT DESTROYER

"Better weapons lead to better and better weapons until the earth is a grenade with the fuse burning."

William Burroughs
Cities of the Red Night

What kind of a nation reacts to an act of terror as we have? In response to a vicious and brutal attack, we mercilessly destroyed one nation (the poorest of the lot) for harboring the terrorists while allying ourselves with those nations that supplied and supported them. We could have as easily bombed ourselves for financing and supplying Al Qaeda, the Mujahadeen, and every other Islamic fundamentalist militant group who served on the front lines in our war against the Soviet beast.

Did we not promise never again to forget the destruction we have wrought and have we not forgotten? We have left Afghanistan with a government confined to its capitol. We have left their country in the hands of the very same war lords who made the Taliban acceptable to a people ravaged and broken by war.

Did we not promise never to forget those responsible for knocking those towers down and have we not forgotten? Osama bin Laden is alive. Al Qaeda is regrouping even in the very same region where we were supposed to have routed and destroyed them. But we have turned our attention elsewhere. We prefer to fight old enemies, enemies we can face on a battlefield, in wars we can televise from beginning to glorious end.

What kind of a nation uses a terrorist attack to justify declaring war on three sovereign nations, however ruthless or despicable their leaders may be, having no relation and bearing no responsibility for the destruction we have suffered?

Can we look at ourselves in honesty and candor and reflect that this is the behavior of an enlightened nation? Are we in truth the great liberator our president proclaims or are we the great destroyer, an avenging angel, champion of the cause of vengeance? Do we carry the torch of liberty or the hammer of wrath? Do our friends and allies welcome us or do they fear not to welcome us?

Place yourselves in the shoes of our adversaries if only for a moment. You are living in Kabul. Your country is decimated, its economy in tatters. You cannot find work or housing, medical care or schools for your children. You cannot leave the boundaries of the city for fear of landmines or warlords or parties still loyal to the Taliban or Al Qaeda. America has spent tens of billions destroying your country but offers only a fraction to rebuild it. An American reporter approaches you to ask how you feel about your liberators. You reply that you love America but in your heart there is no love. You fear America and do not wish to rouse the anger of its government.

Imagine now that you are living in Baghdad. You have suffered under the rule of a tyrant but you know that America helped place him in power, supplying him with the instruments of terror and oppression, and helped keep him in power for as long as the oil field remained open to western control. You have watched half a million of your children die from the American war and its aftereffects and you cannot bring yourself to blame it all on Saddam. When the conquering army marches into your city you cheer and smile and pray that your suffering has come to an end. But within you is deepest, darkest doubt. America has never brought good will or good fortune.

Imagine living in Korea, Iran or Venezuela. Do you pray for American intervention? Do you welcome the great liberator or do you fear her wrath?

It might so easily have been different. We could have responded as an enlightened nation. The world was united in its good will toward us. Americans were ready to be challenged. Instead of challenging the world to brace itself for unending war, our president could have issued the greatest challenge of the new millennium. He could have challenged us to transform our economy from oil dependency to a solar, wind and hydrogen based economy. No longer would we need our troops on the holy lands of Saudi Arabia. No longer would we consume most of the world's finite resources. No longer would we claim the right to poison the world's air, pollute her waters, and destroy her ozone layer. We could have weaned our selves and the world of the inevitable catastrophe of nuclear energy.

Of course we would have had to go after Al Qaeda as well but we might have listened when the Taliban offered to present the accused to an international court of justice. We would still have faced many hardships but Osama bin Laden would not be free and Al Qaeda would be isolated and inoperative. America would not have to stand alone (with none but borrowed and dependent allies at her side) in her crusade against terror.

But is this just a dream? Is it as impossible as it seems? There is no escaping the fact that a different path could not have been chosen as long as the same corporate interests that direct us toward war and oil dependency are in control of our government. Despite our best intentions and desire for peace, the people are paralyzed by a notion of patriotism that requires our support in times of war regardless of the circumstances.

Clearly, the path to a more enlightened nation begins by striking down the dual dogmatism of false patriotism and blind faith in corporate dominated governance. Our economy is dependent on fossil fuels because our government is financed by the profits that fossil fuels provide. We could long ago have achieved oil independence. We need only desire it to make it so.

For the time being we must fight against the forces of war. We are not a war loving people. The dirty underside of war is rarely observed before it slips into the realm of history. It is popular now to lament the plight of the Vietnam veterans but when their story was immediate, when the suffering was living history, America's silent majority did not want to acknowledge it. We yearn for ribbons and parades but we do not wish to hear why so many of our children are disturbed. Even now, as we lament our forgotten soldiers, our mourning cries ringing through the nightmares of history, we have all but forgotten those who served in the last war. The Gulf War Syndrome is more than a soldier's bad memories. In the shadows of the forgotten where no cameras are trained, ten thousand have died and one third of those who served are seriously ill.

The time for our passions, for our sympathy and outrage, is before the suffering begins. We must rise in one voice to challenge the path of war. But as we do so we must not forget that the path to enlightenment begins with a change in government. To free our nation of oil dependency and all the bloody entanglements it demands, we must free our government of the same. We must elect individuals whose only interest is the welfare of the people they represent. Only then will the price of war be too high to pay. Only then will peace have a chance.

Jazz.

COLD WAR RESURRECTION

In the weeks preceding our preemptive strike on Iraq, our president begrudgingly appealed to the United Nations, inspectors reentered Iraq and they were greeted by a great deal of cooperation. In the days before the invasion, Iraqi officials were destroying the Al Sammoud missiles (marginally in violation of the 1991 disarmament accords). The destruction of the missiles (perhaps their only line of defense against the forces amassed on their borders) was not enough to ward off the attack. With the benefit of hindsight, there was nothing the Iraqis could have done. The entire process was a façade, a war dance, and a prelude to the inevitable.

We now know the invasion of Iraq had nothing to do with weapons of mass destruction. We know the war was not related to Al Qaeda or the war against terrorism. We know it was not in retaliation for the attack of September 11, 2001. Well into the occupation, as our president has supplanted Ariel Sharon as the most despised leader in the Arab-Islamic world, we are left wondering why. Through the process of elimination, there are two interrelated reasons: First, the importance of oil to an oil president. Second, a vision of the world by so-called "neo-conservatives."

Let us understand what this vision really is. It is a vision of endless war. It is the vision of a nation so obsessed that the preparations for the next war are in place before the first missile is fired. As vice president Dick Cheney said in the wake of September 11, it is a commitment to forty years of war – a prediction that deliberately and cynically parallels the duration of the Cold War.

To appreciate the scope and horror of this vision, we must revisit the four decades between the end of World War II and the fall of the Soviet empire for these Bush visionaries are the philosophical descendents of the Cold Warriors.

At the onset, understand that the Cold War was never cold. It cost the lives of over 100,000 American soldiers and literally millions of the indigenous peoples of Asia (Vietnam, Laos, Cambodia, Korea, Indonesia, Malaysia, the Philippines), Latin America (El Salvador, Nicaragua, Chile, Cuba, Columbia, Costa Rica, Guatemala, Argentina, Panama, Grenada, the Dominican Republic), Africa (Zaire, Libya, Angola), the Middle East (Lebanon, Iran, Iraq) and elsewhere. The American Cold Warriors recruited, trained, armed and financed the terrorists that now plague much of the world.

The Cold War is a legacy of death, destruction and oppression in the name of freedom. Its culmination was Vietnam, a nation upon which we unleashed a destructive force unrivaled in world history. Yet the Vietnamese did not surrender. They are arguably the bravest people known to humanity, having survived the successive invasions of foreign powers and the most awesome military force on earth.

The great lesson of Vietnam was not only that we were wrong, that we sacrificed millions of lives for an abstraction (Communism and the Domino Theory), but that we could not conquer a people without winning their hearts and minds. We were not the liberators we were supposed to be. We were conquerors. As Daniel Ellsberg put it, we were not *on* the wrong side; we *were* the wrong side.

How strange it was, then, after the conclusion of the first Gulf War, for an American president to proclaim that "the specter of Vietnam" had been "lifted forever." It was clear the American government had not learned the lesson of Vietnam. Perhaps these right wing ideologues secretly lament that we did not drop the big one on Saigon. Perhaps they believe their own propaganda: that the Cold War led to the collapse of Communism.

When the Soviet Union fell it was, above all, a lesson in economics. A state sponsored economy, under an oppressive and corrupt government, was not strong enough to support a system that dedicated more than half of its wealth to military spending. We are now in a position to learn whether or not a free market economy, under an increasingly oppressive and corrupt government, is capable of supporting a similar imbalance between domestic and military spending.

There was a time when our economy was predominantly industrial. Much of that industry – manufacturing, oil and steel – could be directed to the war effort. War was therefore considered a boon to the economy. The new economy, however, is increasingly based on technology. While technology can and does serve the military, its greater application is in the service and information fields. Only a fraction of the new economy benefits from perpetual war and many of them reside in the government, counseling our oil wealthy president. The economy as a whole will suffer from a prolonged economic slump and an alienated world market. In the new economic world order, peace and good will are our best allies.

The Cold Warriors of the Bush administration yearn for war at all costs to the general populace. Having disproved the Domino Theory, they wish to test a new theory of free-market dominance and an American controlled New World Order, but if they are wrong, it may well result in economic collapse.

The Cold Warriors desire an enemy that will rival the

propaganda value of the Communist beast. In the war on terror, they will be the ones to determine who is a terrorist and who is not. It is already clear they have decided that Palestinians are terrorists. They are lining up potential enemies throughout the Arab world. Who will be next? Syria? Iran? Libya? Or will we shift hemispheres and resume our Latin American operations? Venezuela, Argentina, Brazil, Cuba?

It is not for those who oppose the war machine to defend those nations destined for invasion or subversion (though many are worthy of defense) any more than it is incumbent on the proponents of war to defend such allies as Pakistan, Israel, Columbia or Saudi Arabia. It is rather for us all to recognize that the vision the Bush administration is offering is a nightmare of unending destruction.

The Iraqi invasion was not a battle of virtue or principle. It was a prelude to decades of war. It was not a war for democracy. It was a war for dominance. In the final analysis, it is a war America can never win for we lost the battle for hearts and minds at its inception. America has neither the right nor the means to control the resources of the planet. America cannot and should not impose its will on the peoples of the world for the people will never submit.

We must finally come to terms with the fact that we are but one nation and that our wisdom is no greater and our god is no greater than that of any other nation. Though we have come to possess power and wealth beyond the world's imagining, our greatest strength has always been our virtue.

As a nation, we have never had to face the full consequences of our actions. As a people, we have been protected by our government and its propaganda machine. To this day, there are those who believe that a crazed gunman killed our most promising president. To this day, there are those who believe that the Vietnam War, the bombing of Cambodia, and the invasions of Cuba, Panama and tiny Grenada were justified. To this day, there are those who refuse to believe that America sponsored and trained terrorists in the Middle East, Latin America and throughout the world. To this day, there are those who believe that the genocide on our own soil was the manifestation of a Christian god.

Unless we finally come to terms with the crimes of our past we cannot begin to understand the dangers we now confront. We are a nation that desires empire. Those who have studied history already know how it ends. This is the vision of the Cold Warriors as it was the vision of the ancient warriors of Rome. This is their collective promise to the world: An endless cycle of violence, where every act of terror is answered by another, where every voice of dissent is considered treason and every nation that opposes is considered an enemy. Is it any wonder the world has risen against us?

Wake up, America. Wake up before these lords of war and avarice steal our nation's soul. We are still a free nation of proud and virtuous citizens. Now, at the time of greatest need, let us rally that pride and steady our resolve to change the course of history. Americans have no desire to control or dominate the world. Let us elect new leaders who share *our* vision, who will bury the doctrines of first strike and world dominance, and who regard our fellow beings in this world with respect and tolerance.

Jazz.

INFANT NATION

What could be more pathetic than the incessant lament of privileged white men condemning preferential treatment on the basis of race, if not the lament of successful black men and women who appear to have severed themselves from their cultural and ancestral roots?

It is symptomatic of a greater problem shared by all of America and consistently exploited by its congressional, judicial and executive leadership: Americans have pathologically short memories.

From an historical perspective it is undeniable: In the great expanse of recorded time, America is but an infant nation. Given this simple and unquestionable observation our behavior in the world suddenly comes into focus. As an infant nation our behavior is as predictable as the salivation of Pavlov's dogs.

Consider the psychological profile of an infant: An infant knows only the moment. Yesterday is ancient history. An infant remembers only the blow that struck, never the blow that preceded it. An infant believes that the universe revolves around her and only her. An infant's emotions run no deeper than unconditional love and uncompromised rage. When an infant is harmed he strikes back. He is incapable of understanding the complexities of circumstance. To the infant there is no history. There is only now. The infant seeks immediate gratification and blind vengeance. There can be no middle ground. The infant believes that the soft stroke of the moment is eternal love and a terse rebuke cannot be differentiated from utter hatred. The infant relies on simple labels in place of a reasoned response to interpret events. In the voice of her parents "bad" becomes a moral imperative.

I submit that we are an infant nation. We believe what we are told. We rely on push button logic in place of reason. Our leaders create and offer labels that become the triggers to a guttural response. In the McCarthy era, those labels related to the Cold War enemy: communist, socialist, Marxist, red. In the era of mass media we are given a broader array of push button triggers: radical, liberal, Hollywood left, conspiracy theorist, tree hugger, anarchist, actor, extremist. The purpose of these labels is to short circuit the logical process and supplant it with a conditioned reaction based on raw emotion. Thus, when the environmentalist is called a tree hugger, the conditioned response labels her un-American. When the activist is called an extremist, he is labeled unpatriotic.

Our leaders rely on the assumption that Americans have short memories and, to a large extent, the assumption is correct. On the matter of Vietnam, Americans tend to consider it ancient history though the world will tell us it was only yesterday. When we consider it at all, we lament that our soldiers were not well received or that we lost the war. Any reasoned analysis of that tragic, misbegotten war must conclude that the patriots were those who fought against an unjust war. It was the massive protests of the left – not the passive submission of a silent majority – that shortened the war and saved countless American and Vietnamese lives. Yet our leaders would have us believe that protest in a time of war is unpatriotic. Nothing could be more infantile.

Though history tells us that our leaders have habitually misled us when war or military action was involved, we continue to believe that they tell us only the truth. When our president proclaims that he has proof positive of the cause for war yet refuses to reveal it, we are expected to accede. We are expected to go along. We are told that our forces fight only for democracy when, in fact, our government has always preferred to support military dictatorships and right wing despotism. Yet we are expected to accede. We are told that we have always fought for peace though we have planted the seeds of war, creating circles of violence all over the world, with the intent of overthrowing and replacing the governments of sovereign nations. There is no corner of the planet where American interests have not attempted to exploit internal conflict.

I submit we are an infant nation. Once a year we are pledged to remember our soldiers who have died in war but we have never acknowledged the dead of our adversaries: four million Vietnamese, Laotians and Cambodians, four to five thousand Afghanis, one million Iraqis, uncounted thousands of Nicaraguans, Argentineans, Salvadorans, Columbians, Panamanians, Indonesians, on and on. We have given a solemn oath never to forget the three thousand Americans who died in a horribly misguided act of terror yet we are blind to the horrors we have wrought in nations less powerful than our own. We cry out for vengeance yet we fail to see that we are creating an endless cycle of violence that was, in fact, instigated by our own intervention in foreign affairs.

Does it matter that Iraq had nothing to do with the terrorist attack? If this is about creating a model of democracy for the region, let us not forget that we have already conquered, occupied and promptly forgotten a nation in the region. If we wish to create a model of democracy let us do so in Afghanistan. Let us rebuild a country we have devastated. If this is about weapons of mass destruction, let us first look to our own stockpiles.

Let us next look to North Korea and Pakistan. Without oil in the equation it defies reason to attack a nation already defeated in war.

But we are an infant nation. We cannot be expected to find the path of peace. It is difficult to make peace. It requires true compassion built on a foundation of knowledge, tolerance and understanding. It requires digging deeper than hatred and characterizing those who oppose us as evil beings devoted to evil deeds. It is much easier to cry vengeance, to paint everything in black and white, to raise the flag and set the blinders: God, country, rock and roll! It is much easier to make war – unless you are chosen to fight it. It is a crime against humanity that those who must fight and die in war are those least capable of understanding why: the poor, disadvantaged and poorly educated.

I submit we are an infant nation and infants never see the faults of their parents. George W. Bush is the perfect president for this endless "war" on terror. He has little knowledge of world history. He has little understanding of world dynamics. He is incapable of compassion because he clearly believes his own platitudes. He believes that Osama bin Laden and his followers were born hating America. He believes in the Holy War. He believes in the Crusades. He believes that "evil doers" hate us because we are free, because we have McDonalds and Sunday football and wealthy oil companies that hand deliver the American dream to the sons of CIA directors. He does not know what his father did in the Middle East when he was in charge of intelligence. He does not know what his father bargained to make his son Commander In Chief.

I submit we are an infant nation led by an infant king. Jeb had the brains but W had the attributes that counted. He does not ask questions. He does not need nor can he profit from lengthy explanations. He is a "bottom line man." He was never trained to think for himself. He had no interest in history or international affairs. Point him the way, tell him what to say, watch him swagger, wink and stammer. George W is the man of the hour. George W is the answer to the question: Why didn't anyone notice when Ronald Reagan's mind slipped away? The answer: He was not necessary to the policy-making government.

I submit we are an infant nation and nothing is more dangerous than a child who believes he can bend the world to its knees.

I submit we are an infant nation but we are showing signs of growing up. There are times when even a child can rise to the occasion. We are no longer so easily fooled. We are slowly finding the courage and independence required to question our elders, to question the policies of our government. Even now, only two years after the tragedy of September 11, many of us have found our voices. We demand a concrete reason before we destroy another country in the name of democracy. We question the validity of a policy of preemptive strike. We question the doctrine of perpetual world supremacy. We question the motives of a government dominated by oil interests. We question the need for innocent civilian deaths. We question the need for sending our soldiers to war – perhaps to die in combat, perhaps to die from chemical, biological or plutonium poisoning. We wonder why we have lost the trail of Osama bin Laden and Al Qaeda. We wonder why we no longer seem to care.

It may well be that we as a people are growing up faster than our leaders thought possible. In the Enron scandal, the energy crisis, the election frauds, the tax relief scam, the deregulation schemes and so many other disturbing events, we have peeked behind the curtain that hides the real workings of our government. The more you say it is not about oil, the more we are certain it is.

JAZZMAN CHRONICLES

It is the enduring shame of our government that a popular uprising of unprecedented proportions could not stop the relentless march to war but it will be our shame if we do not stop the march to empire. They lied to justify this war just as they lied to justify Vietnam. If the people do not heed the lesson, they will surely lie again. Ultimately, our leaders must have our consent to continue on the path of destruction.

There will likely be an election between Iraq and the next invasion. If we fail to defeat this president, we will have sanctioned the Bush push to empire. Only a small child could believe that this cause is truly righteous. Let us not be fooled again. Let 2004 be the year America grew up.

Jazz.

ABSOLUTION

"To initiate a war of aggression is not only an international crime; it is the supreme international crime, differing only from other war crimes in that it contains within itself the accumulated evil of the whole."

The Judges of Nuremberg

America clings to the belief that she is absolved from all sin, all crimes against humanity, all acts of unconscionable violence and equally unconscionable indifference by the simple recycling of leadership every four to eight years. We are not to be held accountable for our past behavior because the names of those who reside on Pennsylvania Avenue have changed.

It is of no consequence that the leading players in the current White House are the same individuals who committed those crimes under previous administrations. The fact is, regardless the changing cast, American foreign policy since World War II is a continuous line of intervention, self-serving unilateralism, and utter defiance of international law and universal principles of equity and human decency.

The world community has long understood and detested American foreign policy. The people of the world have long understood that a changing of the White House guard does not produce a change in America's behavior in the world. It is only a matter of degree. Ronald Reagan and the elder Bush were the hammers of foreign policy. Presidents Carter and Clinton may have provided a brief respite in the brutal prosecution of American policy but they did not (perhaps could not) change the path that would inevitably lead to the critical impasse we now face.

What is now happening in the world is the realization that its people can no longer endure. The problem is not that the world fails to see the Bush vision. The problem arises from the fact that they see it all too clearly.

The entire world was listening in hushed silence when our vice president declared "forty years of war" in the wake of September 11. They understood what Dick Cheney and Donald Rumsfeld meant when they suggested that the tragedy of that momentous event could be seen as an opportunity to resume the war on Iraq. They understood that those in charge of the Bush administration's foreign policy were cold warriors longing to return to the games of international warfare, subterfuge, corruption and intrigue.

Blessings on Jacques Chirac, for though the French had undeniable interests in the region, France stood to gain immeasurably more by caving to American interests in open defiance of her own people. If we believe in democracy then France and Germany were the world's champions in the United Nations effort to prevent the war. You cannot in good faith advocate democracy while dragging your people into war against their will. Trying to achieve democracy through invasion is like trying to achieve tolerance through intimidation. It is a fallacy and a lie. You cannot champion democracy while lying to your people to win their approval.

If you still do not believe your government lied to you, then read its own statements in the weeks and months following September 11, 2001. There was and is no connection between the events of that horrific day and the regime in Baghdad. The alleged meeting between Iraqi officials and Al Qaeda agents never happened. There was no Iraqi connected Al Qaeda training camp at a specified location in northern Iraq. That Iraq openly supports the cause of occupied Palestine is unquestioned and that is the only connection to "terrorists" this White House has documented.

The administration had to resort to fabrication and falsehood because it failed utterly and completely to make its case for war. What they failed to achieve through diplomacy, however, they attempted to achieve through bribery and intimidation. Against this background of failure and disgrace, America saw fit to demand that the United Nations fall into line or withdraw from international relevance. Nothing could be further from the truth. If, under these circumstances, the United Nations had yielded to American demands it would then have proclaimed its own irrelevance. Like the United States Congress, it would have abdicated its right and lawful duty in world affairs.

If we but examine the American case for war without passion or patriotism we will arrive at the same conclusion the rest of the world already recognizes. America repeatedly noted that Saddam Hussein used chemical weapons against Iran and the Kurds ("his own people") decades before but considered it irrelevant that America knowingly and deliberately allowed corporations to provide chemical precursors and biological elements to Iraq with the clear intent of employing them as weapons.

America condemned Iraqi use of chemical weapons – as it did publicly in the aftermath of the Iran-Iraq war – but it is not to be acknowledged that America protected Iraq from the sanctions of the United Nations. Saddam Hussein was America's man in the Gulf region and

Donald Rumsfeld was on the scene to seal the deal with a handshake.

America claimed that Saddam Hussein openly defied the United Nations for twelve years, yet for eight of those years a successful inspection regime disarmed massive quantities of chemical and biological weapons and dismantled the Iraqi nuclear program. More arms were destroyed in this period than during Gulf War I or the subsequent bombings and no lives were lost in so doing. In the second Gulf War, countless lives were saved by those years of "doing nothing," of defiance and UN failure to act.

We should not forget that the American government (whose president was in political trouble) in fact orchestrated the discontinuance of the inspection process. The ensuing four years of inactivity were in large part the legacy of Ken Starr and a right wing conspiracy – although the president can hardly be absolved.

America claimed that the United Nations did nothing for twelve years yet the UN sanctions – which the US alone continued to support and prosecute – resulted in over a million Iraqi deaths. All the while America fought against the Food for Oil program and all proposals to restructure the sanctions so that they targeted weaponry instead of food and medicine.

America claimed (rightly) that Saddam Hussein was guilty of war crimes and crimes against humanity yet America alone refuses to sanction the International Court of Justice. The truth is: America would stand trial as Saddam's accomplice.

As we stood on the precipice of war, the advocates of the Bush Doctrine argued that we had to go to war because our troops were in place and they could not wait much longer. If ever there was a reason for justifiable war this did not rise beyond the level of contempt. It seems to me our soldiers could have learned to persevere in the deserts of Kuwait and Bahrain in the hope that war could be averted but we had beat the drums of war so long and so loudly (they argued with the curious passion of a child that has lost his favorite toy) that we could not fail to act now! What would become of our prestige, our credibility, and our weight on the world stage?

One thing we can readily agree on without trepidation is that neither the cost of maintaining our troops nor the collective credibility of Dick Cheney, Donald Rumsfeld, Paul Wolfowitz, Colin Powell and Condoleezza Rice was worth the blood of a single American soldier – no less thousands of innocent civilians. Let them eat diplomatic crow and let our soldiers be spared.

Remember: In a last ditch effort to justify the irrational and reclaim their self-proclaimed prominence in international affairs, the warmongers threw up their hands and demanded: What would you have us do? Nothing? Would you allow Saddam Hussein to go about his business? Surely, if he was not developing weapons before the threat of war, he will do so now!

There are in fact many things that could have been done to further contain and disarm this monster of our own creation though doing nothing would have been preferable to the path of destruction we have pursued.

As former Senator Gary Hart suggested, we could have expanded the No Fly Zone to include all of Iraq and continuously monitored his activities. We could have increased the number of inspectors and provided them with all the equipment and intelligence they needed – as required by Resolution 1441. We could have maintained a force in the region while withdrawing most of our troops so that cooperation could be measured without the threat of an imminent attack. We could have restructured the sanctions so that the Iraqi people were no longer denied essential commodities – drinkable water, food, and medicines – while the Iraqi government was denied the materials of war. As an assurance of good will, America could have pledged, in the event of war and occupation, that the United Nations would assume control of Iraqi oil. Finally, we could have sanctioned the International Court of Justice and submitted our case against Saddam Hussein.

All these actions could and should have been taken with United Nations approval and support. The UN behaved admirably in this crisis. They stood the high ground between the world's superpower and the world's people. Under the constant pressure of American demands, the United Nations alone was positioned to make an informed judgment as to what should happen next. The United Nations alone had the authority to act where no nation has attacked another. If the time for war with Iraq had come, the United Nations would have known it and acted responsibly.

If the time for war did not come then we should all have been eternally grateful for the crisis would have been defused, diplomacy would have won the day, Iraq would have been disarmed peacefully, and the world would not have been hurling toward four decades of unending war and violence under the banners of freedom and security.

Jazz.

MEDIA, WAR & PROPAGANDA

And a vast paranoia sweeps across the land
And America turns the attack on its Twin Towers
Into the beginning of the Third World War
The war with the Third World

Lawrence Ferlinghetti

Secretary of State Colin Powell's transformation from an alleged dove to the Bush administration's foremost hawk must lead us to wonder if his prior reputation as a reluctant warrior was nothing more than a media shill.

His sudden advocacy of circumventing the United Nations process by going to war with a "coalition of the willing" betrays his assumed philosophical preference for reasoned diplomacy as an alternative to war. His proclamation that a dozen nations stand ready to join the US alliance in a preemptive strike is misleading and disingenuous. The inclusion of such nations as Bahrain, Qatar, Kuwait and the United Arab Emirates (all remnants of colonial empires and dependent on America or Europe for their defense) make it clear that it is hardly a coalition of the willing but rather an alliance of the coerced. The inclusion of Great Britain (where 70% of the people oppose the war), Turkey and Australia (where the opposition is at least as prominent) leads to a revealing question:

If we are fighting for democracy (and democracy is a representation of the will of the people), then how many peoples in the nations allied with US aggression support the Bush administration's headlong rush to attack Iraq? The answer of course is none.

The people of all nations, including our own, have made their opposition to this act of raw aggression clear. Despite the most dedicated propaganda campaign in history, a campaign that has dominated the corporate media, even Americans have made it consistently clear that we do not support this war without United Nations involvement, consent and support.

Something remarkable is happening in the world of American politics. The more they repeat their platitudes the less convincing they sound. When they remind us of Saddam Hussein's evil deeds we remember that we enabled him. When they belittle the opposition of France, Germany, Russia and China, we consider the moral imperative of our allies. When they remind us of the glory of the Gulf War, we wonder how a nation defeated and destroyed in a matter of days could now threaten the world's security. When they point out how successful that war was, we remember the victims of the Gulf War Syndrome. We know them. They are our friends, our brothers, sisters, sons and daughters. When they speak of precision weapons we remember the lies of 1991. When they tell us that it is a cause for war if the inspectors find weapons and it is cause for if they do not, we recognize a Catch 22. When they smirk and say it is not about oil, we know with increasing certainty that it is.

Something remarkable is indeed happening: The propaganda machine is faltering. But it is not enough to observe and acknowledge its demise for even now they recalibrating. They are certain that once the bombs are launched and our soldiers are thrust onto the battlefield, Americans will once again rally to the constant drumbeat of false patriotism. Mainstream media will launch its new campaign with marching bands, a parade of generals, and Pentagon issued war coverage against a backdrop of the American flag. War protestors will again be derided as traitors and Americans at home will be summoned to support our soldiers in the field. The alternative reality and greater truth that the best way to support our soldiers is to bring them back home will never be aired on America's airwaves.

The sad fact is we have lost hold of one the most sacred principles of democracy. Our founding fathers, in their great wisdom, had a special place for freedom of the press. It was included in the first amendment to the Bill of Rights. They knew the importance of a press not controlled by the government. What they could not have known is that the day would come when the same corporations that manufacture stereo equipment in Malaysia, that supply auto parts and breakfast cereal, and that control much of the world's communications and oil supply, are also the owners and controllers of mass information whether by print or electronics. Had they known then the dangers of a corporate media they would have written the amendment quite differently.

The loss of a free and independent media was one of the primary reasons the Florida election fraud was possible. The real story was the deliberate dis-enfranchisement of over 70,000 African American voters, yet the media story was all about hanging chads and recount procedures. The absence of a free media is also the reason that public discourse has become so limited and so short sighted. The obsession with high-profile trials, shark attacks and child abductions is a means of distracting the people from the real issues that affect their lives. The media defines the political debate as a contest between the major parties so that no one else can present fresh ideas.

The media holds all the cards. It tells us what to believe and defines the context of our belief system. It tells us that a vote for a candidate of independent integrity is a betrayal of democratic responsibility. It tells us that anyone who believes in conspiracy theories, secret societies, and dark forces within and without government is a lunatic on the fringe of society. It tells us that anyone who advocates an end to the drug war and decriminalization of drug offenses is criminally dangerous. It tells us that those who believe in extraterrestrial life are cult members and kooks. It tells us that anyone who criticizes the president or questions the call to war is unpatriotic.

The way to alter this reality is as simple as it is obvious: In the interest of open and free speech, we propose outlawing the ownership of any media organization, be it television, radio or print, by multi-national conglomerate corporations. If you are in the business of providing news, you should have no interest in lobbying politicians for favorable legislation. If you are in the profession that is charged with the sacred duty of providing the free flow of information, you should not have a vested interest in the story.

Such a radical change in policy cannot of course occur until our legislators are themselves cleansed of corporate influence. In the long term, it all depends on a successful independence movement.

Meantime, we have a war to fight and our most pressing concern is to exploit the inexplicable failure of the propaganda machine. Until the drumbeats of perpetual war are silenced, there is little else. We cannot allow our civil liberties to be so compromised in the name of homeland security that we will never recover them. We cannot allow the flames of war to engulf the world.

Colin Powell has lost his credibility by staking his claim with an administration that is dedicated to the path of war despite all facts and in open defiance of the

American people. They have only managed to convince a congress that is tragically dependent on the same corporate interests that stand to gain in the prosecution of war. Democracy is at stake when the expressed will of the people is dismissed as irrelevant on the most critical action a government can take.

Our national interests are not at stake in Iraq. Oil interests are at stake there. Our national security will be enhanced by a diplomatic solution to the conflict and seriously compromised by an act of war. As long as the inspectors are on the ground there can be no danger to the world. As long as inspectors are on the ground, Saddam Hussein poses no threat. As long as inspectors are on the ground Iraq cannot develop weapons. As long as inspectors are on the ground Iraq can take no actions that will endanger anyone within or without the region. Let us keep the inspectors on the ground. Let us keep them there as long as it takes. Let us keep them there until Saddam has died of old age. Let us keep them there forever if need be. The cost and the risks of doing so will be less than unleashing the destructive force of the American military.

Spread the word. Stay the motion. The war is not inevitable and should it proceed as planned, it is not unstoppable. We have arrived at a moment in history where the power of the people may be harnessed to change the course of a world gone mad. There should be no misunderstanding. This administration has announced its intent to wage war on a worldwide scale. They have triggered a return to proliferation of weaponry even while pretending to stand for disarmament. There are powerful forces behind this endeavor. It falls to the people, united as never before, to rise in one voice and claim the most basic of human rights: The right to live in peace.

Jazz.

CODE OF SILENCE

As our troops marched on Baghdad we were not fooled by our president's bravado. We were on the path of a conqueror, a path fraught with danger. As we observed the electronic images of mass destruction, shock and awe, we had to remind ourselves that this was real, that real lives were perishing before our eyes and real people were suffering beneath the plumes of American bombs, but we also strove to observe these events from a broader perspective. We realized that this was but the first official implementation of the Bush Doctrine and we began the search through history for points of reference.

The leaders of this nation would have us believe that the critical analogy is Nazi Germany. If we had known what Adolph Hitler intended, would we not have struck preemptively to prevent the Holocaust and the destruction of World War II?

None but the most biased and demagogic historian would seriously suggest such an analogy. No matter how repressive and horrific the regime of Saddam Hussein may have been (never mind that we were instrumental in placing him in power and facilitating his most egregious crimes against humanity), Iraq was but a third rate power, defeated, disarmed and more effectively contained than any nation on earth. By contrast, despite disarmament after World War I, Germany was the most powerful industrial nation on earth. Its massive rearmament was not a dark secret but an open reaction to rising unemployment. Hitler's aggressive intent was clearly announced in the annexation of Austria and

Czechoslovakia prior to its invasion of Poland. Had we chosen to preemptively strike Germany at any point along this historical line, we would not only have failed to prevent the war, we would have precipitated it with unpredictable results.

Let us not forget that Hitler's Third Reich rose out of a representative democracy. Let us not forget that the transformation of Germany from a republic to a one party fascist state was accomplished with the rationalizations of war and patriotism. Let us not forget that the first clear indication of Germany's imperialist intent was its withdrawal from the League of Nations without and its suppression of opposition within.

Once the bombs had fallen and blood was spilled on the fields of war, our government all but demanded that we honor a code of silence. Are we not a democracy? Do we not retain freedom of speech most especially in times of war? Have we so become what we decry in our enemies that we must impose a military code of silence on the democratic opposition?

We were not silenced then and we will not be silent now. You might as well ask us to severe our hands, cut out our tongues and pluck out our eyes as to demand that we be silent on the opposition that stirs in the depths of our souls.

We cannot remain silent as the nightmare continues, as our soldiers die along with countless Iraqis beyond the scope of military trained cameras, as the specter of Vietnam rises once more from the desert sands of the Persian Gulf.

We have found a new point of reference. The American government may well have made the gross miscalculation that thwarted its horrific campaigns in Laos, Cambodia and Vietnam. Despite the repeated assertion that this is a war against an oppressive government and not against the Iraqi people, it is now clear that the citizens of Iraq do not welcome the invaders of the west. Like the Vietnamese before them, even those who owe no allegiance to the Ba'ath Party and its despotic regime will resist the despotism of a foreign power.

The military revelation of Vietnam, after five years of unprecedented destruction, was that we were not fighting an ideology after all. We were not fighting Communists, Marxists or Anarchists. We were fighting nationalism. It is essentially the same message the Soviets learned in Afghanistan.

No, we will not remain silent.

We cannot remain silent believing as we do that this is but the first of many wars, under varied pretexts, that serves the interests of the oil industry and the international corporations who are already contracted for profiteering.

We cannot remain silent as we watch our civil liberties crumble like the ministries of Baghdad. We cannot remain silent knowing that our freedom is under attack, that our democracy is threatened, that our press and media are muzzled, and that our colleagues may soon become the next casualties of war, prisoners of conscience who will never face trial and will never be seen or heard from again.

We cannot remain silent while the world is divided, international law is discarded, while terrorists strike out in blind vengeance, and war threatens to break out on every continent of the earth.

We are the hearts you cannot rule.
We are the minds you cannot sway.
We are the eyes that see through your lies.
And we will not be silent.

Ours are the dissident voices. We are the voices of

outrage and moral indignation. We are the radicals in that we believe in the most radical form of government ever invented: democracy. We are the heart and soul of democracy. We are the reason for the Bill of Rights. You can take from us our most cherished liberties. You can monitor our phones and Internet activities, our political affiliations, our financial records, and our choices in reading and entertainment. You can detain us without charge, harass us and paint us in the colors of treason. You can accuse us of disloyalty but you cannot shake our faith. We know who we are. We are the defenders of liberty and democracy in America. We are America's last best hope. You can lock us up and throw away the key. You can even shoot us down in the streets and on university squares. But we will not be silenced.

The chain of events we have set in motion with this unwarranted, illegal and immoral war is rapidly catapulting out of control. If we cannot stop it now the world is in peril and we are the root and cause.

It is no longer about Saddam Hussein or weapons of mass destruction. It is about American aggression. It is no longer about democratic ideals. It is about corporate control of our democratic institutions. It is no longer about Al Qaeda and terrorism. It is about an official foreign policy that declares America's right to attack any nation at any time if they dare stand in the way of our mission.

What is our mission? What is the end game? Does it stop with the occupation of Iraq? We have already declared virtual war on three nations. We have already drawn a line in the sand and declared: You are either with us or against us. What is this vision of the world: A world in which all nations must bow to our demands or face annihilation? A world in which international law and international institutions are allowed to exist only so long as they abide our will?

JAZZMAN CHRONICLES

We cannot remain silent now and allow this darkness to descend for it is a darkness that will not lift in our lifetimes. It is a darkness that will haunt generations as yet unborn. Those who remain silent now must face the solemn judgment of conscience in the years and decades ahead. Those who believe as we believe cannot remain silent without sacrificing our souls.

And yet ... in a world where the language of irony is lost like an ancient tongue never committed to tablet, where war is peace, where gods are summoned one against another, where liberty is hailed as rights are discarded, where democracy is sacrificed on the alter of empire, and where freedom of speech is dependent on thresholds of influence, perhaps silence is the most appropriate response.

Even now, as the war mongers and false patriots demand our silence, perhaps the best answer comes in a language they are not familiar with: A March of Silence. Let us then gather together in tens and thousands, to drape ourselves in black, to march in deafening silence, to mourn and dissent in silence, to cry out in the silence of those who can no longer cry out, and to observe the silence of oppression and death.

The choice belongs to every man and woman old enough to know and brave enough to think. Whether it is in silence or more tangible form, our opposition must remain steady and strong. For it comes to this: The future of the world is thrust into our hands. What we do now will be the wonder of future generations who cannot but judge us harshly or well.

The president was right: Either you are with us or you are with them. War or peace? Liberty or oppression? Democracy or empire? We must choose.

Jazz.

THE NEW ENEMY

"Every American needs to believe this: that if we fail here in this environment, the next battlefield will be in the streets of America."

Lieutenant General Richard Sanchez

With the firing of the first missile on the orders of our president, with the dropping of the first bombs from the bowels of the Pentagon, we are confronted with a new and imposing enemy. It is an enemy that has no face, that owes allegiance to no ideology, and that rejects reason as a foundation for belief.

This new enemy wears the mask of anonymity and hides in shadows not unlike the terrorists of Al Qaeda. This enemy accepts no responsibility yet thousand (perhaps millions) may die by its hands. This enemy rallies to the false cry of patriotism, bathes itself in national pride, and invests its faith in war as if the one who leads its cause is the one true god and savior.

Who would Jesus bomb?

They have worn with jealous pride the name of the Silent Majority. They have marched in parades and claimed the heritage of our founders but their true heritage is blissful ignorance for they have never read beyond the headlines of American media, their knowledge of history is pure mythology, their perspective of the world is that of a romance novel, and their understanding of international affairs is that of a child.

How can we fight such an enemy?

We may take some salvation in the fact that we have faced and defeated this enemy before: on the streets of America during the Vietnam War. They were there, just as we were, in the cracks and shadows, hiding behind trees and bushes, hiding in office buildings, hiding behind yellow ribbons, hiding behind flag decals and shallow slogans: America – Love it or Leave It! My Country: Right or Wrong! Support our Troops!

So they stood on the sidelines as the parade marched on and 50,000 of our soldiers died in a war they did not understand. And they watched and cheered as millions of Vietnamese died at our hands, while the silent enemy went to barbecues and John Wayne movies and trotted out the flags for the Fourth of July. They watched and applauded, year after year, as presidents spoke of victory and light at the end of the tunnel, as the body count grew. They watched until their silence turned to sickening horror and they began to whisper among themselves: What have we done? Why?

But they absolved themselves of blame. They washed the blood from their hands and the stain from their memories.

The question that lingers over the decades and the clouds of war must finally be asked: Can we rightfully absolve the crime of silence? Can we forgive the citizens of the Third Reich or the society that enabled the Indian killers of the Seventh Calvary?

Is it enough to say that the ordinary citizen was deprived of sufficient knowledge to rise in opposition? Is it sufficient to acknowledge that our leaders have lied to us? In solemn truth, those lies were not so difficult to detect. For though our media has been horribly biased, the truth has always been there to those with eyes open.

Is it sufficient to acknowledge that our culture is one of obedience and unquestioning loyalty when, after all, our national culture is but in its infancy?

Is it possible that we have been too forgiving of our fellow Americans? We are in fact a democracy and in a democracy the ultimate responsibility – the blame and the glory – belongs to the people.

We speak to you now as we would a wayward brother or sister: You are forgiven your past misdeeds. But if you fail to heed the lessons of the past, if you repeat the crimes of indifference, blind faith and false patriotism, if you refuse to see the truth as it is plainly laid before you, if you continue to hide behind parades and slogans as the blood begins to flow, as the occupation settles in, and as the next war begins, then the blood will be on your hands and the stain will not easily be washed away.

Be mindful that history will not be written by American historians alone. Be respectful of other beings, other cultures, other nations and societies, whose people have endured infinitely longer than we have. When the people of the world rise in unparalleled unity, with undeniable dignity and courage, it behooves us to listen and to understand.

Our declared enemies have long made a distinction between the American government and her people. What will happen if that distinction is no longer deemed reasonable? What will happen if we are held accountable for the actions of our government? Will we be safer then?

Both our military and our government (how long will that distinction be merited?) continue to claim that our wars are not against people but against leaders and alliances and abstract ideals. But it is the people who die and suffer. When precision bombs target civilian infrastructures it is the children who die.

In this age of information ignorance can no longer offer absolution. If your silence or patriotism or blind faith sanctions war, then your soul must accept the blood of the innocent. If you take it upon yourselves, you will not allow it. Americans are not a war loving people. We are just a people who have lived too long in the isolation of relative paradise. We are not alone in the world any more.

Jazz.

AMERICAN HEROES

"In my years as a journalist, I have known only a single time as critical as this, when it seemed that the future of our democracy hung in the balance."

Walter Cronkite

Beneath the spoon-fed, military issued war coverage, as the Iraqi resistance to the American invasion continues to shock and awe, there is an equally surprising resistance emerging from the foot soldiers of the American press corps. It is the struggle to assert independence from government control. This is a resistance we can embrace and support with all our hearts.

The Iraqi resistance tears us apart for we do not wish to see the despotism of Saddam Hussein prevail. We do not wish to see the war prolonged. We do not wish to witness the carnage that a prolonged invasion entails. Yet neither do we wish to see America rewarded for her arrogant and unconscionable aggression. The implications of a successful initiation of the Bush Doctrine are horrible beyond imagination.

However, when we see American journalists asserting their professional pride and thereby reclaiming the fourth branch of a democratic government, it warms our hearts and gives us new hope. When we see Christiane Amanpour stand up to the pundits, the demagogues and the retired Generals who reign supreme on the airwaves of CNN, to assert that the resistance is not only strong but far stronger than any of the politicians led us to believe it would be, we must hail her courage and applaud her integrity. She, along with every other journalist who has thrown off the yoke of embedded journalism, is an American hero.

She is walking a fine line and one that may well determine her future as a mainstream journalist. We observe her demeanor and the shrouds of concern in her expression and we read the message beneath her spoken words: She is demanding that our leaders speak the truth about what is happening on the field of war. She is demanding that our leaders reconsider their war strategy. She is demanding that we recognize the distinct possibility that we have embarked on a path that more resembles Vietnam with every passing day.

You cannot liberate a people if they do not wish to be liberated. As the war presses on and the resistance stiffens, we must recognize that Iraqi people may have chosen the same line that governed American policy toward Iraq for decades: Saddam Hussein may be a ruthless dictator but he is *our* ruthless dictator.

The leaders of this war have challenged us to view this invasion as a brutality of enlightenment. But that enlightenment depends entirely on the support of the Iraqi people. If that support has vanished like a desert mirage or the pipe dream of Iraqi exiles, it is the duty of a free press to report what they have seen. If we have in fact lost the battle for the hearts and minds of the Iraqi people at the inception of this campaign, it is inconceivable that we will reclaim it under occupation.

The obvious and appropriate response to the emerging reality is the cessation of aggression, the withdrawal of our troops, and resumption of negotiations for the disarmament of Iraq. Sadly, it is the one bridge the current administration has burned at its rear. We have a president who is incapable of reflection. We have a president who has never reconsidered an $800 billion dollar tax cut as unemployment rises, as our debt reaches unprecedented levels, as health care is neglected, and as every other child is left behind in our public schools. We have a president that has never paused to wonder if the west coast energy crisis and the Enron disaster might have been the result of government neglect as well as corporate corruption. We have a president who will not be second-guessed and will never rethink his path.

We have chosen a path of war with dogged determinism and we have neither the means nor the character to recognize its fatal flaws. Amidst the signs of mounting trouble and the omens of doom, we will march on with what we hope will pass as courage. Like a madman on a desert highway we are compelled to travel faster and faster toward catastrophe. Like a runaway train we can neither stop nor turn away.

We pray for our soldiers. We pray for the journalists and civilians caught in the crossfire. We pray for the people of Iraq, Britain, America and Australia, whose divisions cut deeper than any pundit dare admit. We pray for the families of those engaged in this battle. But most of all we pray for our leaders to awaken. We pray for our president to find the greatest courage of all: The courage to admit you are wrong.

One of the darkest tragedies of Vietnam was that we could never doubt. We were not allowed to doubt. Year after year, as the death toll rose and the end game became increasingly clear, we could not confront the truth. Even after the war ended with the routing of the south, few Americans came to terms with what happened there and fewer still were willing to accept responsibility.

A once exemplary journalist, who has sacrificed much to his patriotic zeal, has written that the greatest American generation was the one that survived its greatest war. There is something profoundly sad and tragic in the assumption that greatness can only be measured in war. That it might be valid at this stage of our development is more tragic still.

I do not believe in the greatness of war. I believe that the greatest generation – like the greatest government or the greatest society – will be the one that confronts the truth. The greatest generation will stand face to face with the sins of our past and the crimes of those who came before us. That generation will point us on a path of enlightenment and atonement. That generation will rekindle the flames of liberty, reclaim the sovereignty of the people, and light the way to peace. They will be the soldiers of peace and they will be our greatest heroes.

Jazz.

THE CONDUCT OF WAR

"The Bush administration, with the cooperation of the media and the courts, is going back to the pre-World War II period, when there was no serious framework of international law dealing with crimes against humanity and crimes of war."

Noam Chomsky

Thousands of civilian dead, thousands more permanently marred and crippled, yet we are to be consoled that it could be much worse if we had deliberately targeted civilians, if we had not employed precision weaponry, if we had carpet bombed as we did in Vietnam, Laos and Cambodia. It would have been much worse had used the tactics of the Iraqis, dressing soldiers as civilians, using suicide bombers, and hiding in residential areas.

It is relatively easy to sit in judgment on war crimes and crimes against humanity from the antiseptic distance our embedded media provides. It is relatively easy for Americans to say we would never resort to such inhumane measures. The fact is we do not know what measures we would take if we were confronted with the invasion of a foreign army – especially one of infinitely superior force. Would we take cover where the bombs seem certain not to drop or would we march out to be massacred with honor?

JAZZMAN CHRONICLES

It has been said that Americans have no sense of history – not even their own. Those of us who do, recognize that we were once in a similar position as that which confronts Iraq today. At the birth of this nation, confronted with the greatest military force on earth, brave American rebels virtually invented the tactics of guerilla warfare. British Generals complained bitterly that the Americans would not engage them on the field of battle as the code of military convention and honor dictated. It was the Kentucky long rifles that particularly galled them – taking cover behind trees, firing from a distance, employing cowardly tactics.

The Kentucky riflemen were not cowards or terrorists. They were men defending their country in the best manner they knew how and the Continental Army was eternally grateful. But then the Ba'ath Party of Saddam Hussein is not the Continental Congress and George W. Bush is not King George the Third – although there are striking similarities. The question arises: To what extent is the conduct of war mitigated by the nature of the government or the circumstances of the conflict?

War is hell. It cannot and should not be anything else. Yet in a world that is as yet incapable of settling international disputes without war, we have evolved certain humanitarian expectations in the conduct of war. Civilians should not be targeted as they were in previous wars. Civilian infrastructures of water, electricity and health should not be destroyed as they were in previous wars. Prisoners of war should be treated with minimal standards of decency. The role of the media should be respected by both sides, regardless their nation of origin or the content of their stories. Indiscriminate weapons (be they chemical or cluster bombs) should not be employed.

We cannot be surprised that the rules of war have been discarded in the current war. When the aggressor nation, representing an overwhelming force, claims the right to revise them as she goes, there are no rules of war.

For a time we were somewhat heartened. Having demonstrated the political costs of prosecuting an unpopular war, we thought the administration would show restraint. We thought there was a conscious effort to avoid civilian casualties, to avoid the most egregious violations in the conduct of war. But the president is not a patient man. He is an angry man who cannot understand why journalists keep asking the same silly questions: How long will it last? How many must die? How much will it cost? How badly have you miscalculated? He will not be asked such questions for long. He will have his victory and he will have it now. He will demand it at any cost.

It is fitting that the president sought the advise of Henry Kissinger in the early phases of this campaign. It was Kissinger who orchestrated the carpet-bombing of Vietnam and Cambodia. It was Kissinger who brought democracy to Iran (the Shah). It was Kissinger who deposed the evil tyrant of Argentina (Peron). It was Kissinger who befriended Pol Pot and Suharto. And it is Kissinger who cannot travel freely in the world lest he be arrested and tried as a war criminal.

America does not believe in international justice. America does not believe that war crimes apply to her. If she did, she would not threaten her enemies with charges of war crimes. She would be afraid that the killers of journalists and those who targeted a residential area with four 2000-pound bombs in an attempt to decapitate Iraqi leadership would be in line after the Iraqi generals.

We are at a critical juncture in the conduct of this war as well as the wars that will follow. If the American military, stung by political impatience and civilian resistance, decides that it will no longer be constrained, then the cost in human lives will be measured in tens of thousands. What begins with the killing of foreign journalists has no predictable end.

The defeat of the Iraqi military was always a foregone conclusion. But America has little experience in occupation – for good reason. Occupation is the business of empires. Not since Japan and the Philippines in the wake of World War II have we occupied a foreign country and our objectives then were to maintain order and ensure disarmament – not to build a democracy.

We can only hope that international pressures and the continued protest of concerned Americans will be more successful in persuading our government and its military forces to observe standards of common decency than they were in stopping the march to war.

Jazz.

THE LESSONS OF WAR

"The saving of our world from pending doom will come not through the complacent adjustment of the conforming majority but through the creative maladjustment of a nonconforming minority."

Martin Luther King, Jr.

In the confrontation of politics there is a tendency to ignore or minimize those realities that do not support one's cause. The proponents of war – including the mass of American media – have a marked tendency to ignore the dead and wounded of the Iraqi military. The lives of enemy soldiers are not to be valued though the nature of military service under a tyrannical regime is hardly voluntary. Similarly, the proponents of war are very nearly callous in their response to civilian casualties. We are instructed to admire our forces for their determined effort to avoid civilian targets and to treat the attack on foreign journalists as a tragic error when in fact it is a strategic maneuver. How can we demand that our enemies honor the code of war and the Geneva conventions when such an egregious violation is summarily dismissed with hardly a whimper from our embedded press?

By the same logic, those of us who oppose the war must acknowledge the suffering of the Iraqi people under the rule of an oppressive dictator. Though it angers us that America will not acknowledge her complicity in the crimes of this tyrant (nor will she vow never to repeat the pattern), there should be no doubt that the fall of Saddam Hussein could be an important first step toward a more equitable society. We must unashamedly proclaim our sympathy for the oppressed people of Iraq, for the Kurds and Shiites who suffered disproportionately under this tyranny, for the dissidents who were tortured, imprisoned and killed, for the wounded, the dead, and prisoners of war, and for the friends and families who survive to mourn.

Even if we do not believe that the goal of this administration is to achieve a democracy that would surely act against American interests, we can hope that whatever form of government evolves it will be better than what has passed. While we continue to oppose the policies of pre-emptive and unprovoked war, we must also serve to remind this nation that victory cannot be proclaimed until the occupation ends and something resembling democracy is in place. Even as we continue to expose the imperialist designs of the Bush Doctrine, as they lay the groundwork for war on Syria and Iran, we should also press for democratic reforms in all oppressive governments.

It is disarming to observe the reactionary measures of the Castro government in Cuba. It is insufficient to understand that this is the direct consequence of America's policies of aggression. It is inadequate to rationalize that American intelligence may in fact be active within the island nation. Unlawful detention with military-style tribunals to suppress dissidence is indefensible in any nation and international pressure must be brought to bear to reverse such practices before they become the pretense for yet another war of liberation.

Nations of the world beware: The American government is in search of war. Do not hand them an open invitation. With a crippled economy and all campaign promises broken save those to corporate sponsorship, this administration cannot be sustained without fear – without enemies both within and without. Cuba may not possess the natural resources of Iraq or Venezuela but it has long possessed the ire of the right wing ideologues that now hold the reigns of power in Washington.

We plead with the government of Cuba: Undo the damage insofar as it can be undone. We plead with the government of Syria: Return to the policies of greater tolerance and governmental restraint that once held forth promise to your people. We plead with the government of Iran: Yield to the demands of your people for greater representation and liberty. We implore the governments of America's prospective targets, as we implore her allies, to acknowledge the universal nature of fundamental human rights. We plead with North Korea, though it may be the only targeted nation with an effective deterrent: Rejoin the world community and reform. Learn from your neighbors to the south that you can achieve economic strength and social reform without sacrificing your sovereignty. We plead with all oppressive governments: Remove the cause (though it may well be only pretext) before it yields predictable effects.

The lessons of the Iraq war are many and rich with irony. It would be tragic indeed if the lessons taken were those that immediately leap to the fore:

That disarmament is merely a prelude to inevitable war; that only massive proliferation, replete with weapons of mass destruction, can deter American aggression; that severe measures of internal oppression are necessary to subvert the covert operations of American intelligence; that preemptive strike is the accepted norm of international conflict; that international law exists at the prerogative of powerful nations; that nations who do not yield to American policy are to be punished and derogated as cowards or enemies; that the united voice of the world community and the expressed defiance of the United Nations are not sufficient to alter America's path; that economic sanctions can and will be employed as an act of war against civilian populations without accountability; that America's corporate allies will be allowed to profit from war without reproach; that America requires no evidence of its accusations to justify invasion or conquest; that liberation is a relative concept and reconstruction is a secondary priority – if not an afterthought; that acts of terrorism are the only means of striking back at American power.

These are the horrors the Bush administration has unleashed upon the world with its new code of international warfare. There is not a nation on the earth that should not be concerned. Even the incredibly loyal Tony Blair has begun to glimpse the full implications of aggression without moral or legal restraint. Those silent partners who signed on to this war must now be recoiling in their seats of governance. Where does it end? How many nations will fall subject to its decree? How many must die? How much must the world's economy suffer to appease the American thirst?

Rather let us pray that the lessons taken are not the lesson intended. Let us hope beyond hope for the unexpected. Let us do what we can to persuade the target governments to embrace human rights and embark on programs of social reform. Though it would be claimed a victory by the warmongers of the White House, it is in fact the most effective and least costly means of denying and obstructing their true objectives.

For the people of America there are other equally

important lessons. First and foremost, we must vow never again to allow our government to support, finance, train and supply tyrannical regimes for political expedience. Never again should we allow our government to facilitate the use of chemical-biological weapons against a perceived "greater evil." Further, let us finally recognize that our government does not always tell the truth in matters of war and peace. They told us that Iraq was a threat to the world and made comparisons to Nazi Germany. That was a lie. They told us that Iraq was directly involved with Al Qaeda and by implication was responsible for the terrorist attack on this nation. That was a lie. They told us there was no doubt about Iraq's possession of massive stockpiles of chemical-biological weapons. That too was a lie. We should not be surprised. Our government has lied before to justify its wars. They are clearly prepared to do so again. It is time we greeted them with the skepticism they have earned.

We can only hope that something good may come of this nightmare. As we condemn the oppressive measures of enemy governments, we can only hope the same standards will be applied to our allies in Egypt, Saudi Arabia, Pakistan and Israel. We can only hope that this administration will deliver on its promise to establish a Palestinian state. We can only hope that the occupation of Iraq is neither too long nor too brutal.

As we implore the world community to press for democratic reform in other nations, we must not neglect to do so for our own. As America professes to lead a worldwide crusade for democracy, we cannot allow the people to forget that the majority of the electorate did not elect this president. The right and proper response to this outrage, to the spectacle of an election decided by a politicized Supreme Court, and to the blatant display of anti-democratic zeal, should have been the immediate repeal of an antiquated Electoral College system. That such a response was not even considered is a disgrace to our founding principles and a testament to the anti-democratic nature of party dominated politics in America.

The best outcome we can now hope for lies in the emergence of dissent. An army of protestors has risen from the malaise of American politics. We must transform the antiwar movement into a political force. In the end, we can have little hope that the party of complicity will suddenly awaken to become the party of opposition. The Democrats have a long and tortured history of Cold War aggression. They will not fight the war machine for it is not in their interest. They will ask us to be content with domestic issues while the policies of war press on.

Now is the time to create from the ashes of perpetual war a viable political alternative. Now is the time to unite all who oppose this policy of dominance and defiance of international law. Now is the time to unite those who believe passionately in democracy and civil liberties and are alarmed at the swiftness and ease with which our fundamental rights are being stripped from our legacy. Now is the time to channel the antiwar movement into the politics of independence.

Knowing that the odds are overwhelmingly against us, that the stakes are immeasurably high and the commitment is long term, it is nevertheless the best and most promising path we can choose to turn back decades of war and end the appalling decline of freedom and democracy in America.

Jazz.

A VIEW FROM AFAR

"We are truly sleepwalking through history. In my heart of hearts, I pray that this great nation and its good and trusting citizens are not in for a rudest of awakenings. To engage in war is always to pick a wild card. And war must always be a last resort, not a first choice."

Senator Robert Byrd

We have crushed the enemy. We have toppled their government, destroyed their armed forces and broken their will to resist. Whatever lines of authority remain exist at our mercy and to do our bidding. Without the rule of law the people of Iraq face an immediate crisis and future hardships beyond imagining. Without humanitarian aid on a monumental scale the prospects of famine and disease are looming. Without order massive civil strife, mob rule and tribal warfare are certain.

It seems we have been here before. It seems we have repeated history on a grander scale. Remember Afghanistan? How could we so soon forget?

With the resistance vanishing as stunningly as it had arisen in the south only days and weeks before, with American forces transitioning uncertainly from conquest to occupation, a number of questions arise not the least of which is: Will we leave Iraq as we left Afghanistan? Will we establish a dependent government whose authority cannot reach beyond the borders of its capital and charge the international community with rebuilding what we have destroyed?

There are of course critical differences between Afghanistan and Iraq. While the Afghan economy cannot be sustained without opium or international aid, the Iraqi economy is both oil rich and oil dependent. It is becoming increasingly clear that America intends to finance much of the war, the occupation and the reconstruction with Iraqi oil. What is the efficacy of invading a country and exploiting its resources to such a purpose? Will Iraqi debts to our non-cooperative allies (France, Germany, Russia) be cancelled at the risk of setting precedent for other survivors of deposed despots – even those supported by American governments? What are the realistic chances of democracy in a land where democracy may well pose the greatest risk to American interests? Can there be a democracy when the will of the people will only be honored if it is approved by a foreign power?

Clearly, there are more questions than answers and the outcomes will remain in doubt for a very long time. Those who are demanding apologies from the antiwar movement at this juncture are speaking both prematurely and disingenuously. We have not chosen to oppose this war because we thought our forces would lose. We oppose the war because it is wrong regardless of outcome. We do not support the oppression of any people but we believe there must be a better way to defeat tyranny than the employment of overwhelming military force. (As South Africa's Bishop Desmond Tutu reflected on his country's struggle for freedom: We wanted help but we did not want bombs!) We do not oppose the war simply because it was launched on false pretenses but because we believe it is only the first of many wars to be fought under similar pretenses.

If we could remove ourselves from the present circumstances to the safe distance of time, armed with the information that will reveal the truth, we could assume the perspective of objectivity. Future historians will take account of these events for they will have shaped the world to come.

Will they tell the story of a nation's valiant attempt to free an oppressed people and rid the world of dangerous weapons? Will it be the opening chapter in a crusade for democracy? Will it be the explosion that ignited the world's most dangerous region? Will it be the beginning of peace in the world's most ancient lands? Will it be the trigger to a cataclysmic chain reaction reaching around the globe? Will it be the story of noble intentions gone horribly awry or nefarious intentions with predictable results?

All these scenarios with virtually unlimited variations are now in the field of play. Anyone who claims to know with certainty how it will end might as well open shop in Marie Laveau's House of Voodoo for it is something mere mortals cannot know. What we do know with absolute clarity is that a great many will lose their lives.

Believe what you will. Believe in the purest of motives behind those who have perpetrated and sold this war to the American people and you must still answer the question: Is it worth the risk and the cost?

Leave all emotions aside. Suppress all empathy for the dead and dying. Shed no tears for the families of soldiers. Commit all your senses and faculties to the rational pursuit of logic and you must still answer no. For the risks of this war and the policy that gave it birth are so far beyond any reasoned expectations of rewards that it fails miserably the test of logic.

Now allow yourself to feel the full weight of human misery, sorrow and loss. In all fairness, balance the despair of oppression against the horrors of war. Balance the indignity and suffering of ruthless dictatorship against the indignity of foreign occupation and the terror of lawlessness. Observe the carefully edited war coverage of American media, allow it to settle in the pit of your gut, and you will inevitably discover that your heart leads to where your mind has already arrived.

When the parades have long faded and the celebrations are forgotten, the ugly truth will remain: This war is wrong. What was undertaken for false reasons and supported with false facts will end with false victory. When shallow patriotism is abated and misbegotten pride subsides, the dark truths underlying these events will sicken us and fill our hearts with shame. When we hear the truth of wartime profiteering we will shake our heads in dismay. When we hear the whispers of empire and monopoly we will gasp in disbelief. When we see the greed of international corporations exploiting the blood of the innocent we will be outraged. When we hear the story of false diplomacy and deliberate undermining of international institutions we will finally stand to exclaim:

This is not the American dream; it is the American nightmare! This is not our finest hour; it is our darkest day! The promise we once held forth to the world is broken and scattered with the remnants of Baghdad. The promise we now offer is one no nation and no people on earth wish to receive for it bears the mark of hypocrisy and betrays all that humanity holds dear.

Will it be too late? Those of us who have awakened to this nightmare must somehow awaken those around us. We must all of us come to a higher understanding. We must recognize the nature of aggression and ambition before it has gone too far. There is so little time left to alter the course of this nation. The election looms like a wall of darkness on a near horizon. These are hard times for all of us. In such times as these it is all the more difficult to stand against the onslaught of our nation's propaganda but it is all the more important that we do so. As men and women of honor and faith, what else can we do?

So as we mourn our nation's dead and console the families of the fallen, let us pledge to do all we can to ensure that no one else will die in this crusade. It is a cause unworthy of so many lives. It is a cause unworthy of one.

In the name of the founders, in remembrance of our legacy of hope and promise, we must oppose this administration now so that we can stop them at the ballot box in November 2004.

Jazz.

THE PEACE CANDIDATE

In the push to war with Iraq, something extraordinary is happening in the world of Intelligence. All the king's agents, the silent partners in former crimes against humanity – Army Intelligence, Navy Intelligence, and the Central Intelligence Agency –refused to provide false information to support the Bush administration's push to war with Iraq. Even now, in what the administration intends as the last minute of the eleventh hour, Director of Central Intelligence George Tenet states flatly there is no documented link between Al Qaeda and Saddam Hussein.

Why? Could it be that the intelligence community knows something we do not? Could it be that they know what we know: that Saddam Hussein and Osama bin Laden are bitter enemies? Could it be that they do not wish to be tried as war criminals when the truth comes out under the Freedom of Information Act twenty years down the road? Of course, if the administration has its way, the Freedom of Information Act will be repealed or rendered useless by the second wave of the attack on civil liberties. But the intelligence community may wish to hedge that bet – especially since the administration's case is so palpably weak.

One of the greatest casualties in this conflict, in terms of reputation and credibility, is Colin Powell. He knows full well this policy of preemptive strike is an abuse of power yet he presses on like a good soldier. He has singularly defined the new patriotism as a patriotism that requires no reason, demands no rational explanation, and claims no righteous cause. It is the same patriotism that has historically allowed nations to raise and support conquering armies. In its essence, in contrast to the patriotism of a democracy, it is the patriotism of a soldier; it is the patriotism of fascism.

General Powel might have been a great statesman. He might have been a great leader. He has sacrificed all that might have been to serve a false god. He has pledged his loyalty against his conscience. The loss is tragic to those of us who thought he might have become the first president of African descent. Some of us even hoped against hope that he might have become the first to win the White House as an Independent. Such thoughts now pass into the realm of pipe dreams. Were he to win the White House now he would only be another brick in the wall.

The loss is not so severe in the case of Hillary Clinton. Still many of us hoped that she would rise to the occasion. At a time when we are being catapulted into decades of unprovoked war (the policy of preemptive strike) in the rightful name of empire (the doctrine of perpetual supremacy), it is astonishing that not a single prominent Democrat will stand to challenge this White House on the most important issue we will ever face. Even Kennedy is in retreat.

If there is no opposition now, then there is no opposition. The only hope must lie outside the major parties.

The die is cast. The president has not heard the voice of a million protestors. He has not heard the dissent of our allies. Convinced of his own righteousness, he will press on in his crusade to glory. He will never doubt and he will not be plagued by question. He has succumbed to the bane of many presidents: he sees himself the hero of a great historical drama. He will confront any challenge and never falter. He will bear any cost to bend the world to his knees. Unfortunately, it is not the president or the president's children or grandchildren who will die in the march to never ending war we are embarked upon. It is never the elite who are called upon to sacrifice. It is the poor who must fight and the rest of us who must pay.

Has it escaped our attention, while we are focused on the evil of a far away land, that when oil is in short supply, oil stocks and oil profits go up? When the price of gas skyrockets, Americans will pay but the Bush people and the Cheney's and the Enron's and the Halliburton's will make a ton of money.

Again and again and again: The more they say it is not about oil, the more certain we are that it is.

The president demands to know why the Iraqis refuse to let a spy plane map the target area before the bombs begin to drop. The president demands to know why the Iraqis do not trust the inspectors, why interviews must have witnesses, and why monitors must attend the inspector's missions. These are not the whys that demand war. The inspectors have been corrupted by US influence before. They supplied intelligence to the attacking US forces in the 1998 bombing campaign. As for witnesses, inspectors have been known to lie or mislead or, in the vernacular of American politics, to spin – as some believe Hans Blix did before the United Nations Security Council.

Those who have studied the matter know the US position has no more credibility than the Iraqi position. If American and British intelligence are to be believed, why have their leads failed to yield concrete results time and time again? We know that the US infiltrated and exploited the inspectors under Ambassador Richard Butler. We know that the US deliberately undermined a successful inspections regime. We know that the US used the inspectors for intelligence purposes (to track the movements of the Iraqi leader). We know that the US sabotaged the inspections process to justify the 1998 bombing.

Who bears the greater responsibility for deceiving the American public and the world community? Iraq or the US? Why the smoke screen? Why the rhetoric, full of vitriol and misguided passion but lacking in fact? Where is the imminent threat to this nation that would justify a preeminent strike in direct violation to all principles of international justice?

We know that your administration was planning the attack on Iraq long before the war on terrorism. We know that the hawks that guide your thinking challenged you in the days following September 11, 2001 to use the attack as an excuse to go after Saddam Hussein (see Bob Woodward's soft reporting). We know that American hawks have lied to justify their wars before (see the Gulf of Tonkin). Why should we believe you now when you have given us little more than your personal hatred of a petty tyrant?

Of all the half truths and misleading statements uttered by our Secretary of State in the vaulted chambers of the UN Security Council, the most insidious was the assertion that an Al Qaeda training camp was operative in northern Iraq. The question immediately arose: If we know of an Al Qaeda camp in Iraq, in a region controlled by the Kurds under American and British protection, why then have we not eliminated it? The obvious answer is that it was more important to fabricate a Gulf of Tonkin (the lie that committed us to the Vietnam War) for Iraq than to eliminate a direct terrorist threat.

Within days of General Powell's assertion the truth began to emerge: So-called intelligence reports were lifted from twelve-year-old student papers. The alleged terrorist camp did not exist. Journalists inspecting the site found armed Kurds (our allies in this venture) and assorted video equipment. Is this a reflection of British-

American intelligence? Is this the best we can do to justify an illegal, unjust and unprovoked war that has been in the planning stages for years? You may have fooled what passes for journalists in the mainstream media press, but you did not fool the world and I pray you did not fool the people.

Either the General lied or our intelligence was false. With hundreds of thousands of lives in the balance, it will not do.

In these last days of peace before the great campaign, we must steady our resolve and return again and again to the question: What can be done?

There are at least three avenues of recourse and we must bring them all to bear with such unity of resolve that we cannot be ignored: Protest, Boycott, and the Ballot.

On February 15-16 millions of citizens across the globe took to the streets to voice their opposition to war on Iraq. None was larger than the gathering at Hyde Park in London. Tony Blair take note: You have sacrificed the support of your people by siding with the Bush doctrine of preemptive strike and perpetual superiority. It is now abundantly clear that the vast majority of people do not support this war and many, at a time when dissent is characterized as treason, are actively opposed. This is unprecedented in history.

It is becoming equally clear that the proponents of war are undaunted. What lies behind the headlong push to war now? The leaders of the warrior nations are certain that if they can manage to get this war under way, the opposition will be muted and the questions will no longer require answers. It is our solemn and patriotic duty to make sure this does not happen. When the bombing begins – and it seems all but certain that it will – the antiwar movement must grow. Those who have joined the march of protest must resolve themselves to return again and again. We must recruit like-minded friends and new converts to join the movement and march despite the inevitable confrontations that war will bring.

We must also expand our protest to the consumer realm. I am currently aware of the National Green Pages (Co-op America) that offers a comprehensive listing of environmentally and socially conscious goods and services. It is a beginning. I call upon those who possess the required knowledge to produce a boycott list of goods and services that support the war machine. In those instances where difficult choices must be made we must position ourselves to make informed choices. For instance, many of us cannot do without oil products entirely. We can assume that some oil companies (British Petroleum, Exxon) are worse than others. We need information to be able to avoid the most offensive supporters of war. We must apply the same kind of reasoning to our choices in entertainment and media. No one in the antiwar movement should be watching the programming on Fox. We should consider boycotting the products that are advertised on such programs. Keep in mind that these people are not true ideologues but, rather, capitalists. If we can register on the profit margin they will listen.

We must finally begin to prepare for the next election.

Colin Powell's presentation to the United Nations Security Council allowed us to witness what can only be described as a mass media conspiracy. As the world went about the business of debunking Powell's pathetically weak case for war, American media were united in praise. It is the sacred responsibility of a free press to question, probe and investigate. But just as the American Congress abdicated its war making powers, the media abdicated its duty to the White House public relations office.

As Independent Congressman Bernie Sanders of

Vermont recently pointed out, there is not a single nation on earth whose people support this war. Faced with this solemn and largely undeniable fact, how can we pretend to be fighting for democracy? Those on the extreme right who take a peculiar joy in pointing out that we are not a democracy are, in the literal sense, correct. If we were a democracy the opinion polls this administration proudly ignores would be sufficient to stop this war in its tracks. But we are not a democracy. We are a representative democracy (i.e., a republic), which means that our elected officials are supposed to represent our collective will. Clearly, on the matter of war with Iraq, there is a disconnect.

The founders had the foresight to leave the matter of war in the hands of those who are closest to the people. They knew that the people, who would be called upon to sacrifice their sons and daughters, would truly be reluctant warriors. That is how it should be. They did not intend for Congress to abdicate their constitutional duty. The fact that Congress has done so with such unanimity and ease is a clear indication of systemic failure. Our elected leaders do not represent the people. Their true constituencies are the corporate powers that finance their campaigns. It is not surprising that they wish to wipe their hands of an unpopular, immoral and unjustified war. It is nevertheless an act of cowardice.

We cannot look to the dominant parties to stop this march to war. It is however the nature of war that it overshadows all else – especially when the war is promised to march on for decades. If a true peace candidate, like Gene McCarthy or Bobby Kennedy in a former time, were to emerge from the silent Democrats, then we must offer our united support. Such a candidate cannot come from among those who have voted for the abdication of war powers. A peace candidate cannot come from those who have pledged to support the war once the bombing begins. An antiwar candidate cannot come from those who threw up their arms and demurred when Colin Powell gave his Security Council performance. A true antiwar candidate will not be among those who sold out our civil liberties by voting for or supporting the Patriots Act.

There are few Democrats who meet this modest set of criteria and, to my knowledge, only two (Congressman Dennis Kucinich and Former Governor Howard Dean) who have declared for president. We might look to former Senators Gary Hart (an eloquent spokesman for the anti-war movement) or Bill Bradley to emerge. We might look to Representative Sheila Jackson Lee of Texas, Kucinich of Ohio, Julian Bond of the NAACP, Independent Congressman Bernie Sanders of Vermont, activist Medea Benjamin, Congresswoman Barbara Lee of California, Jesse Jackson or Al Sharpton of the civil rights movement, and of course Ralph Nader and Winona LaDuke of the Green Party. Whomever we choose, we must unite behind one candidate. If it is a Democrat and we fail to win the party nomination, we must be prepared for that contingency.

If we turn to the third party or independent route, then we must demand that our candidate and organization pledge to remain true to Election Day. Never again should we be embarrassed by betrayal in the eleventh hour as the Green Party did in the millennial election. We must have the courage of our convictions. We must not exchange one warrior for another.

For those who believe as I do – that the dominant party system is corrupt beyond redemption – the possibility of supporting a Democratic peace candidate and thus breaking the pledge of independence is agonizing. This is the nature of war. The cynical would argue that is precisely why this faltering and illegitimate administration has chosen the path of war. It distracts us from a failing economy. It nullifies all discussion of corporate corruption, environmental assault, inadequate health and medical care, the war on civil liberties, on and on. On this matter, you may count me among the cynical.

I do not believe that the Democratic Party is capable of nominating a true antiwar candidate. I do not believe that the mainstream candidates who voted for the war on Afghanistan, for the Patriots Act, and for the abdication of war powers can now offer a substantive alternative to war. Their arguments are not whether we should proceed on the march to world dominance in the name of the war on terror but, rather, how we should proceed. This is not the impassioned opposition we require. It will not do.

We must therefore be prepared for the continued failure of the Democratic Party to offer a reasoned alternative in foreign policy. If and when they fail to nominate a true antiwar candidate we must be in position to unify behind a third party or independent alternative.

I call upon all independents, Greens, Libertarians and others to act now. Open up the lines of communication. Lay the groundwork. Build the organization. As the antiwar movement has clearly demonstrated, there is an army of volunteers ready and willing to work for this cause.

I call upon all independents, Greens, Libertarians and others to organize an Independence Day Convention with the express purpose of unifying behind a single antiwar candidate. Let the obstinacy, belligerence and arrogance of our current leaders be translated into the most important democratic development since the enfranchisement of women.

What was truly striking about the presentations at the Valentine's Day session of the United Nations Security Council was that those who stood with America in the march to war lacked passion. If this were sincerely a war against evil then the moral outrage would have been palpable. But all the passion of the day was for the cause of peace and international justice.

What becomes clear is that the American president, while bitterly dividing his own people, has united the world against him. Will he claim this as a victory too? Shattered is the unity of the North Atlantic Treaty Organization. Gone is the universal good will that was given America in the wake of September 11th. Gone too is the trust required to combat worldwide terrorism. America stands alone with only those nations who either share her vested interests or are too afraid to tell her she is wrong. By any measure, this administration's foreign policy is a failure. In his quest for greatness, this president may well go down in history as the worst of all American leaders.

It is my fear that we will be at war by the time these words go to print. If so, we must not be silenced by the false cry of patriotism. The lesson of Vietnam is that when our nation engages in an unjust and immoral war, it is our duty to do everything in our power to bring our soldiers back home.

We have it in our power to change the course of history through nonviolent and democratic means. We must embrace it.

Let us not forget that the right candidate to lead this cause, the uncompromised and impassioned candidate, died in an unlikely plane crash in the clear skies of Minnesota. Let us never forget Senator Paul Wellstone. Twice in consecutive elections senatorial candidates have gone down. Will it happen again? Is it unreasonable to expect that it may?

We must be prepared for that contingency as well. No individual is the cause and the cause must march on. They will call us traitors and we must march on. They will arrest and detain us and we must march on. They will persecute our leaders and we must march on. They will curtail our freedom of speech, undermine our right to assemble in peaceful protest, and disenfranchise those who believe as we do yet we must march on. For ours is the cause of freedom, democracy and peace. Ours is the voice of the people and the hope of human kind.

Jazz.

THE WAR PRESIDENT

It is an election year. It is the season when all promises and all actions must be taken with a great deal of cynicism. Having waited three years for an economic recovery to register beyond corporate profits, the president is searching for answers to joblessness and the loss of living wages. Having failed to slow the rising trade deficit or reduce the national debt, he renews his call for permanent tax cuts. Having failed to deliver a prescription drug benefit to seniors, he pushes through a Medicare reform bill written by the pharmaceutical and insurance industries. Having failed to find weapons of mass destruction in Iraq and failed to sell the American public on "program related activities," he promises to uncover the truth after the November election.

Moreover, the president believes the question is irrelevant. It is sufficient that Saddam Hussein had the intention to develop such weapons. It is sufficient that Saddam committed crimes against humanity though they occurred decades ago with the support and assistance of our government. It is sufficient that Saddam was a very bad man.

Given the president's insight into the mind of a "madman," he is confident he did the right thing. He is confident that American soldiers (not to mention Iraqi civilians) are not dying in a mistaken war. He is so confident that he swears, knowing what we know now, that there were no weapons of mass destruction, that there was no documented link between Saddam and Al Qaeda, he would still go to war.

"I'm a war president," he intones with a smirk.

Finally, we have found an issue upon which we can take the president at his word. If by some miracle of incredulity, you were not frightened before, now is the time. Until now, the president has been constrained by the prospect of a coming election. If he were to be reelected, the true war-seeking nature of this administration would be unleashed upon the world.

As the Bush Doctrine clearly dictates, the warlords of this White House do not require an imminent threat. They do not require international alliances or the blessings of international law. They proclaim the right to strike any nation at any time in order to advance their cause of global supremacy. They speak glowingly of democracy but their actions belie their words. Democracy notwithstanding, they are content with controlling the world's resources.

Much of the debate in civil society has been directed at the wars already begun. Considerably less has been devoted to the wars that will follow if the policy of global dominance is allowed to grow and flourish. The possibilities are as varied as moves on a chessboard but the signs are all about and they are neither disguised nor hidden. The warlords are so arrogant that they promote their dark vision openly and without shame. They boldly state their plans for remaking the world but their portraits lack depth; they are not drawn in flesh and blood detail. It is time to take them at their word and follow the lines of their intentions to real world consequences.

Immediately upon election to a second term, the Bush team will confront a monumental problem. Plainly stated, there are not enough soldiers in a volunteer military to pursue their objectives. They cannot continue to abuse the guard and reserves as they have in Afghanistan and Iraq. They will continue to press for international support but it will not be enough. They will expand the use of mercenary forces but it will not be enough. Mark it, post and save: They will find an occasion, real or fabricated, to renew military conscription. Young Americans, many of whom are woefully unprepared to make such judgments, will be compelled to choose between military service and civil disobedience. The antiwar movement will grow tenfold and the guard and reserves will come home to fight the battle on America's streets. The machinery created by the Patriot Act will be brought to bear on its members. More divided than ever, America will be at war.

Undaunted and eager to secure his legacy, the president will be in search of war. The search will begin where the staff has already been planted: The Middle East. Those of us who have listened carefully have come to realize that when he speaks of terrorist ties in Iraq he is no longer summoning Al Qaeda (perhaps he never was). Rather, he is speaking of Hezbollah, the Lebanese organization most prominently known for its efforts to free Palestine from Israeli occupation. Regardless of how one assesses the organization, expanding the war on terrorism to include Hezbollah would engage the entire Arab and Islamic worlds, beginning with Syria, Lebanon and Iran. Saudi Arabia would be forced to take sides: Us or them?

In this manner, the misbegotten policies of one president could easily evolve into a war of centuries, a battle of civilizations, and a march of death and destruction that would surpass anything the world has yet known. While I do not believe it is what this president intends, the ends of warfare are often unpredictable and this administration, despite its vaunted brainpower, has displayed a startling lack of foresight.

The Middle East scenario is the most dangerous we will face. At its worst, it is Armageddon. At best, it is a horrifying waste of human life -- a waste that would not be possible except for the liquid treasure beneath their sand. It is a scenario that engages the second of the president's "axis of evil."

The third member of the exclusive club is North Korea. In the lead up to the war in Iraq, many in the antiwar movement pointed to North Korea with the taunt: Why not attack them? We know that they possess weapons of mass destruction. They felt secure in their challenge because it would be sheer madness to attack a nuclear power whose immediate response would bring death to hundreds of thousands of innocent civilians in Seoul.

To this I could only shake my head in dismay. What would we say if the president accepted the challenge?

It should not go unnoticed that the administration has pushed the development of a new class of tactical nuclear weapons. This alone is evidence that the madness of King George is taking hold and its names are Rumsfeld, Cheney, Wolfowitz and Perle. Given the "bunker busting" bombs we have already demonstrated, it is unlikely that the tactical nuke is for this purpose. It is more likely that they are designed for a preemptive strike that would decimate all nuclear facilities in a target nation before that nation could strike back. While such a strike could be applied to North Korea, it could also apply to Pakistan -- especially in the event of another military coup. Since the destruction would be somewhat contained, America could claim humanitarian motives but the nuclear nightmare would be upon us and the world would shudder in horror.

As terrifying as these scenarios may be, we cannot leave the future wars in faraway lands. Latin America has long been the favorite playground of American warlords. When presidential adviser Condoleezza Rice prematurely expressed satisfaction at the news of a coup in Venezuela, she not only signaled American approval but probable

American involvement. The admission was particularly revealing because Hugo Chavez was a lawfully elected president. Support for a military takeover exposed the lie of our support for democracy. It is also revealing that Venezuela has the richest oil reserves in the hemisphere.

All of Latin America (as in Africa and elsewhere) is suffering under the failed policies of the U.S. dominated World Trade Organization (WTO) and the International Monetary Fund (IMF). Electorates have increasingly turned to progressive, anti-American parties. The people have begun to suspect that the WTO-IMF policies have not failed at all. Rather, they have enabled international corporations, America's partners in global dominance, to take control of their natural resources. Poverty is good business except that it has a tendency to breed discontent. Discontent has a tendency to breed organized opposition and organized opposition has a tendency to be labeled "terrorism."

America has a rich tradition of intervention in the region with only minimal cover. In Chile, 9/11 has a very different meaning: It was the day the CIA overthrew Salvador Allende and supplanted him with a monstrous dictator. Throughout the region, the people are well acquainted with American foreign policy. Under prior administrations, the excuse was always the drug war or the Cold War. Now, it is the war on terror.

If the administration engages in Latin America, it will hope to draw Fidel Castro into the conflict. If it succeeds, the administration will achieve the one goal it cherishes even more than the overthrow of Hugo Chavez: Regime change in Cuba.

These are but a handful of the possibilities that await the second term of a Bush administration. There are many others (Haiti, the Philippines, Liberia, Somalia, Sudan, Malaysia, Nigeria, on and on). No longer will they belong in the realm of screenwriters and novelists. They will no longer be remote and some of them will most assuredly become stark realities.

We cannot afford to test the hypotheses. We cannot afford to gamble the lives of so many soldiers and innocent bystanders. The world cannot afford a war president in the White House. For though we are shocked by the losses already sustained, they are but minor compared to the profound horror the future may reveal.

The lords of war and avarice will go to the ends of the world to maintain their hold on the reigns of power. If we fail to deny them, we will become the generation that lives forever in infamy and shame. Often has it been foretold but never with more urgency: We hold the future in our hands.

For all the derision heaped upon him in a campaign of partisan politics, Howard Dean is right: We have the power.

It is time we used it.

Jazz.

VOLUME III

THE ANTIWAR MOVEMENT

CONTENTS

CONTENTS

PREFACE

THE LONG WARS

Is it enough to fight the good fight? That is the perpetual question to all dissidents and members of the resistance to governments and policies that refuse to change. How long can a resistance movement be maintained when year after year there are no palpable rewards? We march, we fight, we resist, we write and still the wars rage on and on.

The Vietnam War tested our strength and endurance. Many turned away from the antiwar movement to seek what seemed more achievable goals in alternative cultures, environmental awareness, civil rights, civil liberties, on and on. Many of us turned inward and sought to develop our own personalities, skills and knowledge. We abandoned the university square for its classrooms. We did not forget the war; we simply left it behind.

Few of us suspected that the wars in Afghanistan and Iraq would outlast all prior wars. The resistance was more severely tested than ever.

Perhaps because we endured Vietnam and finally saw an end (albeit one ordered by the enemy in Richard Nixon), we did not abandon the antiwar movement. When our pro-war contemporaries went about their business, pausing to remember the war on holidays and special occasions, we lived with war. We remembered. We protested. We marched. We voted.

Still, the war has dragged on so long that the intensity and the numbers in the active resistance had to dissipate. We have lives to live. We have families to feed. We go on with our lives and we do what we can.

These Chronicles represent the sustained resistance to the longest wars America has ever fought. They date from July 2004 to February 2012 when a new president at long last began reducing our military engagements in both wars.

Barack Obama's ascendancy to the White House was achieved partly because of the antiwar movement and the changing sentiment of the American people. He should not forget that his promise to end the war in Iraq and withdraw our soldiers from Afghanistan has not yet been accomplished and neither should we.

Jazz.

IRAQ AND VIETNAM

THEY WON'T KILL THEIR OWN

Confronted with the Tet Offensive in 1968, American warlords publicly professed confidence in our campaign to liberate Viet Nam. There was a light at the end of the tunnel. Secretly, they lamented the ineffectiveness of South Vietnamese forces: Vietnamese would not kill Vietnamese. We know now that the presidency of Lyndon Johnson would not survive long enough to see that light revealed as Vietnamese liberation.

Confronted with the rising tide of Iraqi resistance in the wake of Fallujah, our president assures us it is only the remnants of Saddam loyalists and isolated foreign terrorists. Secretly, our generals know better. They have expanded the targets to include noncooperative journalists (Al Jazeera) and civilians who refuse to collaborate with the occupying force. Like Operation Phoenix in Viet Nam (a CIA operation that killed 20,000 South Vietnamese), we are targeting the very people we are supposed to be liberating. Openly, our warlords lament the ineffectiveness of the Iraqi security force. It seems we must learn again another lesson of Viet Nam: Iraqis will not kill Iraqis – at least not for a foreign invader.

What has become clearer than any light at the end of the tunnel is that there can be no American victory in Iraq. The people of Iraq have delivered a strong and unambiguous message: Victory is an end to the occupation. They do not believe we are liberators. They believe we are there to secure their oil and to establish a permanent military base in the Middle East. As long as our president flatly refuses to disavow such claims, those beliefs will persist and harden into a conviction that will feed the resistance. We cannot kill enough Iraqis to suppress the will of the nation and the more we kill, the stronger the resistance will become.

The president is right for the wrong reason: Failure is not an option because it has already been secured. America will never be allowed to establish permanent bases in Iraq. America will never be allowed to control Iraqi oil. And whatever form of government evolves in Iraq, it will be one of their own choosing.

The Vietnamese fought against foreign invaders for centuries before securing independence. Are the Iraqis so very different? How many lives are we prepared to sacrifice to find out? How many lives must be lost before America can admit we are wrong? How many more must we ask to give their lives for this mistake?

You cannot convert wrong to right by prolonging the occupation. You can only increase the cost in lives, money, and the respect of all nations. You can only fuel the fires of our true enemies and further alienate our true friends.

Let us undo the harm insofar as it can be undone. Let us use our resources not for weapons but to rebuild the nations we have destroyed. Let us make amends as best we can. Let us admit wrong and withdraw our troops. Let us pledge our support to the United Nations. At this critical juncture, we can do little else.

Jazz 21 April 2004.

JOHNNY GOT HIS GUN

David went to Canada, Dick received a college deferment, Charlie was granted conscientious objector status, George joined the National Guard, Sam was classified 4-F, and Johnny got his gun (see Dalton Trumbo's *Johnny Get Your Gun*).

We all remember what happened to Johnny. He was shot down in Nam, a victim of the Tet Offensive, reduced to the unending nightmare of a living, thinking mind trapped in a body paralyzed to the eyes. He learned to communicate by blinking and by blinking he communicated the horror that was his life.

To those who believe that military conscription is the answer to our growing need for soldiers: There never was and never will be an equitable draft. Those who believe that the inequities of the past can be corrected by legislative means have lost contact with reality. The wealthy and elite will never serve involuntarily and those who volunteer will serve in a manner their wealthy and elite parents demand.

The heroism of John Kerry and John Fitzgerald Kennedy belies the greater truth: The commanders of our military forces are neither fools nor morality's slaves. They know who butters the bread and who stands between them and promotion. They will not send the prodigal sons and daughters of the ruling class to glorious death on the battlefields of foreign lands.

Johnny got his gun because he was nobody's son, because he had no pedigree, because he had no connections to members of congress or secretaries of state, and because no one bothered to tell him the truth. No one bothered to tell him there were alternatives. Johnny got his gun because Johnny was a common boy who would never grow into a common man. Johnny got his gun because his life did not matter and his name was not on the social register.

Military conscription is a crime against humanity. Rationalizing the morality of an equitable draft is like condoning slavery or forced prostitution if it can be applied to all victims without prejudice. How is it easier to compel a child to kill than to force a child into hard labor or acts of depraved sex? It is an abomination and one that any mother understands by gut instinct.

Future generations will look back on this practice in wonder and amazement at how primitive this culture was, at how callously we sent our young and innocent souls to their ends, at how carelessly we threw away the best of our species, and how cruel we were to condemn the powerless to horrors beyond belief.

Johnny got his gun and 58,000 of his brothers came home in a box. The Vietnamese did not require conscription yet millions of their Johnnies died by our conscripted hands. Hundreds of thousands of Johnny's brothers came home with broken bodies and hundreds of thousands more came home with broken hearts, broken minds, broken spirits, and souls shattered by the gruesome realities of war.

Will we send our Johnny off to war once again? Will we add our Mary to the parade? Will we explain to them why they must march? Will we explain why they must die? Will we ask them if they have a different mind? Will we disdain them if they do?

There is no greater scourge on society than to have condemned its own children to the hell of war. There is no greater shame a parent can bear than to have sent a child to the killing fields. There is no child that can understand or forgive such betrayal. There is no medicine that can heal such deep wounds.

Cry, America! Weep for your children! For as sure as votes go uncounted in Florida, your children will be compelled to war.

The people who now hold the reigns of power in this nation have begun to change their tune. When once they spoke of decades of war, now they speak of centuries. If we do not stand up to them now, we are condemned to mourn forever. If we do not stop them while there is still time, our great grandchildren will curse our remains.

We know the way to right this wrong, to end this nightmare and to settle this war on terror. It does not require greater armies and greater weapons; it requires greater understanding. It does not require commanders and warriors; it requires diplomats and peacemakers. War itself is the curse of human kind. We must find a better way.

We have no business in Iraq. Let us withdraw and make amends as best we can. Let us devote our resources, our genius, our devotion and raw effort to the development of alternative sources of energy.

If America harnesses the power of the sun, the power of wind and running water, and the power of ingenuity, there is no limit to what we can accomplish. If we no longer need the remains of dinosaurs, Johnny will not need a gun.

And Johnny's mother will not need to cry herself to sleep.

Jazz 17 July 2004.

4F AND OTHER HEROES

I was there. I read the book.

Denied secular conscientious objector status, I fasted for months as I traveled the nation's highways by thumb. By the time I reported for my induction physical, I weighed less that 85 pounds, which at a height of 5'9" met the criterion for disqualification from military service: 4F.

Like the president and the vice president, I was a draft dodger. Unlike our nation's leaders, my actions were a matter of principle. I believed then, as I believe now, that our leaders had led us into an immoral war. I believed that the true metaphor for Vietnam was Native American genocide. I did what I had to do to avoid serving in a cause I considered nothing less than sanctioned mass murder.

It was 1972. The option that Dick Cheney exploited five times (student deferment) was no longer available. The National Guard was booked. Only the elite could excuse themselves from a low lottery number. Mine was 31 – until then, it had been my lucky number. In 1972, it became my ticket to hell.

Some shot themselves. Others refused to step forward and accepted the legal consequences. Some went to Canada. Others went to jail. Some ended up in Nam. Some fought and others got high. Some were wounded and others died.

In the early days of the war, volunteering was understandable. We were Americans. Our values were defined by coaches and cheerleaders. Our history books glorified war. America was always right. Our soldiers only fought for freedom and democracy, never for lesser motives. By 1972, however, that façade had fallen. The truth was a neon sign on every corner. It screamed from every college campus. It marched in the streets and declared itself in music, theater, culture, politics, books and lifestyles. By 1972, the deeply disturbing reality of Vietnam was clear for all to see.

I was in the army of resisters and not one of us was a coward. We were young and angry. Our government had betrayed us. We knew better than to kill for all the wrong reasons. Vietnam was neither our country nor our cause. If we were Vietnamese in those tragic years, we would have fought against the foreign invaders. We knew about Operation Phoenix (20,000 South Vietnamese rounded up and executed in a CIA black op). We knew about My Lai. We saw soldiers come home unfit to live in civil society. It was not because the country had turned its back. It was because they were trained killers in a world where killing human beings differed little from killing cockroaches. So many of the Vietnam veterans were disturbed because what they had done in the name of their country was disturbing.

Was it a crime for John Kerry to testify about the crimes against humanity that clearly happened in Nam? Or was it a crime that our government sanctioned them? Like Abu Ghraib squared, Vietnam was the ultimate modern-day demonstration of the dehumanization process. What began as dehumanizing the enemy ended up dehumanizing our own.

When the troops came home, we did not treat them as heroes because neither they nor we regarded what they had done as heroic. Contrary to popular mythology, spitting on soldiers was not a common occurrence. Those who opposed the war extended our hands in sympathy and, in return, many of the returning veterans spoke truth to power. They joined the cause that ended the war and saved both American and Vietnamese lives. Among them was John Kerry.

Where was young George Bush? Was he opposed to the war? Apparently not. Did it bother him that hundreds of thousands of his contemporaries were compelled to serve in a faraway land? Apparently not.

We may have a difference of opinion regarding those who opposed the war and still served. We may have a difference of opinion regarding those who opposed the war and refused to serve. We may even have differing opinions regarding those who supported the war and served. The one thing we can all agree on is that those who supported the war and yet avoided service – whether by conscientious objection, student deferment, exile or the National Guard – were motivated more by self-preservation than by any sense of duty.

Is such a man qualified to be president and commander? Should we consider what happened decades ago as a measure of a man's character? Only the people can judge – beginning with those who were there, not only in Nam but also on the streets of America in the hour of greatest need.

We took a vow back then and we have never betrayed it. We will not forget Nam. Ever.

Jazz 27 August 2004.

THE UNTOLD STORY OF WAR

On Sunday, January 9, 2005, nineteen-year-old Andres Raya shot two police officers, killing Sergeant Howard Stevenson of the Ceres Police Department, and was himself killed in the ensuing gun battle.

Raya had served seven months in Iraq with the 2nd Battalion, 4th Marines of the 1st Marine Division. Though he served in the infamous Sunni Triangle, the military denied he had participated in the assault on Fallujah.

Andres Raya and Howard Stevenson will not be entered on the official casualty list for the war in Iraq but they are both casualties of the war as certainly as the Iraqi civilians who were not targeted by American bombs but died under them just the same.

Characterized as a possible suicide by cop, the story of Andres Raya made national news because it was captured on the surveillance tape of a local liquor store. It is symbolic of the untold story of war. In the coming years, thousands of similar stories will unfold in towns and cities across America. They will not make the national news wires. They will not be featured on television newscasts. They will not usually be so dramatic: Stories of domestic abuse, alcohol or drug related rage, homelessness and crime statistics. They will only be reported as local interest stories, buried in the back pages where few will notice – like the fallen soldiers themselves.

The untold stories of war fall under the category of collateral damage. Hundreds and thousands of trained killers survive their missions only to come home to a life for which they are no longer prepared. They have seen what men and women should not see. They have engaged in operations that brought them face to face with the death of innocents, women and children. They have lived in an environment where no one could be trusted, where the father of a smiling, waving child could be the enemy, where local hatred for the occupying army is ubiquitous, and where they learn to hate and kill indiscriminately, before an unknown enemy strikes first.

The untold story of the first Gulf War was sickness and infirmity, a debilitating syndrome neglected and denied by both the government and the military. The untold story of Vietnam was a lost generation of soldiers not unlike Andres Raya, whose family and friends agree, did not want to go back to Iraq.

Raya was recruited at Ceres High School where Staff Sergeant Robert Tellez pegged him as a possible career man. He knew what he was signing up for but, when he returned, as Araceli Valdez told *San Francisco Chronicle* reporters Meredith May and Matthew B. Stannard, "That man on the liquor store surveillance cameras wasn't our cousin. He wasn't Andy anymore."

According to the Marines, while Raya's battalion was engaged in the assault on Fallujah, his unit was not involved and Raya saw little direct combat.

According to Alex Raya: "He told us about going into homes and shooting them up. He said he wouldn't pull the trigger a lot because he didn't want to kill anyone. He kept saying it was a war that had no point, that it was all for oil, and it made no sense that we were after bin Laden but went after Saddam Hussein instead."

He had nightmares, often staring into space and locking himself in his room for hours.

As Marisa Raya said, "How can you see the things he saw and not be affected in your soul?"

To those who continue to ignore the deceptions and

lies of our government because of their overriding need to support our troops, take a good hard look at Andres Raya. He was a Marine, strong and tough as they come. He wanted to make a life for himself. He wanted his family to be proud. He was not so different from any other mother's son or daughter until he came home from the war.

At a time when the military is hitting our high schools, malls and soda shops, looking for fresh recruits, talking tough about patriotism, honor and duty, who will tell the story of Andres Raya? Who will give testimony to the dark side of war? Who will talk about the Gulf War Syndrome, the soldiers who threw their medals away, or the veterans who could no longer endure? Who will tell them why daddy turned to drugs or ended his own life? Who will tell them about *Hearts and Minds* or *Johnny Get Your Gun*?

It is time to get the military out of our high schools or, if they will not, it is time to call on the veterans of war for the other side of truth. If we send our kids to war without giving them the full and unvarnished picture of what they will face, we are almost as guilty as the warlords themselves, who never served, who never risked their own lives or the lives of their loved ones, but who are perfectly willing to raise the flag for the Fourth of July parade.

Jazz 12 January 2005.

THE GATES OF HELL
OCCUPIED IRAQ

"All hope abandon, ye who enter here."

Dante Alighieri

"The way down to hell is easy. The gates ... stand open day and night. But to retrace one's steps and escape to upper air – that is toil, that is labor."

Virgil

On March 22, 2003, the Department of Defense announced the identities of two Marines killed in action in Southern Iraq. Second Lieutenant Therrel S. Childers of Mississippi and Lance Corporal Jose Gutierrez of California became the first Americans to die for the ambitions of the White House warlords and the little man with an inferiority complex who should never have become president – even in his dreams.

History is a strange and fascinating tale. What historians make of this president will be a fiercely fought battle between those with integrity and those with a political agenda. While past presidencies have been held somewhat in check by the knowledge that historians will hold them to account, the current lot believes it is immune to historical judgment. They are determined to control the pen with which the tale is told. They will discredit all accounts contrary to their interests and reduce history itself to the basest form of propaganda.

If it were not so tragic, it would be amusing to observe the machinations of media in reporting the war and occupation of Iraq. In the absence of compelling distracter stories, they seem to have awakened from a long slumber (if only momentarily) to discover there is still a war going on. They pretend that the latest series of attacks represent a sudden upsurge in response to political events. In truth, the violence has been a steady rumble, geared only to opportunity, and the media treatment is a cover for their collective failure to report on the ongoing disaster.

On April 20, a fifth attempted assassination of interim Prime Minister Ayad Allawi fails, four Iraqis are killed and thirteen wounded in Baghdad. Three police officers are killed, nineteen bullet-ridden bodies are identified in Haditha, and fifty bodies float down the Tigres, confirming rumors of mass hostage taking and executions.

On April 22, a car bomb near a Baghdad mosque kills eleven and wounds 20, the bodies of nineteen soldiers are found near Baiji, a government official in Mosul is assassinated, and fourteen mercenaries are killed when their chopper is shot from the sky.

On April 23, a roadside bomb kills nine soldiers and wounds 20 outside Baghdad, another kills a civilian in Samara, another on the road to the Baghdad airport kills one and wounds seven, more bombs kill two soldiers and injure three in Yusifiya, two civilians are killed in Baquba, and two more are killed in Basra with two children wounded.

President Bush appeals to Congress in his weekly radio address for another $81.9 billion for the war effort. His voice is confident and his words are optimistic. Progress is being made. The Iraqi security forces outnumber US forces. "Like free people everywhere, Iraqis want to be defended and led by their own countrymen."

On April 24, bombs in Baghdad kill fifteen, wounding 40, while bombs in Tikrit kill six police and wound 35 unidentified others.

The march of death continues unabated, unaffected by the words of the president or the latest moves of the Iraqi government. The end of April and the beginning of May bring a torrent of violence, death and bloodshed. News stories roll out a daily death toll of mostly anonymous victims: 50, 70, 120, 140, 200, 245 dead and at least twice that many wounded. Occupation forces round up the usual suspects but indiscriminate mass arrests have no discernable effect. The violence continues. The civil war is on. A reporter reveals it now costs $35,000 for a six-mile taxi ride to the airport. Lacking a small mercenary army, you cannot get in and you cannot get out.

Welcome to Baghdad: The Gates of Hell are open for business.

Like the fall of Saddam, the appointment of an interim government and the election, itself, the christening of a new ministry did not have the desired effect. The vast majority of casualties on the side of the occupying forces are no longer American soldiers; they are allied Iraqis, police, militia and contractors – the euphemism of choice for mercenaries. How much is a man paid to enter the Gates of Hell and descend to its lower depths like Dante and his guide Virgil? It is a closely guarded secret and one reason for the extraordinary cost of this endeavor. There is a special place in Dante's inferno for those who perform evil deeds for money and an even crueler place for those who paid the hired torturers, killers and assassins so that their hands would remain unstained.

Iraq may not approach the mind-numbing destruction

of Vietnam but it is more resembling Algiers with every passing day. For those who require historical review, Algiers was the last stop for French ambitions of a new Napoleonic era. At the beginning of the Muslim uprising, the insurgents were demeaned as terrorists and thugs. The insurgency would never last. The people of Algiers loved their French masters. The people of France, though never directly consulted, supported the continued occupation. The Battle of Algiers raged on for six years. At every turn, the French proclaimed imminent victory. At every turn, they were wrong. Indiscriminate killings, mass imprisonment, torture, bombs carried in baskets by women and children, assassinations, strikes, and the insurgency refused to die. It would calm until the occupiers grew complacent and then it would erupt again. After six years of costly failure, the endgame was clear (in fact, it was always clear) and the verdict in French public opinion finally sealed its fate. Though they left a nation torn and tattered, impoverished and divided, the occupation of Algiers failed. Historically, the only occupations that ever succeeded were those that employed mass murder and genocide (i.e., the conquest of North America).

The occupation of Iraq will reach the same inevitable conclusion as Algiers. It is only a question of how long and how costly. Much depends on the verdict of the American people. We have been shielded from the daily horrors of Iraq but we cannot escape our fair share of responsibility. It would be too easy to fix all of the blame for the atrocities of this war at the president's feet but it would be neither just nor accurate. He has had his collaborators, beginning with Tony Blair and ending with those who sold out at first sighting of the purple finger of fate.

The White House has the excuse of rose-colored glasses. They were blinded by their own twisted sense of destiny. The turncoats should have known better than to believe in the value of a media controlled event. They would have known if they were not so eager to cut and run. It is difficult being right in America today. It is difficult to maintain a career in the media and oppose governmental outrage. It is difficult proclaiming the obvious: that both dominant parties are wrong, have been wrong, and will continue to be wrong as long as money is on the table.

"All we like sheep have gone astray." Isaiah (53:6).

Critics of the Bush administration are wrong when they claim that the warlords are victims of their own faith. If they had any faith at all, they would dismantle the Gates of Hell now while it is still possible. If they believed in the sanctity of life and the rewards of virtue, they would have ended the suffering long ago.

"Long is the way and hard, that out of hell leads up to light." John Milton.

I did not know Therrel Childers or Jose Gutierrez. I did not know their friends, loved ones and families though I am relatively certain they had them. I did not know their mothers or fathers or the enduring grief they must live with as the years of absence accumulate. I do not know the names of the first Iraqis to die in this war but I am no less certain they had friends, loved ones and families as well. I am certain that their sorrow and grief is no less enduring. I am certain that their numbers are far greater and their nightmare is the ongoing hell of their daily lives under the occupation of their native land.

Jazz 5 May 2005.

IMPEACH BUSH: US OUT NOW!

"Our focus is not on the past. It's on the future."

Scott McClellan, White House Spokesman

How convenient to focus on the future when the past is a compelling indictment of criminal and immoral behavior. If it were an adequate explanation, then Richard Nixon would have completed his second term, Lyndon Johnson would have sought reelection, and the Nuremberg trials would not have been convened.

Beyond the incredulity of the president's response to a growing body of evidence that his administration cooked the books to justify an illegal and unjustified war, the crime is not limited to the past. It is ongoing and has no end in sight.

When you are caught in the process of committing a crime, whether it is a common burglary or a war of naked aggression, you do not ask leave to consummate the act. Should this be any less apparent when there are hundreds of thousands of lives in the balance?

This nation went to war on allegations our leaders knew with absolute clarity were false and malicious. Stubbornly clinging to the lie while slandering those who bring the truth to public light only compounds the crime with arrogance and obstruction – the very crimes that ultimately ended the reign of Nixon.

Under the leadership of this president, America is

directly responsible for the massive destruction of an innocent nation's infrastructure, a monumental waste of desperately needed resources, and the loss of more lives than we are willing or able to count.

The defenders of war and the White House may be right in one respect. The Downing Street Memo is nothing new. It is like waiting for an autopsy to confirm a death. After a steady stream of revelations and testimonials from impeccable sources such as Ambassador Joseph Wilson, counter-terrorism analyst Richard Clarke, and former Treasury Secretary Paul O'Neill, as well as the targeted leaks of the CIA, British intelligence and the State Department, anyone who did not know that the war was ordained at Bush V. Gore, was not following the news. Anyone who did not know that intelligence was shaped to policy is deliberately uninformed.

Unfortunately, the White House press corps (also know as the American mainstream media) has become very adept at obscuring the truth with subterfuge. Like a mantra, the lies of war are repeated until they become accepted truths. Our leaders were betrayed by a massive intelligence failure. Like an illusionist, the war propagandists offer up an endless parade of dazzle, titillation and outrage. The bug-eyed runaway bride gains more attention than the affairs of state (The people want to know!) and Congress follows suit by calling a special session to decide the fate of Terri Schiavo.

It has become necessary to repeat the truth over and over again until the most reticent of news outlets can no longer ignore it. As it was in the days of Watergate, so it is today. Both the media and the political powers are entrenched. Their primary motive is not to reveal or embrace the truth but to secure their power base by any and all means.

At the time of Watergate, however, it was the

blessing of this nation that the Washington Post was an island of integrity in a sea of indifference. The blessing now is that the internet has given birth to an alternate universe of knowledge, information and analysis. Neither the Times nor the Post has the power to ignore Memogate to a quiet death. The bloggers gave it wings and they will keep it flying. Members of Congress are jumping on board not out of courage or a sudden resurgence of conscience but of desperation. The truth is coming out. Like the bulging waters of a broken dam, those gutless politicians who are not braced for impact will be swept away like yesterday's news. Those who voted for the war, the Patriot Act and the continued occupation, who christened Freedom Fries and chastised the antiwar movement for treachery and fanaticism, are scrambling now for higher grounds. The warning has sounded; the tsunami is upon them.

Those of us who recognized the truth and opposed the war from its inception owe it to the collective conscience of the nation to continually point out that it was never difficult to decipher. George Bush may be charming at a certain level to a certain segment of society but he was never good at hiding the truth. He wanted war so bad he flaunted it like a chest-thumping gorilla. He ordered Shock and Awe while the disarmament of Iraq was literally in progress just so he could mark the anniversary of Daddy's War with his own. It could not have been more obvious.

Those who wish to jump on the antiwar, anti-occupation bandwagon now, you are long overdue and welcome but do not ask for special recognition. Let it be recorded in history that America's political leaders (with the exception of the Congressional Black Caucus and very few others) were slow to act and that they deferred until shifting public opinion made it tenuous not to declare opposition.

As for those who continue to support the president, his wars, his occupations and his doctrine of perpetual war, may whatever deity you confide in (for I am told you are people of faith) forgive you. As you stood with the president, so may you fall. It is very late in the day and there is a price to be paid in blood, treasure and political capital for every moment we continue to prolong the inevitable.

We have lost another war we should never have begun. We have darkened the dignity of the nation. We have dimmed the light of freedom and democracy. We have lowered the flag in mourning and in shame and we have held it to public ridicule.

We cannot regain what we have lost by continuing to prosecute the occupation and expanding the war to other nations under the familiar Vietnam fantasy that just a little more will turn the tide. There is no winning an endless war and the enemy we have chosen to fight (ultimately, the entire universe of Islam) will never yield. We can only hope to limit the damage, make amends and reparations.

Let us begin now, before another life is lost or another dollar cast to the wind, by announcing the withdrawal of all American troops and simultaneously removing the fundamentally flawed Commander-in-Chief that led us tragically astray.

Jazz 18 June 2005.

LIGHT AT THE END OF THE TUNNEL

"I think they're in the last throes of the insurgency." Vice President Dick Cheney.

When Dick Cheney's optimistic assessment of the war in Iraq was greeted with derision, he responded by suggesting that his critics needed to consult a dictionary on the meaning of the word "throes."

Throes: 1. Pangs, spasms. 2. Hard or painful struggle.

The vice president's problem is that his critics were not responding to the meaning of the word "throes" but to the adjective preceding it.

Last: Final, having no successor; after all others in time or order.

No one disputes that there will be violent upheaval in the days and weeks ahead. A day without eruptions of violence in Baghdad, Mosul, Tikrit, Fallujah or anywhere else where American troops are engaged, would be shocking indeed. Only today, the media report dozens dead from suicide attacks in Mosul while mortar attacks in Baghdad claim another eight lives, including the Baghdad Chief of Police, and the official death toll for American soldiers climbed another notch.

The vice president is either hopelessly naïve or

deceitful beyond belief. This from the same man who brought us "We will be greeted as liberators" and "We know where the weapons of mass destruction are" and "Saddam is in league with Al Qaeda" and "We have to fight there so we won't have to fight them here."

A day in the life of a Baghdad resident is filled with gridlock, triggered by waves of violence and counter violence, as Operation Lightning gives way to Operation Thunder, as bombings, suicide attacks, assassinations and executions kill countless innocents and not so innocents alike. Life goes on or it does not and the last throes of a Christian fundamentalist crusade can last a thousand years. In a war zone, mourning is brief and constant.

The last (as in "most recent") time we were referred to the dictionary it was that master of circumlocution, Secretary of Defense Donald "Rummy" Rumsfeld, directing us to look up the meaning of the word "slog." I did. It has two meanings. One is to hit hard and the other is to plod as in to proceed slowly and tediously. Apparently, the Secretary meant that we were going to hit the insurgency hard, not that we were facing a protracted struggle against a determined enemy.

As our soldiers come home in boxes, guarded from media coverage, are we supposed to take comfort that the leaders of this war are expert in parsing words? Are we supposed to be impressed, if not by their war strategy, then by their vocabularies?

Neither the soldiers nor the Iraqi people are comforted by the optimistic views of American politicians or Generals. They have learned to recognize a smokescreen and simply walk away.

General John Abizaid suggests on CNN that we are at the 21st mile of a marathon. He insists we are fighting with the Iraqis, not against them. Place yourself in the boots of an Iraqi soldier. How did you arrive at this place? There are no jobs in Iraq but security. Police are even more vulnerable than soldiers. Who is the enemy? Will you storm the homes in a Baghdad neighborhood on the orders of an American commander? Will you fight against the insurgents? Little wonder that so few Iraqi soldiers are considered capable of fighting without American "support." In this context, "We've got your back" has an entirely different meaning and one that does not require reference to a dictionary. If you ask them before the embedded cameras, they will give the words the Americans want to hear but they, along with all of Iraq, are praying for the occupiers to leave.

"I would say we have been relatively successful in reducing the violence in Baghdad," says Major General William Webster. Relative to what: the Gaza strip?

"It seems we are reaching a point of no return," says Abed Qadeer, a Baghdad resident.

"The insurgency is in its last throes." Look it up in the dictionary.

The president goes on the road to exploit his bully pulpit, to spend his political capital, to practice the fine art of persuasion. No one – not even Karl Rove – has the heart to confide the truth. He is a lame duck. He has no pulpit. His capital is spent. His account (like the nation's) is beyond empty and his art is beyond lost.

I am once again reminded of the former opposition leader to Tony Blair in old Britannia, who ended every round of questioning in the House of Commons with "and nobody believes a word you say."

There is no need to look it up in the dictionary. We are not losing the war; we have lost it. Any member of Congress who does not join the cry for immediate withdrawal (even as we negotiate with the insurgent leaders) must feel the pangs of popular uprising. You are in the last throes of your reign. We must not allow the party of opposition to offer up a softer version of pro-war. If the occupation is not over by the midterm elections, there is only one issue and it is not social security.

As the weeks roll by and the body counts rise, the last throes seem more and more like the light at the end of the tunnel and the light at the end of the tunnel appears more and more like a desert mirage. Iraq is Vietnam. Look it up in the history books.

Jazz 28 June 2005.

SCHIZO SCHERZO: THE LAST WALTZ

Schizo: Split, irrational, bizarre.

Scherzo: A playful movement in a symphony.

The psychological theory of cognitive dissonance holds that two incompatible thoughts cannot be held in one mind simultaneously – or rather, they cannot be held without damage to the psyche.

For example, if you believe that good people do not do bad things and that Joe is a good person and then learn that Joe hit his wife, you are confronted with a dilemma: Either Joe is not a good person or good people do bad things. Something must give.

A recent poll suggested that nearly 70% of Americans no longer support the war in Iraq. They do not believe that the war was necessary, justified or worth the cost. A subsequent poll suggested that fully 60% of the people believe we must stay in Iraq to a successful conclusion.

Curiously, these polls mirror the position of the mainstream Democrats and support the current policy of the Bush White House (though they object to certain administrative details). It is a portrait of two parties in spasmodic harmony, waltzing in blissful ignorance while the flames of war rage just beyond the sight and sound of our fearless patriotic leaders. It is the portrait of a mythology-pathology designed for cinematic rendition and set to the tune of Schizo Scherzo in B flat major. It is strangely reassuring and hauntingly stimulating but it is not founded in reality. Something must give.

With all due respect, the consensus position is a hybrid of incompatible beliefs. We are in effect saying we oppose the war but support the occupation. It is like acknowledging that we raided the wrong house but we might as well finish the search. More accurately, it is like slaughtering half a village only to learn that the victims are innocent. Rather than acknowledge our mistake, apologize and make amends, we wipe out the survivors so that no one lives to tell the tale.

This is the American pathology and it has never been more dangerous than it is today. To us, Iraq is like a walk in the park – even if the park is a little risky at night. To the Iraqis, having lost over a million people, more than half a million children, to the western liberators over the last decade, it is an endless nightmare. Not only do we destroy and occupy their country, laying contractual claim to their bountiful resources, but we expect them to be grateful as well: Schizo Scherzo.

It is time we confronted our own dark truths. We have been allowed to shelter ourselves from responsibility by pretending that we have faith in our leaders. We are not to blame if our leaders deceived us. We were told Iraq was the enemy. We were told they posed a threat to the world. We were told they conspired to knock down the Twin Towers. We were ill equipped to distinguish between the lies, the deceptions and the ultimate truth.

The truth is the polls do not tell the story they pretend to tell. They pretend to be a snapshot of public opinion at a given time. They are no such things. We have taken our cues from our leaders. It is not what we believe but what we say we believe that matters. The polls are nothing but a façade, a masquerade, so much puff and stuff.

We Americans are neither stupid nor ignorant. We did not believe in the weapons of mass destruction fantasy. We did not believe even for an instant that Saddam Hussein knocked down those towers. We did not believe that diplomacy was played out at the United Nations. Rather, we simply required something to tell our children and grandchildren now and in the future. Our leaders gave us the lies so that we could hand them down through the decades like Manifest Destiny and absolve ourselves of blame.

The fact is, like Cheney and Wolfowitz and all the president's men, we believed it would be a cakewalk. We believed that no matter how many Iraqis died in Shock and Awe, they would be grateful and no more than a handful of our soldiers would pay the price. We believed it would be a long weekend in the desert (like the first Gulf War) and when it was over there would be parades and parties and medals of distinction.

We believed that the world would salute in awe and allow us to play the Cowboy King one more time. Just another episode of Duke Wayne, the Lone Ranger, 20 Mule Team Borax and How the West Was Won. We're the best and the brightest. We've earned our stripes. When the chips were down and all the cards were on the table, we picked ourselves up by our own bootstraps, summoning every last ounce of courage and willpower, gave it one last college try, and won one for the Gipper. Why? Cue music (Queen):

We are champions, my friend!
We'll keep on fighting 'til the end!
No time for losers 'cause we are the champions ...
of the world!

What a shame it is not a movie. We could demand a better ending. As it is, we are saddled with the reality we have helped to create. There is no more pretending. As we stand with the president and his vision of endless war, we will find no redemption. The blood is on our hands now and all the waters of the Tigres and Euphrates will not wash the stain from our collective soul.

We have lost our senses. We have gone mad. What is the world to do when its most powerful member has wandered over the rainbow to the dark side of the moon?

It's a waltz and we're spinning our way through history like Scarlet O'Hara and Rhett Butler, pretending that the war is about honor and not slavery, like Charlotte Corday with a dagger to the heart of Jean Paul Marat, convinced that Marat is the source of all evil, like brave Colonel Custer at the Little Big Horn, Chivington at Sand Creek and the eighteen recipients of the Congressional Medal of Honor for the slaughter of 350 unarmed Lakota at Wounded Knee.

It's Schizo Scherzo and we all have our parts, dancing continuously in the flames of war and bathing in the waters of penitence.

Jazz 2 July 2005.

LONDON AND MADRID
REFLECTIONS ON THE WAR ON TERROR

A year ago in March, when the innocent people of Madrid were attacked by terrorists, their government lied about the nature of that attack and the people responded by removing the government from office. Among the first acts of the new government was fulfilling its promise to withdraw from the American alliance in Iraq.

The people of Spain are not cowards.

When one is attacked – even by fanatics that take the law into their own hands – it is not cowardice to look inward as well as outward. It requires strength and courage to recognize that the attackers may have cause. It did not diminish the Spanish resolve to bring the terrorists to justice but to recognize the error of their ways and correct their course required a strength of character unknown to the American government in the post-911 environment.

Sadly, the leaders of the American war on terror have reissued the same deceptive clichés we heard in the wake of September 11, 2001. They speak of cowardly acts, a test of resolve, evil in the hearts of our enemies, and proclaim: "We will not be intimidated."

Contrary to these views, geared to stimulate passion and pride, the terrorists did not attack London because they hate British freedom. They did not attack London because they wish to impose Islamic rule in the heart of Europe. They certainly did not attack London to capture the publicity of the Olympic designation or the G8 Summit. They attacked London because England is

America's ally in a war of aggression in the Middle East. They attacked London because they fear a revived western crusade.

Let me be clear: Terrorism is the enemy of all civilized nations and civilized beings. Our hearts go out to all the victims of this horrid crime. Our hearts go out to all the British people who had absolutely nothing to do with the actions of their government. The people of Britain (as the people of Spain) have made their opposition to the American led war overwhelmingly clear. Even in the last election, confronted with a regressive opposition party and relative prosperity, the British registered their distaste for the foreign policy of Tony Blair.

However, civility also requires self-examination. Because the enemy employs indiscriminate violence against innocent civilians does not mean that they have no cause. They have attacked our people, our friends, our colleagues, our brothers and sisters, and it is not shameful to admit that they have caused us harm. To see the innocent killed and bloodied arouses our passion, our rage, our instinctive need for vindication but when the rage subsides, let us bow our heads, mourn our losses, and finally take account.

Inevitably, if we are a righteous people, we will recognize that our governments have also brought great harm, death and destruction, to people who are no less innocent than the people of London, Madrid and New York. The rage, the passion and the deep sense of loss is not lessened because they are inflicted by missiles and invading armies.

Inevitably, if civilization is to survive and prosper, this self-perpetuating mutual hatred must end. The beginning of the end will come when both sides look inward. For our part, it begins by recognizing that while we have been wronged we have also done wrong.

JAZZMAN CHRONICLES

The sad and ironic fact is that one horrific day in London is not unlike a very bad day in Baghdad, the key difference being that in Baghdad there is no morning after. There is something obscene about the disconnect between the cause of this tragedy and its effect. There is something obscene about the rally cries of the radio warmongers, the stock market reaction, and the posturing of politicians who should know better. There is something obscene about the media cutting off voices that speak the obvious truth and parading others who speak the party line.

The cause of this tragedy is war. When Tony Blair eagerly signed on, knowing that it was an illegal war of aggression founded on false and distorted intelligence, he made his country a target. He knew it going in, so now that it has happened, it is madness to use the tragedy as a vindication for the war.

No one is asking the British, the Americans or the Australians to alter their way of life. We are asking our governments to change our foreign policies. We are asking the people to resume the march for peace.

One by one, the leaders of the war on terror stepped forward on this tragic stage not only to express their heartfelt condolences but also to declare that we must never alter our course in response to a terrorist attack. In this, they are right. We should alter our course because it is the right thing to do.

That is the path of courage and strength. It is the path of compassion and righteousness. It is the path the people of the world have long since chosen though our leaders lag far behind.

For now, it is a time of mourning. For now, the fates in this never-ending conflict have chosen the city of London, a city of light and shadow, a city of art, literature and civil society, a city of tolerance and enlightenment, a city of a thousand cultures, to express the world's rage.

Tomorrow, it will be another.

As the days of sorrow unfold, as the rage gradually subsides, take time to reflect on our role and standing in this world. Take a long, hard look at our reflection in the actions of our government and come to a deeper understanding.

Jazz 7 July 2005.

AGAINST THE WIND
THE INEVITABLE END OF THE IRAQI OCCUPATION

"Every senator in this chamber is partly responsible for sending...young Americans to an early grave. This chamber reeks of blood. Every senator here is partly responsible for that human wreckage – young men without legs or arms or genitals or faces or hopes. There are not very many of those blasted and broken boys who think this war is a glorious adventure. Do not talk to them about bugging out or national honor or courage. It does not take any courage...for a congressman or a senator or a president to wrap himself in the flag and say we are staying...because it is not our blood being shed."

George McGovern, September 1970

Regardless of where they began in the tragic chain of events that led to the current quagmire in Iraq, the vast majority of mainstream politicians (we can no longer call them leaders) have arrived at the consensus opinion that we must stay the course no matter the cost in lives, limbs, treasure and international esteem.

The question that stymies otherwise rationale beings is: What happens when we leave?

Unless we intend to remain in Iraq in perpetuity, it is

the wrong question. We will leave Iraq not because we want to and not because we have given our word but because we must. We will leave Iraq when the cost has finally become too great to bear. It is as inevitable as the tides. Whether it is tomorrow or twelve years from now, we will leave and there will be an explosion of violence when we do.

The only unifying force in Iraq today is the occupation. It unites disparate groups, tribes, communities and sects that otherwise would have very little in common. Ironically, the longer we stay and the more we prop up a government that can never be representative of the Iraqi people (how can it be when collaboration with the occupier is prerequisite?), the greater the ensuing period of violence will be. We can build them an army and supply them with all the tools of oppression (technology, prisons, weaponry, intelligence, terror and death squads) but they will never shake the stain of collaboration and they will fall. It is as inevitable as the wind.

Observing the media over the last several years, we have learned that an "expert" can be found for every cause and every opinion. Cut out the demagogues, ideologues and party loyalists, however, and there would be no one left in the studio but the camera operator. There is not an objective military expert who, in his considered opinion, will claim that this war is winnable. There is not a legitimate political expert who, in her considered opinion, will testify that whatever government we install is sustainable.

If you find a military analyst who says we can still win the war, you can be sure he is on the take. No one has disgraced himself more in this endeavor than Generals Tommy Franks, John Abizaid, and Lieutenant General Ricardo Sanchez (the man ultimately responsible for Abu Ghraib). Having observed Colin Powell under similar circumstance, we understand the strict limitations of a military man but these individuals have crossed the line. They have become politicians or worse, servants to politicians, and have lost the respect of their soldiers.

A day after the vice president declared that the insurgency was in its "last throes," the Secretary of Defense assured us that it might take ten or twelve years. Who are they kidding? There might be someone in the White House who believes we can pull back, let the cities go to hell, and defend the oil fields from our strategic military strongholds but even that is pure fantasy. Not even Karl Rove can devise a political strategy for defending such a blatant theft of another nation's resources and not a single ally in the vaunted coalition would stay the course.

In recent weeks, military commanders have conveniently tossed the ball into the political field of play. Knowing that a military victory is no longer in the equation, they ask us to hold out for a political solution. Little wonder that Paul Wolfowitz, the mastermind of this disastrous foreign policy, jumped ship to become president of the World Bank. He saw the writing on the wall. Anyone who believes that the government we impose, no matter how many elections we stage for embedded cameras, will last a day beyond our departure has been divorced from reality for a very long time.

The joke in Baghdad is that all the men in power (for they are all men) are never in Baghdad. They are in Jordan, Lebanon, Iran, and Saudi Arabia – anywhere but Iraq.

Roughly one third of the Iraqi National Assembly recently signed a petition demanding a timetable for American withdrawal. Unfortunately, that democratically elected body is not authorized to take up the singularly most important issue in Iraq. They can collect a million signatures. They can file as many petitions as they like.

The National Assembly cannot ask the Americans to leave.

Another recent development is equally revealing. According to Al Jazeera, the Iraqi Defense Minister Sadoun al-Dulaimi agreed to sign a military cooperation agreement with America's avowed enemy and a charter member of the Axis of Evil: Iran. If we had any doubt that the situation is completely out of control, we need look no further than this. Our hand picked Minister of Defense would rather sign on with the Iranians than stake his claim with the occupation.

Unlike Senators Joe Biden and John McCain, I claim no expertise in foreign affairs but I do know this much: there are no political or military solutions to this mess and "quagmire" is a generous descriptor for what we find in Iraq today.

At the current stage of chaos and confusion, we could revive the draft (perhaps it is fortunate we did not elect Kerry!) and send 500,000 troops. We would still not win. We could litter the landscape, from Tehran to Damascus, with tactical nukes. We would still not win. We could hunker down for a hundred years. We would still not win and the cost of delivering Iraqi oil to the western world would not be worth the price.

There is only one objective left in this misbegotten venture and it is not worth the blood of a single man, woman or child: Saving face.

In Vietnam, the record is clear: Our president and his esteemed advisors knew that the war was unwinnable yet they allowed the war to claim tens of thousands more American lives and hundreds of thousands of Asian lives before they finally found an exit in the Paris Peace Accords (January 1973). Though the war would drag on for two more years (the last American soldiers to die for a lie did so in April 1975), that face-saving gesture lasted little more than half a minute when our forces were withdrawn. There was indeed an explosion of violence yet no one but the intellectually perverted would suggest that we ought to have stayed the course.

If we learned nothing from that experience, then all those American lives, whose names are immortalized on the Vietnam memorial wall, as well as the millions of Vietnamese, Laotians and Cambodians, really were lost in vain.

We have ripped apart a nation that never really existed, that was drawn in the sand by the British Empire and held together by the iron fist of an American supported dictator. If there were any good intentions supplanting our glutinous need for oil and arrogant desire for empire, they were sadly misinformed. If there was any chance of creating something better than what was before, we have failed.

We have eliminated all options but one: Timely withdrawal.

We are not the solution; we are the problem.

We must implore the international community to take charge of a disaster area on par with the recent Indian Ocean tsunami and the scourge of poverty and disease in Africa. Either way, leave or stay, it will cost us a great deal – as well it should.

London, Madrid, Casa Blanca, Istanbul and Bali are all collateral damage to our arrogant dream of world domination. Let it end here and now.

Jazz 11 July 2005.

IRAQI RESISTANCE
THREE YEARS AFTER SHOCK & AWE

"For misleading the American people and launching the most foolish war since Emperor Augustus in 9 BC...Bush deserves to be impeached and, once he has been removed from office, put on trial."

Martin Van Creveld
Israeli Military Historian

"Five to seven years. No less. In five to seven years, Iraqi army is OK."

Iraqi Army Officer,
San Francisco Chronicle, March 16, 2006

On 15 February 2003, I joined the largest worldwide protest in history on the streets of San Francisco. I carried a simple sign reading: BUSH/ENRON/WW III. Thirty-three days later, without United Nations approval, our president christened the invasion of Iraq with the infamous Shock & Awe campaign.

Three years later, we are more shocked than awed.

The president issues yet another call for perseverance in the war effort. As yet another offensive is unleashed upon the inhabitants of the Sunni triangle, he asks for American patience and Iraqi unity against the resistance.

The truth is the Iraqi resistance is the only cause that can unite the Iraqi people.

Meantime, Senator Dianne Feinstein charges that the war is more difficult now because of the administration's incompetence. One more round of a familiar Democratic refrain: More troops, better planning, better equipment and more allies to prosecute an immoral war.

The truth is the war in Iraq was doomed to failure from the very moment Congress handed the president a blank check and a loaded gun to initiate the doctrine of preemptive strike. Would we really be better off now if we had sacrificed more soldiers and punished the Iraqi resistance with even greater deadly force?

Message to Senator Feinstein and her war-loving friends: The problem is not the efficiency of the killing machine; it is that the cause is morally bankrupt.

The truth about Iraq is: We have become the front line of the Shiite militias. Of course they want us to stay and secure a Shiite government. When the mission is complete and the Sunni resistance is crushed, they will give us a choice: Leave or face a new resistance. They will seize control of the resources we have contracted to international corporate profiteers and they will take possession of the monstrous military installations we have constructed for permanent occupation of the oil fields. They will form a new alliance with Iran, establish a variation on Shari'a law, and say goodbye to their former allies. (If you believe that Russia, China or even India will take our side in the new equation, you may well be catastrophically wrong.)

If we refuse, we will be compelled to pick up the pieces of the Sunni resistance, change sides and fight alongside the same soldiers we currently condemn as terrorists.

The truth about Iraq is: There are no terrorists – none. Even if we accept the neocon definition of terrorism (which conveniently exempts sovereign nations – otherwise, Shock & Awe would be the operative model), an act of terrorism requires the intent to terrorize. In Iraq, the intent of roadside or suicide bombs is not to terrorize the most powerful military force on earth but to exact a price on the enemy occupiers and their collaborators.

Whether we accept it or not, the Iraqi resistance is engaged in a civil war because the occupying nation has taken sides. If we had been told three years ago that we would sacrifice American blood and treasure to establish Shiite rule in Iraq, we would have had no part in it.

All this lip service to the cause of democracy is a charade, a deadly farce, and a perversion of American ideals.

Democracy is not a cause for war. Like foreign occupation, it is a cause for rebellion from within. Democracy in America has a very different meaning than democracy in Iraq. In America, it means that two parties controlled by the same corporate interests alter the rules of the game until the majority will of the people is virtually obscured. Democracy in Iraq means total Shiite dominance and inevitable civil divide.

You do not impose a state of war on any nation for any reasons other than a real, direct and imminent threat or an ongoing process of ethnic cleansing or genocide. (Clearly, this was not the case in Iraq where the vilified dictator is facing trial for crimes committed fifteen years before the invasion.) If your only reason for war is to change the form and nature of government, you have denied the people the fundamental right of self-determination – a right that includes the choice between peace and rebellion.

Any reasonable criteria for justified war would disallow the invasion of Iraq, an aggressive act of war perpetrated by a deceptive, corrupted and ideologically driven administration. (Such criteria would also preemptively prohibit an act of aggression against Iran, a nation infinitely more threatened than threatening.)

We may not favor the form and nature of any number of governments around the world but it is not for us to determine by military means which will stand and which will fall. We have embraced far too many despots to defend such a distinction as grounds for war.

As the Bush administration continues to promote its dark doctrine of military supremacy and preemptive strike, at this juncture of international affairs, there is not a single nation on earth less peaceful and more threatening than our own.

The truth about Iraq is: We were wrong at the inception of the war; we have been wrong for three years, and we continue to be wrong today.

For the first time since the Bush administration took office, we should appeal to the international community without a covert agenda. In the humility of a nation that has willfully violated the cardinal principle of international conduct (aggressive war), we should request that a neutral body negotiate a simultaneous truce between the warring factions (Shiites and Sunnis with Kurdish engagement) and the withdrawal of all occupying forces. The only acceptable condition of withdrawal is the safety of our soldiers and their replacement by a legitimate peacekeeping force.

Save for a continued occupation, all options should be on the table, including shared oil revenues and civil divide.

We have inflicted great harm upon the world and we have paid a great price yet our sacrifice is little when compared to what the people of Iraq have endured – even if we allow for the demise of a ruthless dictator.

We are not miracle workers; we cannot change water into wine. We cannot transform the sands of Arabia into a democratic Garden of Eden and we cannot expect to profit from our gross and criminal misdeeds. We can only hope to make amends.

Let us begin by ending the occupation and beginning the long process of transforming our own political system so that disasters like the presidency of George W. Bush never happen again.

Jazz 21 March 2006.

THE PROPAGANDA WAR
REVISITING AFGHANISTAN ON 9-11

There are two kinds of propaganda. One is guided by principle and strictly adheres to what it knows to be the truth. The other is guided by a political agenda and does not hesitate to distort, misrepresent and obscure the truth whenever it conflicts with that agenda.

The former is an honorable tradition in the service of justice and democracy, a legacy distinguished by Tom Paine, Cesar Chavez, Martin Luther King and so many other less-trumpeted American heroes. The latter is the refuge of political hacks and demagogues exemplified by Karl Rove, Rush Limbaugh and Joe McCarthy.

While the demagogues and partisans are invariably financed by the most powerful institutions in the nation, inheriting permanent seats at the table of mainstream media, the purveyors of truth face a constant struggle until finally their numbers are so many they can no longer be denied.

On the fifth anniversary of the twin towers attack, all Americans need to be reminded that there is a war going on within the nation. It is a propaganda war, pitting truth versus power, and its outcome is anything but certain. In the balance of this struggle for the hearts and minds of America lies a future of constant war, fear and loathing, against an alternative vision of enlightened leadership.

Five years after the attack on the twin towers, we remain fearful and angry because we have been denied the essential truths that would allow the healing to begin.

The government propaganda machine kicked in

almost immediately after the 9-11 attack with the omission from news reports of our president's inexplicable seven-minute paralysis in a Florida kindergarten classroom. Within hours, Osama bin Laden was identified as the perpetrator as his image was cast over the still simmering ruins of Ground Zero. Within days, we had determined not only to attack Al Qaeda but also to overthrow the government of Afghanistan for complicity in the crime. We delivered an ultimatum and when they countered with an offer to deliver the accused to a neutral country, we turned them down. Within weeks of the attack, we launched a full-scale invasion.

At the time, Americans were so determined to back the president on the path of vengeance that we were not allowed to ask the questions that needed to be asked. We were not allowed to question the government's account of what happened on September 11. We were not allowed to ask: Why not accept the Taliban's offer? What more might we have learned with bin Laden in custody, facing trial by an international tribunal?

Once the necessity of military action was determined, why did we choose to attack the nation as a whole rather than Al Qaeda? Why did we strike a deal with the opium-driven warlords of the Northern Alliance, choosing one evil over another, rather than concentrating on our real enemies? Why did we choose to destroy and occupy an impoverished land if it was not necessary to our objectives?

To this day, Afghanistan is considered the good war because the issues have never been raised and the assertions of power have never been questioned.

We left Afghanistan a broken nation with a crippled government, eventually handing the job off to an inadequately prepared NATO alliance, in order to embark on the bigger war our government wanted all along.

The deceptions, distortions and lies employed by the

propaganda machine in the push to war with Iraq are too well documented for any serious observer to deny. The partial release of the Senate Foreign Intelligence Committee report on intelligence in the buildup to war shreds any remaining doubts that there was ever any connection between Iraq and Al Qaeda.

There was no intelligence failure in Iraq. The intelligence community got it right. Saddam Hussein was an enemy of our enemy in Al Qaeda. There was virtually zero probability that Iraq would ever use weapons of mass destruction against our allies or us even if it possessed them. There was no connection to 9-11. There was no threat.

The propaganda war is still raging. As the old myths crumble, new ones are hoisted up in their place. The latest are that Al Qaeda and their kind are the great threat of the next century and that, if we fail in Iraq, the Al Qaeda types will absorb the greater Middle East.

That these are mere puff and stuff to propagate the continuation and expansion of war should be self-evident. In the event that it is not, consult those who have knowledge of Al Qaeda and the Middle East. Ask those who have no dog in this hunt. Ask the intelligence community when it is not serving at the pleasure of the president.

Before we embark on yet another war, let us take a good look at where the path of vengeance has taken us. The war in Iraq is already lost and the occupation of Afghanistan is in shambles. Tens of thousands if not hundreds of thousands have been sacrificed over and above the thousands that we lost on September 11, 2001.

The central front in the "war on terror" is where Al Qaeda and Osama bin Laden still reside. When we withdraw from Iraq (as we must inevitably do), owing to the gross incompetence of our leaders, we will have little choice but to return to Afghanistan – not to occupy but to complete the job and get out.

The legacy of 9-11 should not be a perpetual reign of terror in which we are the great destroyer, the purveyors of violence and deception. Rather, the legacy of 9-11 should be a new awakening that will eventually serve to protect us all from such tragedies.

The victims of that solemn day and their survivors deserve better. We all deserve better. In fact, we should demand it.

Jazz 11 September 2006.

A DANCE OF DEATH
THE HANGING OF SADDAM HUSSEIN

An American in the French Assembly before the Revolution became the Reign of Terror, spoke out against the execution of the royal monarch of France. Those who knew him were not surprised at his courage, conviction and strength of character. It was not a popular stance and he was no friend to the monarchy. He was in fact its greatest foe yet his principled position landed him in the Bastille and very nearly cost his life.

His name was Tom Paine, without whom it is unlikely that the great experiment we call democracy would ever have been launched on the American continent.

Saddam Hussein was hanged until the spark of life drained from his flailing limbs.

It is not politically astute to defend the fallen dictator any more than it was for Paine to plea for the life of the French monarch, yet there are occasions when principle must speak.

I am no more sympathetic to tyranny, despotism, oppression, brutality or crimes against humanity than Paine was to the monarchy, yet I felt only shame in observing the morbid dance of death surrounding the execution of Saddam.

Granted, the head of state is ultimately responsible for the crimes of the nation.

Saddam Hussein was executed for causing the death of 150 men and boys in the city of Dujail after an attempted assassination.

Only history can decide if he is accountable for genocide and other horrific crimes against humankind. The record is sufficiently clear that the great dictator was by no means an innocent man. The best that can be said, in light of what has transpired since the fall of his government, is that the divided, artificial and dysfunctional nation of Iraq required the brutal hand of a dictator if only to survive.

(I do not believe this is true. I cannot believe that tyranny and oppression are ever justified but the evidence is mounting with every corpse deposited on the streets of Baghdad or plucked out of the rivers Tigres and Euphrates.)

Consider the actions of our government.

There is compelling evidence of a conspiracy to deceive the American people and extort Congress into a cause of war.

There is compelling evidence of that an aggressive act of war, in direct violation of the cardinal principle of international law, was committed against a non-threatening nation with premeditation and little regard for the bloody consequences of our actions.

There is compelling evidence that the tactics used in this war – from Shock and Awe to Fallujah, where every man and boy of fighting age was prevented from leaving before the siege, from the use of cluster bombs and white phosphorous to spent uranium munitions – were used with full knowledge of the massive civilian casualties that would result.

There is compelling evidence that over 200 Iraqis have died for every American soldier who has fallen during this war. Even without consideration for the events of Haditha, Abu Ghraib and countless other atrocities that have no names, the war itself is a crime of genocidal proportions.

So if the head of state is ultimately responsible for the

crimes of the nation, why isn't our president facing trial?

This was not the heavy hand of justice. It was state sanctioned revenge. It was the justice of the conqueror, of emperors and kings.

For those who suggest that the dictator did not deserve a fair trial, I am compelled to remind you that justice is blind. That justice which is reserved for the good and virtuous is only a masquerade. It is the path to trial by drowning. Justice considers all who come before her with absolute equality. There can be no exceptions to the rule and process of law.

What we witnessed in the execution of Saddam was the killing of Iraqi justice by the poison of vengeance. It was a morbid dance of death.

The hanging of the dictator, however justified, however gratifying to those he victimized in a reign of terror that would not have been possible without the collaboration of western powers, was yet another crime against humanity for which our president must eventually be held accountable.

Jazz 30 December 2006.

BUSH TO AMERICA: WAR!

Faced with a collapse of popular and political support, the president's response in an address to the nation was astonishing: Not only will the war effort go on unabated; it will be escalated and expanded.

The first question that arises is: Why was it necessary to don the mask of deliberations, dancing silently through two months of weighty consultations, for this?

This did not represent a change in strategy. It did not represent a change in thinking. Rather, it was open defiance: Damn the election; load the munitions! It was a barely discernible rephrasing of the same old tired lines:

"We must not fail" but we have failed.

The war is "noble and necessary" when in fact it was a war of choice founded on repeated lies and deceptions.

We are engaged in "the ideological struggle of our time" when in fact we have prosecuted the oldest imperial strategy in history: a war for greed and dominion.

We are "advancing liberty" by ripping a nation apart at the seams.

"We have to fight them over there so we will not have to fight them here" when in fact we have created more enemies by our actions than we can possibly count.

On and on, the president stands firm, lock-jawed and determined. He will not back down. He is a war president: Once a war president, always a war president.

He will send another 21,500 American warriors into door-to-door, urban battle in the midst of an exploding civil war.

He will push Iraqis to take up arms against Iraqis and

position our forces in the crossfire.

He has dispatched a carrier strike group to the Persian Gulf with vague orders to engage Iran on the high seas.

Like the commander who cuts off the head of an emissary and returns it in a box, he has discarded even the hint of real diplomacy and hurled another volley of threats to Iraq's neighboring nations.

Having replaced every commander and advisor who dared, however belatedly, to speak truth to diminishing power, the president has barricaded himself in a tower of stone. He cannot hear our protests. From his high perch, he can barely distinguish us as human beings.

What is the truth he cannot bear? Spurred on by a radical fringe of power hungry, oil greedy, unconditional Israeli loyalists, he defied the history of the world by attempting to become the first western power to successfully conquer, occupy and establish permanent dominion in the heart of the Middle East.

The most dangerous mythology to have evolved over four years of a catastrophic war is the one that holds: We could have prevailed if only we had committed sufficient troops from the beginning. History instructs otherwise. We could only have prolonged the catastrophe in a rising tide of Iraqi and American blood. To believe that the indigenous powers of the region or indeed the world would stand idly by while we seized the planet's most illusive treasure is naïve in the extreme.

The second most dangerous myth to have evolved from this river of shame is the one espoused by Democratic spokesperson Dick Durbin (Senator, IL): That we have given the Iraqis enough. What have we delivered to the Iraqi people if not a broken nation, a legacy of death and a future as dark as a torture chamber in the basement of Guantanamo Bay?

No one wants an end to the war more than I do but not at a cost of blaming the victims. The Iraqi people did not invite us to invade and destroy their country. That invitation was culled from a corrupt circle of power hungry exiles – bloodsucking leeches of the neocon dream.

We cannot be absolved from responsibility for committing the cardinal crime of international law (aggressive war) either by prolonging the suffering or by proclaiming our nobility as if by birthright. To promulgate either deception would be to announce to the world that we have learned nothing from our egregious crimes and that we are fully capable of repeating the offense.

The fallacies of the president's plan for success are too clear for any honest analyst to ignore. Throwing our soldiers into the crossfire, imbedding them with alien forces, engaging the Mahdi army, baiting Iran and threatening Syria can only result in an exponential increase of violence, resistance and civil divide.

The idea that we failed by placing "too many restrictions" on our soldiers will come as a shock to the citizens of Fallujah, Ramadi, Haditha and the detainees of Abu Ghraib.

The president's war plan is a stunning prescription for horrors beyond anything we have yet witnessed or contemplated.

The only elements of his proposal that even remotely make sense are those for political reparations (inclusion, oil sharing) and taking the fight to Al Qaeda in Iraq.

Unfortunately, it is a little late in the game for reparations that should have been accomplished years ago. The Sunni insurgents would have welcomed them then but now they will greet them with scorn.

As for Al Qaeda in Iraq, it owes its existence to the American occupation and it will inevitably owe its demise to America's withdrawal.

In short, the only role American presence can serve in

Iraq today is the same role it has served for the past four years: destruction and death.

The most notable omission in the president's address is more telling than what was included. There was not a single disclaimer of our intent to maintain permanent military bases.

The debate is over. The war president will escalate and expand the conflict until his term of office expires or Congress stops him. By now we should all understand that Congress has the constitutional power to impose conditions of withdrawal on the funding of the war. It is precisely this circumstance that the founders envisioned.

It will require only a modicum of courage to expose what could be the last lie of the despicable warlords responsible for this nightmare: Stopping the war will by no means compromise the safety of our troops in the field.

Stop the posturing. To surge or not to surge is not the real question. The lives of our soldiers and the moral founding of the nation is. End the war...now!

Jazz 11 January 2007.

PETRAEUS BETRAYS US

"Policy makers have a right to their own opinions
but not their own set of facts."

Former DCI George Tenet,
At the Center of the Storm (2007)

"In the push to war with Iraq, something
extraordinary happened in the world of Intelligence.
All the king's agents...silent partners in former
crimes against humanity... refused to provide false
information to support the administration's claims.
Even in the last minute of the last hour, Director of
Central Intelligence George Tenet flatly stated there
was no documented link between Al Qaeda and
Saddam Hussein."

Jack Random
The War Chronicles (2004)

The lies to launch war have been supplanted by the
lies of war itself. The trail of lies is as long as the trail of
Iraqi blood and tears. The lies of weapons of mass
destruction, Al Qaeda connections and Middle East
democracy have given way to the lies of civilian
massacres, the lies of military heroism, the lies of Abu
Ghraib, the lies of the Samara mosque bombing and the
lies of progress in securing Baghdad.

When former DCI George Tenet accuses vice president Dick Cheney of misleading the nation to war, he is sculpting the truth to his own benefit. The vice president did not have the power to declare war and he could not have succeeded without the assent of a feckless commander and the silent complicity of those in the White House who should have spoken out. That evasion of responsibility continues to this day with the newly appointed field commander in Iraq, General David Petraeus.

The General claims there is measurable progress in Iraq if you do not count car bombs or sensational attacks or attacks outside of Baghdad. Just as the White House cherry picked evidence to justify war, the military will select facts to prove the security plan is working when the soldiers on the ground know otherwise.

Like George Tenet, Colin Powell, Condoleezza Rice and Donald Rumsfeld before him, General Petraeus has betrayed us, along with every soldier under his command. His mission is not to secure victory in Iraq – a "victory" that would only further secure America's place in the annals of infamy. His mission is to continue the chain of lies to perpetuate an illusion of success that will enable the worst president in history to pass his catastrophic war along to a new president.

In a spirit of unbridled cynicism, the neocons that launched this campaign of never-ending war are counting on a party of opposition so inept that it will parlay almost certain victory into electoral defeat by stammering, stumbling and falling on the word "peace."

As witnessed by the recent group debate-a-thon, the Democrats have become so conditioned to aggressive posturing that they cannot oppose an unqualified disaster and wholesale waste of life without ceaseless qualifications and pontificating on the virtues of aggression in lesser wars (Afghanistan, the Balkans) and potentially greater calamities (Iran).

General Petraeus, the anointed savior of the Bush war strategy, betrayed us from the moment he ascended to his post as director of the Baghdad theatre of blood. He is not so much a commander as an illusionist, not so much a strategist as a front man for a magic act.

Watch the right hand while the left covers over a pile of fresh corpses, the latest yield in an orgy of sectarian conflict, resistance and revenge. Poof, the war is manageable! Poof, the violence has ebbed! Poof, the Iraqi government is taking charge! Poof, the war is winnable!

It is a dog and pony show (rated R for blood) but the players only come out at night. It would be too easy to see through their masks and detect their slight of hand in the light of day.

We started the wrong war for the wrong reasons and we continue to fight only to cover the lies and the greed that placed us in the center of a sinking hole.

Nothing could have empowered our enemies more than a dim witted, poorly planned and poorly executed war of attrition on foreign terrain and nothing will continue to empower our enemies more than a march of lemmings over the Arabian cliff.

As the surprisingly frank Senator from Alaska suggested in the presidential debate, Osama bin Laden must greet every dawn with a prayer of thanks to George W. Bush.

The warlords, who have never faced an enemy on the field of battle, think it amusing to throw accusations of betrayal and treason at those who acknowledge the reality of defeat but who was more loyal to the troops: the officers who advised General Robert E. Lee that the war was lost after the slaughter of Gettysburg or those who advised him to press on?

To those obstinate holdouts that still support this

cowboy commander and his calamitous war, wake up and smell the battlefield. The air is filled with deadly fire, toxic smoke and the scent of scorched flesh. It is filled with foreboding and a promise of further horrors beyond our immediate view.

Wake up because it is you that enable the horror to go on. Your blind allegiance and false patriotism is all that stands between the lies of victory and the beginning of reparations. Your irrational support is all that props up a failed war president.

The Democrats, with their pandering and posturing frontrunners, will not stop this war or the wars to come unless the people demand it with one voice.

Jazz 29 April 2007.

A GENERATION LOST
FOR WHOM THE BELL TOLLS

"If Colin Powell and George Tenet had walked out …in February 2003 instead of working together on that tainted UN speech…they might have turned everything around. They might have saved the lives and limbs of all those brave US kids and innocent Iraqis, not to mention our world standing and national security."

Maureen Dowd
New York Times, May 2, 2007

The truth is a twisted sister and rarely sets men free. The cold bloody truth of the war in Iraq is like a toxic cloud that poisons everything it touches.

If former Secretary of State Colin Powell and former Director of Central Intelligence George Tenet thought they could find absolution in their post-complicit years, they are as delusional as the little man who dreamed of empire and betrayed a nation. If they believed the armor of loyalty and patriotism could shield them from the harsh blow of accountability, they have been drinking from the well of Shakespeare's Queen Mab.

How now that trinity Medals of Honor awarded Tenet, Paul Bremer and General Tommy Franks have stained the heart of integrity and transformed the very words "presidential honor" into an oxymoron.

Everyone who has grasped the hand of our self-anointed war president now feels the sting of humility and disgrace. Powell is gone. Rumsfeld is gone. Wolfowitz is gone, spiraling down the rabbit hole, wrapped in his own arrogance and cronyism. Ashcroft is gone and Condoleezza Rice has all but vanished from the stage.

The latest diplomatic initiative came and went like a whisper in the night, a token gesture from a token neocon, a one-time renaissance woman who sacrificed the promise of greatness when she consigned her soul to a rabid brain trust bent on the path of war.

As it is for Condoleezza Rice, who might have been a concert pianist or Nobel prizewinner, so it is for the generation that nurtured her and blessed her with the promise of hope.

Shame, where is thy blush? It hides behind masks of honor, loyalty and patriotism.

Among the forgotten coalition of the coerced (our allies in the conquest of the Middle East), Asnar of Spain was first to fall, Musharraf of Pakistan is hanging by a totalitarian thread, and Britannia's Blair is cursed to live out his days in the shadow of the Bush wars, as his companions shake their heads and wonder what might have been.

As it is for Tony Blair, so it is for the generation of new and bold ideas.

The bell chimes and we think of Rice, Powell and a loss of innocence. The bell tolls and we think of Camelot, the Bay of Pigs and a president who at least knew when to cut his losses. The bell rings out and we remember Rudy Giuliani's 9-11 testament: "Thank God George Bush is president." The bell sounds and we think of patriotic boys and girls who will never become fathers and mothers.

The bells echo in the chambers of our collective soul and we wonder if we have finally learned enough to spare future generations the sorrow of an endless cycle of violence and destruction.

As we step forward and look back upon our selves, we reflect that we were the generation with the greatest promise, the greatest moral founding, the greatest hope and vision for transforming the world we inherited, yet we squandered that bountiful promise for the darkest vision an American president has ever advanced.

While we launched a campaign of aggressive war, wars of dominion and economic conquest, our allies in Israel, Pakistan, Philippines, and Russia wandered further from the paths of justice and democracy.

While we led the campaign of denial, the world marched toward global catastrophe.

While we pushed our armed forces to the brink of implosion for a fool's campaign of horror, we allowed genocide in Darfur to roll on as if the community of nations was obliged to tolerate inhumanity in dark skinned populations.

While we squandered half a trillion in fortune on the destruction of other nations, we allowed a great American city to wallow in virtual ruin, transformed as much by indifference as by an act of nature.

When we hear the bells, we reach inside and mourn a generation lost. We hear and we contemplate the words of John Donne: "Any man's death diminishes me because I am involved in mankind: And therefore never send to know for whom the bell tolls; it tolls for thee."

As of Saturday, May 12, some 3,391 men and women of the American armed forces had died in the Iraq War. They all had names and faces and families who mourn their loss.

Jazz 14 May 2007.

THE LIES OF WAR
LEAVING IRAQ, REMEMBERING VIETNAM

"You are part of an unbroken line of heroes spanning two centuries – from the colonists who overthrew an empire to your grandparents and parents who faced down fascism and communism to you, men and women who fought for the same principles in Fallujah and Kandahar and delivered justice to those who attacked us on 9/11.

"The most important lesson that we can take from you is not about military strategy; it's a lesson about our national character. Because of you we are ending these wars in a way that will make America stronger and the world more secure."

President Barack Obama
Address to Troops, Ft. Bragg, December 14, 2011

The lies of war are forgotten as easily and readily as the wrappings of Christmas or the resolutions of a new year. Like a child still in diapers, the lessons of war must be learned again and again until finally they are taken to heart.

The lies of the war in Iraq are so easily buried that six out of seven Republican candidates for president of the United States have publicly pledged to go to war in Iran based on the identical unsubstantiated claims that led us to war in Iraq. The lessons of that ill-fated war, the largest strategic blunder since Vietnam, are so readily put behind us that even before that colossal disaster officially ended, six of seven Republican candidates pledged his and her allegiance to the same neoconservative brain trust that guided us into the snake pit. And the White House is not far behind.

Those of us who remember the war in Vietnam and the years we committed to ending it will find the bipartisan rationalizations of the Iraq War all too familiar and profoundly disturbing.

The lie that drove the Vietnam War was the Domino Theory: If we lose one nation to the red menace of communism, then we will lose them all. On that basis, three generations of western powers (Britain, France and America) chose a little country on the doorstep of China as their playground of war.

It required over three million lives to prove that a child's game was not a legitimate basis for a foreign policy. It only made sense because it fit on a bumper sticker and because our leaders were dominated by military minds in search of power, glory and the spoils of empire.

The great postwar lie of Vietnam was that we lost the war because we were never fully committed. The politicians in Washington held our generals back. Between 1965 and 1968 we dropped over a million tons of missiles, bombs and rockets on North Vietnam, Laos and Cambodia but we were never fully committed. We sprayed 12 million gallons of the deadly chemical defoliant Agent Orange over wide swaths of Southeast Asia but we were not fully committed. At the height of the war in 1968 we deployed over half a million soldiers, including the first conscripts since the Korean War, but we were not fully committed.

Short of nuclear bombs, we were as committed to that unjustifiable war as any nation could have been yet the lies of war survive. The lies of war take on mythological characteristics and believing them becomes a ritual of patriotism.

Little wonder we commit the same strategic mistakes, the same errors in judgment, the same acts of criminal inhumanity, the same ultimately desperate and self-destroying measures over and over again.

In the wake of Vietnam, America's leaders were confined to small-scale interventions until George Herbert Walker Bush, former Director of the CIA, conspired to wage war in Iraq. Though the Gulf War was short-lived, its military success inspired President Bush to announce: "The specter of Vietnam has been buried forever in the desert sands of the Arabian Peninsula."

Forever was not a long time as his eldest son was to initiate two wars that brought the specter of Vietnam back into focus. One was the ongoing ten-year war in Afghanistan and the other was a return to his father's war in Iraq.

Few will recall the lies of the father but the lies of the son are too fresh to be so soon forgotten. They include not only the infamous weapons of mass destruction but also the later claim that virtually all the world believed the lie. For the record, we lost our appeal before the United Nations Security Council to justify military action on the basis of Iraq's weapons of mass destruction. The International Atomic Energy Agency thoroughly debunked our claims and the measure was withdrawn when it became clear that the Council would vote overwhelmingly against our cause for war.

Members of the Bush administration falsely claimed that Saddam Hussein was a party to the terrorist attack of September 11, 2001. They falsely claimed that Iraq harbored and worked with Al Qaeda operatives. These claims were so clearly and demonstrably false that even President Bush was forced ultimately to disavow them.

The lies of war had served their purpose. Once the first bombs lit up the Baghdad skyline, supporting the war became a matter of patriotism.

The next lie was that our actions had nothing to do with Iraqi oil and everything to do with establishing democracy in the Arab world. That lie was exposed when our first action was to protect the oil fields. Well before an Iraqi government could be established we contracted Iraqi oil to the highest corporate bidders. Mission accomplished.

The lies of war are really not that difficult to detect. It only requires an open mind, an appetite for facts, and a willingness to think.

The lies of the Iraq War will survive unless those of us who witnessed them, from the soldiers who sacrificed to the citizens who supported and opposed them, unless each of us vows to accept the truth and pass that horrid account forward to future generations.

We can be grateful that a president elected largely on the promise of ending the Iraq War has officially done so, though we remain mindful that thousands of American-hired mercenaries remain behind to guard the largest diplomatic embassy on earth.

We understand at our stage of development that a president cannot apologize for the harm done in the name of our nation.

We understand the wisdom of separating the war from the warrior.

We know the president cannot inform our soldiers that they were fighting the wrong war for the wrong reasons.

But when the president announces that we have created an opportunity for the Iraqis to thrive and prosper as a democratic nation, he is not only being disingenuous; he is perpetuating the lies of war. When the president declares that our fight in Iraq was for Iraqi freedom and international justice, he is paving the way for another unjust war in America's future. He is attempting to bury the specter of Vietnam.

Leaving Afghanistan for another day, we should all agree that the Iraq War was wrong from its inception. It was never about democracy. It was never about justice. It was always about oil and strategic advantage.

Wrong is wrong.

Jazz 30 December 2011.

VOLUME IV

ECONOMICS:

FAIR TRADE, AUSTERITY AND

THE RIGHTS OF LABOR

CONTENTS

PREFACE

PROGRESSIVE ECONOMICS

Americans like to believe that we are a nation that values fairness and constantly strives to achieve it for all our citizens. At the core of the American Dream is the idea that anyone willing to work hard can rise up the economic ladder to success and prosperity.

Given our history over the last half century we have failed miserably to live up to that dream. In fact, under the current economic system, the American Dream is nothing more than a myth propagated by antiquated history books that should be filed under Popular Fiction.

The sad truth is: We are evolving into a system that crushes the poor, impoverishes the once thriving middle class and consolidates wealth in the hands of the elite.

We've all seen or heard the numbers. Here are a few from the Economic Policy Institute:

- Between 2009 and 2012 the top one percent took 95% of America's income growth

- Between 1979 and 2007 the one percent claimed 53.9% of income growth

- Income inequality has reached its greatest level since 1928 and the Great Depression

- Unionization is at its lowest level since before 1928

- From 1979 to 2007 wages and benefits for middle-income workers remained stagnant; from 2007 to 2014 real income for the median 20% actually declined.

Those are the numbers and there are many more but

the numbers do not tell the story. For every Bill Gates or Steve Jobs, toiling in the garage until they emerge at the very pinnacle of multi-billion dollar success, there are literally millions of common Joes and everyday Eves who work long hours at low wages and struggle to keep food on the table and a roof over their heads. They are one misfortune away from joining the burgeoning mass of the impoverished and homeless.

There are many reasons for this middle American tragedy but none are more important than this: Both political parties have sold us out. While the Republicans have long given the working class its collective middle finger, the Democrats have only pretended to represent the cause of the financially challenged.

A Democratic president with a Democratic congress delivered health insurance reform, a compromise measure that helped the uninsured but left the middle class wondering where the benefits went, when they should have given us universal healthcare, entirely eliminating the insurance industry whose only function is to deny benefits while siphoning trillions from actual healthcare. They gave us the Lilly Ledbetter Act, a positive measure closing a gap left by an egregious Supreme Court decision, when they should have delivered the Equal Rights Amendment.

They speak of a federal minimum wage while they carefully skirt the critical issues of trade policy, public works, job training and the rights of labor. Until our government addresses these issues our middle class will continue to shrink and the wealth gap will continue to grow. Until we recognize that the problems are systemic and designed by an elite few who control the money that elects officials, nothing will change.

Jazz.

MAY DAY

THE RISE & FALL OF THE MIDDLE CLASS

On a quiet evening in 1884, the American Federation of Organized Trades and Labor Unions passed a common sense resolution declaring that, as of May 1, 1886, eight hours would constitute a day of labor. The call went out for a general strike to achieve that modest, humanitarian objective.

One hundred and twenty years later, the demand for an eight-hour workday no longer seems radical but, before the rise of the labor movement, workers were virtual slaves to their industrial masters. Job safety was not economical. Child labor and immigrant exploitation were commonplace. Employees typically worked 10 to 12 to 14 hours a day, six days a week, without compensation. On-the-job injuries were tough luck and wages, even for highly skilled workers, were barely adequate for subsistence.

In the years before the rise of the labor movement, there was no middle class. American society was divided between the poor, the working poor and the elite.

On May 1 1886, behind their fortresses of greed, their towers of avarice, the ruling class was quaking in their shining leather boots. They sensed what was at stake. Like the feudal lords of old Europe, they were confronting their first great challenge. Give them an eight-hour day and there would be no end to their demands. The rallying cry of a living wage would not long be silent.

An army of thugs, police and militia, was amassed to

confront the leaders of the labor movement in Chicago. On May 3' police fired into a crowd of strikers, killing four and setting the stage for a mass demonstration the next day in Haymarket Square. By all accounts, the assembly was peaceful when the police closed in and ordered the crowd to disperse. An explosion rang out, a policeman was killed, and the entire labor movement was charged with cold-blooded murder.

To this day, no one knows who committed the crime but we do know that those who were tried, convicted and executed were innocent (see note). Seven of the eight were not in attendance and the eighth was on the speaker's platform at the time of the explosion. The police were not interested in details and the authorities were blatant in their appeal to the public's fear of lawlessness. It was a time when anarchists were blamed for everything from food shortages to natural disasters. The accused were guilty of being radicals and in the atmosphere of May Day 1886 that was crime enough.

The Haymarket Affair fueled the passions of a generation of dissidents and rallied the industrial world to the cause of American labor. It was an assembly in Paris that first declared May Day a day of international labor in tribute to the Haymarket martyrs.

Despite the relentless and brutal efforts of industry and capital, the labor movement grew and prospered, giving birth to the American middle class and setting the prerequisite conditions for a relatively affluent consumer economy.

On May Day 2005, it is a good time to reflect on the many who gave their lives in the cause of organized labor so that future generations of workers would enjoy a living wage, an eight-hour day, worker's compensation, decent working conditions, basic job security and standards of safety.

Of equal and greater importance, May Day 2005 is a

critical time to consider that what has been gained through generations of blood and sweat can easily be lost through negligence and fear.

What the elite have always failed to understand is that a vibrant middle class is the foundation of a strong economy. Without a strong middle class, there are not enough consumers of goods to sustain the whole. Houses are not built, mortgages are foreclosed, automobiles remain on the showroom floors, small businesses fold, plants close and the system eventually collapses.

Today, the workers of all nations are under siege. In America, good paying jobs are outsourced to foreign labor. Forced to take low paying jobs, our wages are in perpetual decline. State by state, unions are under attack with "right to work" laws and cleverly worded regulations to negate overtime pay. More and more workers, under the burden of mounting debt, are compelled to take second jobs, rendering the eight-hour day obsolete. Fearful of losing our jobs, workers are willing to sacrifice health insurance and reluctant to report unsafe conditions or unjust practices.

It is fashionable to blame migrant and foreign workers for all our myriad woes. It is easy to fix blame on those who have even less say, even less power, than we do. It is also wrong.

Blaming the migrant for job loss is like blaming the child for child labor. Blaming the foreign worker for exportation is like blaming the slave for slavery.

The army of migrants, who must annually run the gauntlet of a harsh environment, unscrupulous coyotes, bandits, crooks, border patrol and vigilantes, are victims of this systemic exploitation as much and more than we are. The indentured do not volunteer for their servitude; they are compelled to it. They do not choose to steal American jobs because they despise us; they come because they too must survive.

The same is true of the workers in foreign sweatshops (a generous term for working environments in many third world nations), whose conditions of employment are every bit as deplorable as American labor in the nineteenth century.

The answer to this seeming conundrum is a Kyoto Accord of Labor: an international recognition and confirmation of the fundamental human right to a living wage.

Once firmly established, the principle itself will shame those governments who, under the cover of free market economics, allow and condone the disgrace of labor exploitation. Moreover, it will shame those collaborator nations and international corporations who encourage these inhumanities with their cooperative silence and implied consent.

It does not require a master of economy to foresee a dim future if we do not alter the regressive path we are on. It makes no sense to continue blaming migrants and foreign laborers for our problems for, in the end, we are all on the same sinking ship.

There was a time when no nation on earth was allowed trade with slave nations without severe consequences. The modern version of slavery proceeds with impunity. When international complicity ends and the exploiting entities are fully exposed and brought to account, the practice will end and the world will witness the birth of a global middle class, which in turn will form the foundation of a just and prosperous world economy.

Those who were derided as the radicals of Chicago's Haymarket Square were right all along: The workers of the world must unite. There is no other way.

Jazz 29 April 2005.

JAZZMAN CHRONICLES

Note: Albert Parsons, August Spies, Adolf Fischer and George Engel were hanged 11 November 1887; Louis Lingg committed suicide in jail; Samuel Fielden, Oscar Neebe and Michael Schwab were pardoned in 1893.

THE LIE OF A STRONG ECONOMY
Beneath the Towers of Avarice

A man born with a silver spoon, who failed at every business venture he ever attempted, can no more understand the hardships of economy than a man who avoided military service (yet charaded as a fighter pilot for the cameras) can understand the hardships of war.

The president tells us the economy is strong and assembles a chorus line of neocon ideologues, charading as economists, to tell us he is right, yet none of these silver spoon pretenders live in the economy they have created.

If they can find numbers that tell us how fortunate and prosperous we are, it is the final proof that numbers lie – or rather, that the unscrupulous can bend them to any purpose.

The numbers the administration and its shameless promoters use to inform us of our good fortune are job creation, the unemployment rate and income relative to inflation. Using these numbers to document a strong economy is analogous to recalculating the casualty rate in Iraq by expanding the definition of "non-combat" death and discounting those soldiers who are mortally wounded in the war but die in a German hospital.

The key to interpreting these numbers is: We've been down so long it looks like up to us. Unfortunately, for most of us, it only looks like up if you're living in castles of privilege behind the walls of greed.

It is fascinating to observe this president speak and to realize that he actually believes the things he says.

Despite photo opportunities with a chainsaw on the Crawford ranch, he has never worked an honest day of labor in his life. He has never needed or wanted beyond the most grandiose ambitions. His idea of a crisis is having to ask daddy to ask the Saudis for another bailout or losing a congressional election. His tight circle of neocon advisors informs him that everything is rosy and he believes them. It's his job to believe them. No one is so pleased with the accomplishments of little George as little George himself.

For those of us who live in the world, the picture is infinitely darker and less fulfilling. No matter where you live in this nation, take a good look around: How many of your friends and family members are finding good paying jobs with decent benefits and a realistic chance of a career? By contrast, how many have lowered their expectations, settling for that job at Wal-Mart, K Mart or Starbucks – sales, service or retail? How many are content with their jobs and wish to make it a career?

After nearly six years of George W. Bush, most Americans are reaching the point of desperation, buried in debt, mortgaged to the hilt, unable to cope with the high cost of housing and gasoline, petrified that a crisis will leave them at the mercy of friends or family, who are themselves faced with the same desperate circumstance.

The administration has reduced the unemployment numbers by cutting the length of benefits (after a fixed period, the numbers magically vanish but the people they represent do not). They cut the inflation rate by conveniently omitting housing and energy costs though the burgeoning commuter swarms swallowing our freeways can hardly do the same. By the same distortion, they claim that wages are outpacing the cost of living but the purchasing power of real people, by any objective measure, has dramatically declined while our savings have been consumed by high-interest credit card debt.

Beneath the towers of avarice, the future is clouded and dark. We must eventually come to grips with the solemn fact that things will not get better without systemic change. The improvements trumpeted by politicians with a vested interest will be illusory, temporary and insignificant. Organized labor (owing partly to their own corruption) has been marginalized and the working people are being transformed (through the magic of neo-liberal policies of corporate dominance) from a middle class, consumer society to a low-cost labor force.

Like the family farmer, the middle class worker is facing extinction. Like the farmer, they have buried us in debt and when we can no longer pay, they will take our homes, our land and everything we have of value.

It is a serpent that swallows itself. When the consumer society has vanished, who will be left to buy their corporate goods? No matter: He who dies with the most toys wins.

The ten-ton elephant looming just over the horizon is the real estate market. When the workers evacuating the great urban centers have reached saturation and can no longer afford their new homes in the commuter kingdom, the vultures of finance will swoop in for the final kill. Because there are no buyers left, either the price of housing will collapse or the money will stagnate for lack of a market to move into. Either way, the darkness will lower upon our house.

We will allow the Asian giants to gobble up our vital resources because, in the end, we will have no choice. What then?

The neocons and neolibs are globalists. To them, there is no nation; there is only the corporation. To them, the rights of labor to a living wage and decent working conditions are barriers to be overcome – an objective they have very nearly achieved.

JAZZMAN CHRONICLES

If the new globalists have solved the conundrum of the vanishing consumer, they have not let us in on the secret. Like an occupation without an exit strategy, we can be sure it will not go easy for the foot soldiers.

Yet the president assures us that the future is bright. He knows because his advisors have told him so. When have they ever led us astray?

Come down from the tower, Mr. President, and smell the decay. It is the stench of a dying American middle class. Won't you at least attend the funeral?

Jazz 12 August 2005.

HOW TO BUST A UNION
Pataki & Bloomberg

The New York City transit strike is over and millions of residents and tourists in the five boroughs are relieved that they will no longer have to suffer what the governor and the mayor characterized as an act of blatant lawlessness.

Soon the discussion will shift from who was right and wrong to which side lost and won.

The great shame is that the debate that should have happened, the debate the people of this nation so desperately need to hear, never occurred. Every major media outlet gave only cursory coverage of the transit workers' case. They uniformly preferred to give free reign to Mayor Michael Bloomberg and Governor George Pataki, buying prologue to epilogue their condemnation of the strikers as thuggish, law-breaking, ungrateful laborers turning their backs on the hard-working citizens of New York.

It is perhaps unfortunate that the strike came in the holiday season, when those who are still watching the news were engaged with other concerns, including drilling in the Artic wildlife reserve, developments in the Jose Padilla case, the latest round of WTO talks, the Iraq election, renewal of the Patriotic Act, and the NSA domestic spying scandal. We had hardly recovered from the torture rendition scandal and the execution of Tookie Williams. Outside the greater New York area, few saw the transit strike coming and fewer were prepared to defend the beleaguered Transit Workers Local 100.

JAZZMAN CHRONICLES

Beneath the constant drone of our ambulance chasing, gore seeking, "breaking news" addicted press, we are trapped in a perpetual three-day news cycle, inundated by a never-ending series of attacks on our liberties, our sense of justice, and our economic well-being.

In this context, perhaps we should be forgiven for not rallying to the cause of the New York transit workers. The problem is: They are us. They are all of us. They are the working class of Bolivia, fighting against the privatization of water and public services. They are the jobless of the Gulf region and the homeless of New Orleans. They are the family farmers of Arkansas, the teachers, nurses and firefighters of California, the perplexed senior citizens in a maze of pharmaceutical options, the high school student whose last option is military service, and the family struggling to hang on to a lost way of life.

Nothing emblemizes the American tragedy more than the transit workers of NYC, caught in a vice grip between a union-busting mayor, with all the power of government behind him, and a working class public numb and dazzled by a pandering press and the image of an All American city recapturing hope from despair.

The real tragedy is that the heroes of September 11, 2001, who braved the storm and kept on marching, are the same working class stiffs who are being shunted aside by big government and big corporations today. It was not the Rockefellers or the elite of Wall Street who were called upon to pay the price of tragedy. It was the firefighters, the beat cops, the teachers and public employees.

Never mind that the NYC Mass Transit Authority had a billion dollar surplus this year, Mayor Bloomberg made a great show of indignation at the illegality and selfishness of the strikers. The fact is union busting has been going on in New York and throughout the nation for a very long time. When the National Labor Relations Act was passed in 1935, ten percent of the working force was unionized. In subsequent decades, union representation rose to 35% before beginning a long decline in the mid to late sixties, as employers realized that legal remedies to union busting were weak and unenforceable. Today, an estimated eight percent of private labor is unionized (less than it was in 1900). It is hardly coincidental that real wages have declined accordingly, including those of nonunion workers.

The sad truth is Mayor Bloomberg wanted this strike. Like Ariel Sharon playing the Right of Return card on the last day of a peace summit, Bloomberg played the two-tiered pension card knowing it would be a deal breaker. The two-tiered system asks the union to sell out future workers by asking them to pay more than current workers. Like a poison seed, it inevitably divides the working force and leads to disintegration.

Pataki, Bloomberg and their lackeys on the MTA left the union with only one way out. They knew how it would play in the media.

What Middle Americans fail to understand about George W. Bush, common New Yorkers fail to understand about Pataki, Bloomberg and his predecessor. They do not represent New Yorkers. They represent the wealthiest of the elite and Bloomberg is among them. Like Giuliani before him, both wish to establish themselves on the Republican play list as world-class union busters.

What is happening to the transit workers in New York is happening to all Americans from coast to coast. It is the reason thousands of Californians spend hours daily commuting to work: They can no longer afford to live where the jobs are. It is the reason the true family farmer is all but extinct. It is the reason households must have two incomes to get by. It is the reason we are drowning in debt. It is the reason a growing number of working people have neither health care nor retirement benefits. It is the reason the middle class is itself a dying breed.

If you believe that is a preposterous proposition, imagine that credit cards were abolished tomorrow. How many of us could continue to pay the bills, support our families, take care of emergencies, and keep a roof over our heads?

What is happening in America is that we are losing what our fathers, mothers, grandfathers and grandmothers worked so hard to achieve. We may have issues with the labor movement, but they are essential to the maintenance of our society. Without them, we will return to sweatshop labor and slave wages.

When the overlords of capital lecture us on the fundamentals of a global economy, we must answer: the world needs unionization as well. When America, by far the largest consumer on the planet, refuses to trade with nations that fail to meet minimum standards of wages and working conditions, the equation changes overnight.

The transit workers in New York were being fined two days wages for every day of the strike. The union was being fined a million dollars a day. Union leaders were being threatened with incarceration.

When was the last time a union leader in America was jailed for doing his job?

We are understandably perplexed by the roller coaster news cycle, the virtual absence of fair and in-depth reporting, and the endless barrage of tragedy, horror and injustice on our televisions. We are tired, frustrated and we have come to believe there is nothing we can do to alter the course of events.

In the case of the New York City transit workers strike, those of us who remained silent were wrong.

The one thing these hard-working men and women needed from us in their time of trial was the one thing we all have to give: Support. They still do.

So do we all.

Jazz 28 December 2005.

THE WAY OF THE DOW
Voodoo Central

The year was 1987. Cocaine was the drug of choice. Ivan Boesky and Michael Milken were the leading names in a widespread insider trading scandal. The Tower Commission held Colonel Oliver North and President Ronald Reagan accountable for the Iran-Contra "arms for hostages" scandal. Mark McGwire and Barry Bonds played their first full seasons in the major leagues.

It was also the year of a precipitous decline in the Dow Jones Industrial Average: On October 19, the same day US warships shelled an Iranian oil platform in the Persian Gulf, the Dow dropped 508 points.

In and of itself, the crash was not unique. What was unique, in the wave of reforms that followed, was that the New York Stock Exchange instituted a braking system to slow the process of panicked stockholders selling en masse. It was hoped that the newly designed, computer controlled system was "crash proof" but of course that was not the case.

In the reform of 1987 inside operators gained access to the inner workings of the market. More than ever, the New York Stock Exchange became Voodoo Central for a market that has long depended on conjuring illusions of prosperity.

Ostensibly, the exchange was empowered to halt trading for up to two hours in a collapsing market. In reality, we observe the workings of the braking system every time we watch the ticker with a decline in progress. The numbers do not flow as one would expect in a free flowing market; rather, they stutter, stumble, stop and often freeze like a digital display losing its pixilation power.

When the market seemingly froze late on the trading day 27 February 2007 and then suddenly burst like a broken dam, a stiff 250 point drop was revealed to stunned traders. What we actually observed was a foot slipping off the brake.

The market is and always has been a house of cards. It was in fact the business model for the Enron-Anderson mega-corporation. Its function is to generate capital and protect the interests of its most powerful members. Like Enron, the market produces no useful product yet it thrives on the belief that its services are essential. Just as deregulation was the key to Enron's excesses and ultimate collapse, an unregulated stock exchange has produced every imaginable variety of gaming, fraud and manipulation.

When the market crashes, as it inevitably must, the biggest losers are always the small investors. Going back to the Panic of 1893, when JP Morgan consolidated wealth and redesigned the nature of money in America, the power players are always protected. The eventual beneficiaries of every crash are the surviving elite, the only ones standing to pick up the pieces of shattered economies and shattered lives at bargain basement prices.

Always the one with the least to lose loses all. That is the way of the Dow.

Today's economy has been wonderful for the wealthiest investors and a well-timed crash will only increase their net holdings.

Every market crash shares certain characteristics: overvalued stocks, under-funded debt, irrational optimism, and underlying economic weakness. There is one unique feature in the current crash (whether it is manifest in the coming days or further down the line): It is the first triggered by a foreign market. In 1987, there were concerns that Japan was too heavily invested in American assets but those concerns are dwarfed by the current ownership of American debt by foreign governments – most notably China.

What is happening now is a perfect storm that will soon blow away the house of cards that is the American financial marketplace. The combination of national debt, individual debt and the looming implosion of the housing market is a deadly convergence.

The American president, already known for the worst foreign policy blunders in history, may soon have to account for the worst economic meltdown since the Great Depression. Like Iraq, Afghanistan and New Orleans, he is ill prepared to deal with the crisis.

He is a free market man. That is the way of the Dow.

As always with these dire predictions, I hope I am dead wrong. I know the people who would suffer most. I am one of them. I am not an economist, only an observer with eyes wide open.

I see the clouds, dark and foreboding on the western horizon, and I know there is a powerful storm heading this way. I see the writing on the wall and I know how to read.

How long will it take our leaders to see what I see, to read as I read, and begin to make fundamental changes?

Jazz 4 April 2007.

BLAME SHIFTERS
Immigration and Free Trade

Nothing could be less genuine than the posturing of Pat Buchanan, Lou Dobbs and the coterie of rightwing blame shifters working to transform fear of the "migrant invasion" into political advantage or viewer dividends.

What makes this carefully orchestrated, plotted and planned strategy all the more depraved is that the very same global labor exploiters who ripped the heart out of the American working class (beware citizens of France for you are embarked on the same path) now wish to pin the blame for their crimes on the exploited.

Having watched these race-baiting bigots operate under the umbrella of populism for too long, I have no doubt the strategy is deliberate. The blame shifters tried so very hard to play the immigration card to save them in the midterm election but they came up short because of the ironic reluctance of the Rove-Bush machine that was hoping to parlay the president's affinity for Mexican politics into future Republican dominance.

The philanthropic side of the free trade equation is a sham − a con so thinly veiled it can only fool the foolhardy and uninformed. Scapegoating racists have always supported blame shifting politicians to their own demise. As former president and supreme leader of the World Bank Paul Wolfowitz found out, the con does not work on sincere and educated public servants dedicated to fulfilling their mandate.

The blame-shifting scheme is all the more nefarious because it pretends to help those it most grievously injures. On the global scale, it promises to lift up third world nations but in practice it strips those nations of natural resources while gutting social services and shamelessly exploiting labor with slave wages and inhuman working conditions.

In America (as in other elite nations), it promises cheap goods and an ever-shifting economic base that will enable us to leap ahead of our competitors. It promises superior education and training but it cuts funding for both and saddles public education with unachievable goals in preparation for its role in the next blame-shifting strategy.

When the promises inevitably flounder, it is blamed not on trade policy, not on foreign labor exploitation, not on greedy corporations with unconscionable profit margins, but on the impoverished migrant labor force.

The much publicized immigration policy compromise, embraced by the mainstream of both major parties and offering a convoluted route to legalization and citizenship with a price tag that few could ever afford, is yet another means of evading debate on a bipartisan trade policy that richly rewards international corporations while decimating the workforce worldwide.

The policy allows the blame shifters to continue their assault on immigrant labor while continuing to ignore both the short-term remedy (strict and cost prohibitive penalties on employers) and the core solution: Fair Trade.

For those defenders of CNN's Lou Dobbs, who more than any other mainstream pundit parlays race baiting, anti-immigrant venom into media ratings, why is it that he turns every discussion of immigration solutions into border defense and ultimately a multi-billion dollar boondoggle wall that sponsors insist (like the Israelis) on calling a fence?

Dobbs knows and has admitted that harsh,

unforgiving and strictly enforced penalties on employers of illegal immigrants would stem the tide at a fraction of the cost, yet Dobbs and his Republican blame-shifting compadres know a cash cow when they see one. They do not want a real solution. They would rather focus on a wall that would mock our founding principles and further a transformation of the American dream into a façade – a guarded refuge for the privileged, a gated nation fearful of its own neighbors, and an object of international pity.

Ancient China built the Great Wall, Berlin had its wall of isolation, Israel has its wall of oppression and America will join that history of ignominy with its wall of fear.

What more could we do to impress the world with our fall from grace: State sanctioned torture? Suspension of Habeas Corpus? Aggressive wars on false pretense? Indifference to the plight of the poor and dark skinned victims? Scientific regression and denial of the world's most pressing problem? Incarceration of the homeless, disabled, dispossessed and destitute? The forgotten ruins of the American city that most embodies our multicultural heritage?

"Give me your tired, your poor, your huddled masses, yearning to be free…"

Let us send Lady Liberty back to France. We have forsworn her and France needs to be reminded of her enlightened ideal.

Jazz 21 May 2007.

WHO KILLED CALIFORNIA?

The decimation of the California economy was a long-term project. It began in earnest in 1978 with the passage of the infamous Proposition 13 (the People's Initiative to Limit Property Taxation). Like the current Proposition 16 (a proposal that protects private utilities while pretending to uphold the right to vote), Prop 13 was perhaps the first use of the most brilliant means of circumventing democracy ever devised.

Embodied in the state constitution that appropriately numbered ballot proposition not only set a limit on property taxes at one percent of value but it also made it virtually impossible for the state to raise sales or income taxes by requiring a two-thirds vote in both legislative houses. Since property taxes were the primary source of funding for education, Prop 13 was the poison pill that sickened and eventually killed the future of education in the state once known as golden.

By crippling the state's revenue raising mechanism it was only a matter of time before economic events would bring California to its knees. Those events would come at the turn of the millennium when the west coast energy fraud followed in the wake of the great technology bust. The latter was largely the product of Wall Street brokers who oversold high tech stocks on the theory that the rules regarding assets and earnings no longer applied. Fortunes were made by clever investment managers who bet against the very stocks they sold to the public. Investors including California's public pension funds lost and the balance sheet began to turn red.

The west coast energy crisis represented the first returns from bipartisan deregulation in the energy industry. It was that deregulation that enabled companies like Enron to fabricate shortages where none existed and run up prices to absurd levels that state and local authorities paid to prevent blackouts from crippling the economy. An estimated fifty billion dollars was transferred from California to a handful of Texas based oil and energy companies. Enron would eventually pay a price but the rest got away with the cash. It was and is a foolproof business model: Steal billions in profits and pay millions in fines.

Politically, Governor Gray Davis paid the price (though he was no more responsible than any other witless politician) and California was treated to the spectacle of a recall election to elevate Hollywood action-hero Arnold Schwarzenegger to the governor's palace. As Californians would soon learn, Davis was not the problem and Arnold was not the solution.

Despite its fall from grace and utter collapse, Enron was in fact the business model that Wall Street would adopt as the bipartisan march of deregulation moved on unabated. The collapse of the real estate market (an unprecedented economic phenomenon) was not only predictable but inevitable. Opportunity and greed is a deadly combination. Because it could and because no one was home at the sheriff's office, the world's largest and most ruthless arbiters of wealth decided to transform the economy into a Ponzi scheme. Economics ceased to be a science and became a plaything of the corporate elite. Like the alchemists of old, spinning gold from common nickel, corporate mystics spun value where none existed.

They were playing with our lives. They were tempting fate. They were inviting an epic catastrophe. But all along they knew the game was rigged. In his last act as president, George W. Bush initiated the bailout that would eventually transfer a minimum of a trillion dollars to the very criminals who caused the collapse. They gambled with other people's money and won. We paid the price.

No one paid a greater price than California. The state is ranked third in home foreclosures with an even more dramatic decline in the value of real estate. In the fourth quarter of 2009 nearly two million California homes were valued less than the outstanding mortgage (Bloomberg.com). A decline in property value means a decline in property tax revenues. A twenty billion dollar budget deficit combined with over eighty billion in long-term bond debt means that California is effectively bankrupt without any visible means of recovery.

So now the Republicans step forward with a promise to save California by running it more like a business. They never mention that it was Republican policies (even when embraced by Democrats) that destroyed the economy. They simply promise to run it more like a business. Someone should ask former CEO's Meg Whitman and Steve Poizner what they would actually do with a business whose revenue-raising potential was frozen at 1978 levels. Ask them what they would do with a company whose income was insufficient to finance its debt. The answer is they would liquidate and that is precisely what they intend.

In the 1970's and 80's there was a breed of Wall Street bottom feeders who dealt primarily in junk bonds and made vast fortunes buying up companies whose value was less than the sum of its parts. It was not good policy. The victimized companies were often sound and profitable businesses. Bought and sold on the scrap heap, workers lost good jobs and industries folded or moved out of the country but the brokers and bankers made money.

It was the age of greed and nobody seemed to care who got hurt. Now we have an entire nation in the process of liquidation and California leads the way. They won't give up until they've sold off our parks, our redwoods, our waterways and public buildings.

Unfortunately neither the people nor anyone in a position of power seems to have a clue. Berkley professor George Lakoff wrote a simple proposal at the heart of the matter. It said, "All legislative action on revenue and budget must be determined by a majority vote." It would have effectively repealed Proposition 13 and rendered Proposition 16 void. It would not have resolved our deepening crisis but it would have been a start.

The Democratic Party killed it with an assist from Attorney General and gubernatorial candidate Jerry Brown on the grounds that it would have been electoral poison.

Respecting Brown's political moxie there must be some truth in it but the greater truth is that Orwell's nightmarish vision has come fully into focus. Our perceptions are so dominated by corporate dictates that we can no longer distinguish our interests from corporate interests. If the Democratic Party fears to take a stand in favor of majority rule then democracy itself is imperiled.

So the California Democracy Act will not be on the ballot but Proposition 16 will and if it passes it will effectively prohibit localities from starting or expanding their own local electrical services to avoid falling victim to the kind of corporate manipulations that hit them during the west coast energy fraud of 2000-2001.

Whenever we are asked to vote on a proposition we should be skeptical. If the proponents pretend it is about one thing when in fact it is about another, we should automatically vote no. When its sponsors include the Chamber of Commerce we should recognize that the

Chamber is nothing but a fence for corporate funding. When it requires a two-thirds vote instead of prohibiting what it intends to prohibit we should revolt.

California is in trouble and there is no easy solution in sight. Like the nation as a whole we must somehow rebuild our industrial base. We must invest in quality jobs. We must invest in education, rebuild our infrastructure and lead the world in green technology.

How we get there from here is a mind-numbing proposition. The one thing we should all agree on, however, is that we should not reward the persons and policies that put us in this untenable position.

Jazz 20 April 2010.

OBAMA SELLS THE FARM
THE CLINTON PIVOT

"Take a tally. Look at what I promised during the campaign. There's not a single thing that I haven't done or tried to do."

Barack Obama

If Barack Obama truly wanted to be a transformative president he would have pushed to break the senatorial filibuster at the very beginning of his term in office. As a former senator he knew full well the power and inclination of a senate minority to obstruct all legislative initiatives.

There is not a syllable in the constitution that empowers a minority in the least democratic branch of government with an absolute veto over all legislative action. That usurpation of power was accomplished by senatorial rules of conduct, which are subject to change by a majority vote at the beginning of each congressional session.

Had the Obama administration been able to lower the filibuster threshold to 55 votes or required senators to hold the floor as they once did or limited its duration to 27 calendar days, the incoming president would have been empowered to usher in an era of progressive change, the very change for which the electorate thought it was voting. He surely could have passed Medicare-for-all with a ten or twenty-year phase in. He could have restructured the tax code and fully financed an emerging green economy. He could have rebuilt the nation's infrastructure and established an interstate mass transit system, achieving something very close to full employment.

There is no end to what Obama might have accomplished had he been willing to take that first bold step. With the economy moving again, he might well have reversed his party's fortune in the midterm elections. But that bold president, the one that would have summoned the spirits of Franklin Roosevelt and John Kennedy, was nowhere to be found.

It was never what Barack Obama had in mind. It seems he was playing from the Bill Clinton handbook all along. Even now, as we approach a new session of congress, there is little talk of reforming the filibuster. With the Republicans taking control of the lower house perhaps we no longer think it important. But the lower house is closer to the people and closer to the next election. Any representative who refuses to extend unemployment benefits with the unemployment rate near ten percent will almost certainly guarantee the wrath of his or her constituency and an abbreviated tenure in Washington. No, the Senate will remain the leading source of obstructionism and the problem should be addressed. But that is not in the Clinton handbook.

Never was I so reminded of Slick Willy as when Obama with a passion rarely summoned in his presidency challenged his progressive critics to name a single instance where he has failed to keep his word: "Look at what I promised during the campaign. There's not a single thing that I haven't done or tried to do."

While managing to project himself as an antiwar candidate, he never promised to withdraw all troops from Iraq. He promised to escalate in Afghanistan and that he has done.

Winning the support of organized labor, Obama promised to sign the Employee Free Choice Act but it never reached his desk. He never promised to support Fair Trade but he appeared to support labor provisions in Free Trade agreements. He advocated exacting a price on those who export jobs but it has never made the Obama short list.

He advocated health care as a right rather than a responsibility but he never promised a public option. He never promised universal healthcare or that health insurance rates would be mediated. He did oppose an insurance mandate but few have held him accountable on that ground.

From Don't Ask, Don't Tell to immigration reform and the repeal of the Bush tax cuts, Obama has always chosen his words carefully. Considered in context, his words are consistent with his actions. He never claimed to be progressive so he cannot be held accountable for failing to live up to what that label entails.

Obama ran as a pragmatist and he has governed in that fashion. What he does not seem to understand is that we really don't care how carefully he parsed his words. We don't care if we were fooled by the audacity of our own hope. We frankly don't care if he is a man of his word or not.

We are living in hard times and we'd like to know he is out to help us. If the president truly believes his compromise on tax policy is in the public interest, fine. Let him state his case. We respectfully disagree and we'll state ours.

Obama has made it clear he is not beholden to the left for having rallied to make him president. Neither are we beholden to him for having done so. While few of us would argue that he is worse than George W. Bush or John McCain, that's a little like saying a plunge in freezing water is better than a dip in raw sewage.

From a pragmatic point of view, we could have chosen to rally around Hillary Clinton in the primaries. Why didn't we? Because we knew what to expect from another round of the Clinton administration. We witnessed Bill Clinton's pivot to the right after his party lost the midterm elections. We witnessed welfare reform and bipartisan agreement on free trade (job exportation) and deregulation, all major Republican initiatives. Even after winning reelection, Clinton held to the right in a bold attempt to dominate electoral politics by eliminating the left from the equation. (In the end, he didn't even have the guts to pardon Leonard Peltier. Yes, some of us still remember.)

We could not rally around Hillary because she showed no inclination to govern differently than her husband. We could not support a third-party candidate because the stakes were high and no candidate rose above the level of symbolism. We rallied to the Obama camp because he was perceived as antiwar and relatively progressive. It was better to gamble on the unknown than to stake our hopes on the highly improbable.

We did not want another Bill Clinton but it seems that is exactly what we got. We gambled and lost but that does not mean we must sacrifice our voices and convictions by continuing to support a president that has not earned it.

The strangest thing about this sudden rightward pivot on tax policy is the urgency with which it was presented, as if the opportunity would be lost once a new congress was seated. As all must recognize by now this is an overwhelming Republican victory. (The president's supporters can produce all the graphs and charts they want. The Republicans favor all the tax cuts. The president sold the farm for an extension of unemployment benefits.) Rushing the proposal through a lame duck congress before the Bush tax cuts expired was not only unnecessary but it also worked against the president's interest.

Had the tax cuts been allowed to elapse the power would have shifted to the White House and a still Democratic Senate. A Republican lower house of congress could do absolutely nothing without Democratic consent. With unemployment near ten percent, there is not a working family in the nation that is not affected. With every vote against extending benefits, the Democrats could have rolled out ads in every district: Joe Worker lost his job when his plant was shipped to China. He took a job as a janitor and was laid off in the Great Recession. Now he's lost his unemployment benefits. Congressman Right says he's lazy. What do you say?

As for tax cuts for the middle class, how many times could the anti-tax party say no without losing all credibility?

The Republicans were playing a bluff and either the president was fooled or he did what he intended to do all along: the Clinton pivot.

The American two-party system functions to the extent that it does by managing a delicate balance between corporate interests and the public good. When the right goes too far by gutting that part of government that serves the public good, the left assumes power to restore the balance. When both parties represent essentially the same policies, balance is never restored. The result is a reversal of centuries of progress, an unraveling of the New Deal and the Great Society, a process that predictably ends with the decimation of Social Security, Medicare, environmental protection, public education, civil rights, labor rights and all regulatory agencies.

It is a prescription for disaster because it favors the

rich to the detriment of the middle class. When the working people can no longer afford to purchase goods and the middle class is impoverished, the system no longer functions.

Barack Obama is no Franklin Roosevelt. He never intended to be. He is a pragmatist, a man everyone can love once they get to know him. He is Bill Clinton without the personal charm.

It's not all bad. There is something to be said for intelligence and good management. There is a reason the crash did not happen on his watch. Had Clinton been president instead of George W. Bush, I'm certain he would have acted long before the global economy was on the threshold of total collapse.

Nevertheless, the elements creating the conditions that inevitably led to systemic failure were put in place by Bill Clinton. Unfortunately, Barack Obama shows no inclination to make the necessary corrections.

Jazz 14 December 2010.

AUSTERITY BRIDGE
MADE IN CHINA

In 1989 the Loma Prieta earthquake brought down a section of the San Francisco Bay Bridge, weakening the structure to such an extent that rebuilding the 1936 monument to engineering was inevitable. When completed in 2013 the bridge, like virtually everything stocked in Wal-Mart, Target or any other mass merchandise chain, will bear on its underside the insignia: Made in China.

If ever there was a clear example of what is wrong with the American economy this is it. The state of California claims it will save $400 million on an estimated $7.2 billion project for its betrayal of American industry. The state does not say how much of that $400 million could have been saved by applying for federal funding which would have required the structure to employ American manufacturers.

Let it be clear: This has little to nothing to do with Free Trade. China can overcome the cost of transporting a bridge 6,500 miles not only because it employs cheap labor but also because the Chinese manufacturing industry is government owned and subsidized. If our government were to subsidize manufacturing it would be decried as a violation of the principles of Free Trade. Indeed, it would.

The fact is: Free Trade does not exist. International corporations and their proxies in government employ the principles of Free Trade selectively to justify labor exploitation and to maximize profits.

JAZZMAN CHRONICLES

In the fantasy world of Free Trade all parties operate on an equal playing field according to the laws of supply and demand. In the real world everything a government does or fails to do creates imbalance. If government provides universal health care as they do in Europe it creates imbalance. If government provides incentives to drill for oil or produce ethanol it creates imbalance. If government guarantees a minimum standard of living wages and decent working conditions it creates imbalance. If government owns an industry and guarantees its success the imbalance is obvious. If it sanctions indentured servitude and neglects slave labor the imbalance is equally obvious.

The fact is: In a civilized world that recognizes the fundamental rights of labor, exploitation of labor is itself a subsidy and all nations that embrace those rights have a responsibility to punish nations that do not. They can do so by enforcing trade sanctions or by subsidizing their own industries.

In a perfect world, all merchants would enjoy equal opportunity while bearing equal responsibility. In the beginning there was equity. But then greed took hold and one merchant decided he could buy out the competition. Monopoly trumped free enterprise and the system became imbalanced and dysfunctional. Employers were empowered to require workers to work longer hours at lower wages under increasingly difficult conditions. Sweatshops and child labor became common. Retirement and medical assistance were nonexistent. If a worker was hurt on the job he became unemployed.

As the abuses mounted it became mandatory for a democratic government to act. Child labor was banned, working standards were mandated, and minimum wage was instituted. Monopolies were broken apart to restore competitive balance and workers gained the right to organize. Unions became the counterbalance to the power of big business.

The system flourished. For the first time in history, working people joined in the prosperity of the nation, laying the foundation for a middle class. Working people were empowered to buy goods and services beyond the necessities of life. Each generation looked forward to a better standard of living for the next. Businesses prospered on middle class consumption.

Social Security and Medicare answered a basic need while relieving employers of the burden.

The system worked not because businesses, industries and corporations were allowed to do as they pleased but because unions and government struck an equitable balance.

Now we have lost the balance because one party decided to serve their corporate masters exclusively and the only viable alternative decided it was easier to go along than to fight for the working people. When the economy went global it provided an opportunity to reset the table and labor was not invited. We no longer hear the term Monopoly but now we have corporations that are considered too big to fail. We have politicians who would prefer to see the economy collapse and working people suffer if it will give them a competitive advantage in the next election. We have governments at the state level declaring war on unions even though organized labor is but a whisper of the roar it once was. We have bipartisan agreement that the national debt is our dominant priority though real unemployment exceeds ten percent and those jobs that are available no longer offer a living wage.

We are badly out of balance and our government is as dysfunctional as our economic system. We are sustaining wars on multiple fronts while we are being told there is no choice but to welcome an age of austerity.

In the case of the Bay Bridge, the deal with China

was struck in 2006 when the economy was relatively strong. The federal government was willing to make up at least some of the difference by subsidizing the project but the state of California under the leadership of Governor Arnold Schwarzenegger placed no value on American jobs and American workers. Schwarzenegger and his co-conspirators in government ran the state like a corporation and corporations have no values, no sense of justice, and no principles of fair play.

As a result, when the new Bay Bridge is opened for business it will represent far more than a triumph of engineering; it will symbolize the systematic degradation of our economy. It will stand as a monument to the corporate world of greed and profiteering. It will be a magnificent memorial to the once-prospering middle class.

It will be a bridge to the age of austerity. In other nations it has begun in earnest and the people have taken to the streets in protest by the tens and hundreds of thousands. In other nations they have come to the realization that they were sold a bill of goods. They have watched the moneychangers run their economies into the ground while they escaped with all the loot. The ordinary working people are angry, fed up, and they are not going to take it lying down. What is happening now in Greece and Spain is a preview of what will happen in America if the austerity hysterics have their way.

When will we begin to wake up? When will we realize that we are all in this together? When California turns its back on workers in the steel mills of Michigan, we all lose. When union busting becomes a government mandate, working itself from state to state, every worker in America loses.

When our elected officials throw up their hands and claim they can do nothing about the exportation of our jobs to cheap labor markets because the capitalist bible of

Free Trade economics forbids it, we must ask ourselves: Who do they really represent?

We are at a crossroad. What we do now may well determine the kind of world future generations will inherit. Will it be a world in which only the wealthy can pursue higher education? Will it be a world that sacrifices the elderly and infirm so the elite can enjoy ever-lower tax rates? Will it be a world in which fathers and mothers must work two jobs just to pay down the debt?

Yes, we are at a crossroad and the only real power we have left is the vote. If we choose to squander it on politicians who preach austerity and raise the flag of Free Trade, then our cause is lost and our future is bleak.

Jazz 1 July 2011.

THE TEXAS ECONOMIC MODEL
A RACE TO ROCK BOTTOM

"If you care about putting people back to work when nearly 14 million are unemployed, maybe Texas has something to teach us."

Rick Wartzman, *Los Angeles Times*

The same economic geniuses that gave us the Great Recession and nearly crashed the global economy are back with a vengeance and a new message: We ought to be following the Texas model of job creation.

Those of us who have memories longer than an Alzheimer patient will recall that these are the same chefs who cooked up the deadly brew of Free Trade, deregulation, evisceration of anti-trust laws and unlimited corporate power. To everyone on the working end of the economic strata it was an unmitigated catastrophe and one that may haunt us for decades. But to those whose idea of labor is handing down dictums from the executive suite it all worked out fine. We paid the bill and they got multi-million dollar bonuses.

Those of us with memories longer than a crack addict on pot will also recall the last time the nation adopted the Texas model: Based on a fictional success derived from skewed data, the country was saddled with No Child Left Behind.

To everyone engaged in public education NCLB is a

disaster on par with Free Trade economic policies but to those who created and promoted it as reasonable reform it is working as designed: As it destroys public education it opens the door to privatization.

As it is with education so it is with Texas economics.

The crux of the current argument is that in these difficult times Texas is the national leader in job creation. The argument is as flawed as a high school engineering project. On the global scale, China and India are the leaders in job creation. Should we adopt the Chinese model?

The reasons jobs are migrating to Texas, Mississippi and North Dakota are the same reasons American jobs are moving to India: Low wages, minimal health and retirement benefits, an unregulated working environment and a virtual prohibition of unions.

Texas is among twenty-two Right to Work states and according to the US Bureau of Labor a disproportionate fifteen of those states are among the top twenty-five in job creation over the last decade. The exceptions to the rule are the rust belt states that continue to hemorrhage jobs regardless of Right to Work status.

For the uninitiated Right to Work is the most effective legislative means of union busting ever invented. In a Right to Work state no worker can be required to join a union, pay union dues or pay an equivalent amount to charity. Because unions depend on worker unity in negotiations with management, Right to Work laws have a crippling effect. Since it would be discriminatory and therefore illegal to pay some workers a different wage than others, under the mandates of Right to Work, a non-union worker is allowed to freeload on the backs of union workers. When a union engages in collective bargaining, all workers benefit. If a union goes out on strike, non-union workers can break the strike and scabs can be hired without consequence beyond the individual conscience. The union is rendered powerless and therefore less able to attract new members.

Just as non-union workers benefit at a cost to union workers, Right to Work states are empowered to steal jobs from states that honor the Rights of Labor (including the Right to Organize in the workplace) by offering lower costs to corporate employers.

Ultimately, Right to Work as public policy is a zero sum gain. If all states followed the Texas model, job creation would be spread evenly but there would be no net increase in jobs. It would however unleash a race to the bottom as organized labor ceased to exist and jobs would offer ever lower wages and benefits.

Like a serpent that discovers its tail and consumes itself, the Texas model on a national scale would end catastrophically because the already dying middle class would be dead and buried and consumption of unnecessary goods would shrivel like a raisin in the sun. Our consumer-based economy would inevitably collapse.

Do we really want to become a nation where corporate treasures are built on the backs of cheap labor?

This is a classic case of pound-foolish and penny-wise. It is the age-old strategy of dividing workers against themselves. It is Starve the Beast in its most cynical form.

The difficulty with economic issues is that the language required to explain them is so convoluted it becomes incomprehensible. It is like the variable rate home mortgage loan with a bubble payment that no one would sign if it were properly explained.

It should be sufficient to say that these Texas model pimps are the same folks who screwed us out of our homes. These are the same brain trusts that shipped our well-paid jobs overseas and replaced them with minimum wage labor. These are the same folks who gave us mass foreclosures and rendered our properties less than worthless for their own gain. These are the same people that crushed the American Dream and replaced it with a nightmare of debt, default and depression.

Now they want to finish the job and Texas will show us the way.

The Texas model is a Trojan Horse. It is paraded before us in all its sequined glory. We are expected to bow down and pay tribute. On the surface it appears to offer great rewards but once we let it in the gates, the enemy inside will emerge to destroy us.

Texas is a place where government is controlled from the corporate boardrooms and the only function of government is to do corporate bidding. Instead of following Texas on the road to ruin, the twenty-eight states that still believe in the rights of labor should take counter measures.

In so many ways we have been following Texas for far too long. Texas gave us deregulation of oil and gas and the $50 billion west coast energy fraud. Texas gave us Enron and Anderson Accounting. Texas gave us Karl Rove and George W. Bush. Texas gave us war for oil in the Middle East. Texas gave us chemical-hydraulic fracturing to extract natural gas deposits deep in the earth, poisoning drinking water throughout the west. Texas gave us No Child Left Behind.

It seems to me Texas has been waging a cold war against the rest of us for a very long time. Maybe it's time we started fighting back.

Governor Rick Perry made some cavalier comments in April 2009 about Texas withdrawing from the union to which I reply: Go ahead. Make my day.

Jazz 14 July 2011.

LONDON CALLING
CIVIL UNREST IN THE AGE OF AUSTERITY

London calling to the faraway towns
Now that war is declared-and battle come down
London calling to the underworld
Come out of the cupboard, all you boys and girls

The Clash

To all those British intelligencia who attributed the recent riots that rocked the streets of London, Birmingham, Bristol, Gillingham, Nottingham, Manchester and Liverpool to hooligans, you're as wrong as the myriad free enterprise economists who swore we had nothing to fear from a deregulated marketplace. You're as wrong as the killing of an innocent man. You're as wrong as holding the poor accountable for the errors of the elite. You're as wrong as an economy that creates an ever-widening gap between the haves and have-nothings.

Prime Minister David Cameron finds fault with everyone but the policies of his ruling party or indeed the increasingly conservative policies of his predecessors in the opposition.

In the prevailing world of British politics, entrenched poverty does not fit into the equation of civil unrest. It has nothing to do with thirteen million impoverished citizens but rather to do with discipline in the schools. It has nothing to do with low wages and rising unemployment but rather to do with excessive tolerance for aberrant behavior. It has nothing to do with the deprivation of ethnic minorities and everything to do with moral depredation.

As income inequality rises to levels unprecedented in the modern era, Mister Cameron promises a crackdown on the rising turpitude of the ungrateful poor in Britain's booming slums and the polite society applauds as if to acknowledge a fine golf shot.

What the Prime Minister and his colleagues are desperately trying to deny is the relationship between the riots in England and the events in Cairo, Tripoli, Damascus and Athens. The combination of inequity, inequality and poverty is a potent brew that leads inevitably to civil unrest. The only difference is a matter of degree.

London is calling and Washington should be listening. By every measure the circumstances are worse in America than in Britain. The poor are poorer, the disparity between the rich and the rest is greater, the social safety net is less intact and the burden of poverty falls even greater on minorities.

Everywhere across the globe the tide of suffering rises and governments have decided that the only solution is to shift the burden downward. The European Union has become an enforcement mechanism for an age of austerity. Budgets for relief of the afflicted and assistance to the poor are slashed to protect the corporate profit margin. In America a presidential candidate complains that the poor do not pay income taxes. Convinced by their own propaganda machine that the poor are unworthy leaches on society, legislatures in Florida and elsewhere order drug testing to qualify for unemployment insurance. Increasingly draconian laws are passed to further stigmatize immigrants at the bottom of the economic spectrum.

Blame the victim has become the mantra of the financial elite, passed down to the working ignorant, spreading like a plague on the nation.

When we have punished the poor all that we can, when we have pushed the once thriving middle class into poverty, when we have evicted families from their homes, when we have forced the family business into bankruptcy, when we have stripped the undocumented of all rights and deported as many as we can, only then will we begin to realize we have been duped.

Civil unrest is the last recourse and the natural consequence of austerity.

Fear not. The authorities are prepared for this contingency. Stripped down security forces will be mobilized to protect gated communities. Violence will be contained in the poor neighborhoods. Slums will burn. Crowd control will become increasingly brutal. Blood will flow on the streets of poverty. Violence will beget violence in a vicious circle of disorder and ruin.

As in Britain, whoever is president will decry the decay of moral fiber and pledge to fight gangs and criminal elements to restore law and order.

There will be no more discourse on economic policy. There will be no more talk of universal healthcare. There will be no more protests against job exportation, free trade agreements or deregulation of industry or financial markets. We will dutifully elect leaders who promise to crack down on lawlessness. Our elections will become contests on who can project ever-greater toughness. We will look for someone to play hardball with the unruly masses.

The erosion of civil rights and civil liberties that began long before September 2001 will continue to accelerate. The right to privacy is the first casualty. City streets and public squares will be under fulltime surveillance.

Telephone conversations and communications media will be monitored. The right to speak freely will come under attack. The right to assemble in protest will be relegated to obscure and closely guarded locations far from public access where the eyes of the corporate media never travel.

There will be no more mass protests against wars of choice and wars for oil as more and more of our sons and daughters line up to fight – not out of patriotism but as the only means of escaping destitution at home.

For all the unrest, for all the violence and destruction, there will be no revolution. The government of the United States will not be threatened. Unlike Tunisia, Egypt and Libya, there are no overlords of justice that will come to our aid. We the people will stand helpless before the most powerful government in the history of the world.

We will rise up and we will be beaten down. We will rise again and the government's response will go beyond what any democratic state can bear. What then?

What is happening before our eyes is that the governments of the world in concert with their sponsors in the corporate empire have devised a plan to revise the social order.

It has taken me longer than it should have to imagine what the end game of the new world order looks like. The corporate mind is unscrupulous and greedy but it is not ignorant or foolish. I have speculated that corporations were so fixated on short-term profit that they refused to see the long-term consequences of their actions. By destroying the working middle class they were eliminating the very consumers on which they depend.

But it seems to me they have discovered a new consumer class. Because of the sheer numbers in China and India, they can prosper for decades without a working consumer force. They intend to replace the working middle class in Europe and America with a management middle class in Asia.

It is the only way it makes sense. It is a plan laden with risk and it demonstrates an incredible disdain for working people. It is risky enough depending on the stability of a corrupt democracy in India and an authoritarian state in China. It is even more risky to create a permanent class of the working poor in the democracies of Europe and America. There will be pushback.

In the end their plan for a corporate world will fail because the spirit of self-determination, the desire for freedom and the yearning for democracy will prevail. We will ultimately press our cause at the ballot box. Despite all the technology and resources mobilized to control our minds, we will overcome. Whether it takes a decade or a hundred years, we will prevail because we are on the right side of history.

Jazz 3 September 2011.

OCCUPYING WALL STREET
The Revolution Started without Me

"[Occupy Wall Street is] a diffuse and leaderless convocation of activists against greed, corporate influence, gross social inequality and other nasty byproducts of wayward capitalism not easily extinguishable by street theater...."

Ginia Bellafante,
New York Times, September 23, 2011

In the summer of 1968 I had finished my freshman year in high school. By chance, I journeyed to San Francisco with some older fellow students, checked the scene at Haight-Ashbury, partied with the cast of Hair and ended up on the beach in Big Sur talking philosophy. I was offered a hit off a joint but declined.

Later that year a friend and I hitched to a New Year's concert at the Fillmore West. As Cold Blood, Boz Skaggs and the Voices of East Harlem marked the hours to midnight, joints passed freely among the audience. This time I accepted though my friend declined.

I had come to understand that marijuana was far more than a recreational drug. It was a sacrament to the Cultural Revolution. It signaled openness to change and a willingness to finally throw off the constraints of our upbringing.

In the ensuing years, I spent many weekends hitching

to the Bay Area, breathing it all in, learning and engaging from the Haight to Washington Square to Telegraph Avenue, Peoples Park and Sproul Plaza. It was an awakening and an apprenticeship.

We were the children of the Rockwell fifties when life was easy, hair was uniformly cropped, and ideology was a well-manicured lawn. We did not question authority and we were constantly assured that our lives would be secure and bountiful if only we went along.

Like so many generations before us, the people who ruled over our lives and controlled our perceptions lied to us. In the mid-sixties, we began to tear at the mask. They were sending us off to war against people we never knew existed and whose crimes were an impenetrable abstraction. They rejected capitalism/colonialism and somehow this made them our enemies.

They were sending us off to war, to kill and be killed in ever-growing numbers, and we were sick of it. We demanded change. We wanted more than an end to war. We wanted a transformation of the very fabric of society.

I was a revolutionary in training but by the time I came of age everything had changed. Jimi, Janis and Morrison were dead. The nation's original terrorists had taken the lives of Martin Luther King Jr. and Bobby Kennedy. The National Guard had gunned down student protestors Allison Krause and Jeffery Miller and bystanders William Schroeder and Sandra Scheuer at Kent State University. Ten days later police shot and killed Phillip Gibbs and James Green at a protest at Jackson State in Mississippi.

We were effectively served notice that if we continued to engage our constitutional right to gather in protest we would be shot down in the streets. We had moved from the hope and exhilaration of Woodstock to the disillusionment and despair of Altamont.

Berkeley and San Francisco were still happening

places but the movement was undergoing a transition from the external to the internal. The revolution was over.

My time came and went. The revolution had started without me and by the time I was ready to take my place on the front lines it was over.

Four decades later, when I read about the Occupy Wall Street movement, I am reminded of the movement that was born in San Francisco circa 1967. It too was belittled by the mainstream media. It too was criticized for its lack of a cohesive message. It too refused to be defined or guided by political voices or appointed leaders. It too was brutally attacked by the very officers who are supposed to protect its citizens.

I do not know where this movement will lead but I applaud its creation. Like it or not, for better and worse, the late sixties cultural revolution defined a generation either in sympathy or in opposition. Those who were fortunate enough to be there when it formed and as it spread across the nation were an important part of history.

The difference between this movement and the antiwar protests of the Bush era is that the latter had a clearly designated beginning and an end. They were highly organized weekend events, licensed by the authorities and proceeded along a prescribed route. When they were over, the protestors went home. There was no attempt to occupy, no camps and no real opportunity to build relationships on common interests.

In the late sixties, the counter culture occupied People's Park and Telegraph Avenue. People came to San Francisco and occupied the Haight. Students occupied university buildings and campus grounds. The people built a movement on the grounds where they lived and found a way to survive with underground economies.

The authorities will never be afraid of a movement

they can license and control. They will never be afraid of resistance that plays by their rules. They will never be afraid of the Tea Party or an antiwar movement that stages events, that provides portable toilets, that sells tee shirts and hands out pamphlets only to go home at the appointed time.

The Occupy Wall Street movement has the potential to become a living, breathing cultural revolution because it is leaderless and inclusive, because it is creative and diverse, and because it attracts young people and university students who have been betrayed by the economic system they have inherited.

Young people were told they had to complete higher education to compete in the new global economy. Now all but the elite are being priced out of their universities. Now those who take on exorbitant loans are graduating only to find there are no jobs even for them. The high-paying, high-skill jobs have also been sent overseas. Now they have found common ground with the rest of their generation because they are all out of a job, out of luck and out of hope.

They will come to the movement because they have a personal interest. They will come because they know the sting of betrayal. They will come because the only way forward is to fundamentally change the system.

They are not socialists but they know what socialism is. They are not capitalists but they know what capitalism is. They include both socialists and capitalists because they know they must form an economy that incorporates elements of both if they are to serve both society at large and the individual.

They are open to ideas and will not be bound to one ideology. This is their time and they are trying to create something new and suited to their technological world.

I salute them and appeal to all university students and young people everywhere. Join the cause and see what you can make of it. This could be the defining and formative movement of your generation. If you do not take hold of it and engage, the time may come when you regret not taking your place in history.

Do not let the revolution come and go without you.

Jazz 10 October 2011.

OMISSION IN OSAWATOMIE
A Line Obama Will Not Cross

Like the sirens to Odysseus, President Obama's address at Osawatomie, Kansas, was pleasing to the progressive ear but if you allow its seductive tone to capture you, it could well prove fatal to the cause.

We have heard this song before. It takes us back to the soaring oratory that uplifted the masses and propelled a one-term senator to the presidency. Then as now, the president correctly and brilliantly deconstructs the problem: The middle class is under siege, hemorrhaging skilled and unskilled jobs to cheap labor markets overseas, resulting in depressed wages and declining benefits, depleted retirement funds, union busting and unregulated industries.

But, then as now, his solutions fail to approach the heart of the matter. Proclaiming a new world economy based on innovation, he advocates government funding for research and education, science and engineering, progressive taxation, regulation, consumer protection and a commitment to building and rebuilding the nation's infrastructure.

These are all worthy ideas that the president strings together with a rising intonation in order to avoid the obvious, central and core solution. Consequently, he builds to a dull crescendo, sounding a sour chord and all too familiar refrain: Technology and innovation will save us.

The president prides himself on his knowledge of history, so much so that he summoned the memory of

Theodore Roosevelt in this address. Unfortunately, history does not uphold his case. Technology and innovation have never sustained the middle class. They have created fortunes and whole industries but how it affects the working people depends entirely on where the industries are located and how the workers are paid.

Take a good look at the major innovations of the Free Trade era: The personal computer, the laptop and the smart phone are all made in China and serviced in India. Solar technology created advanced solar collectors and panels, creating a thriving industry in China. Hybrid vehicles may be assembled in America but by-and-large they are constructed in foreign nations where the cost of labor trumps all other concerns. Even our bridges are made in China.

Within the parameters of a global Free Trade economy, there is no innovation that can revive American industry. The idea that innovation and education are going to create jobs for 300 million Americans is a pipe dream, a fantasy and, in this case, an excuse not to address the heart of the matter.

The obvious answer and the one that perpetually evades the president and the majority of his party is Fair Trade. American workers can compete and win on a fair playing field but no one can compete with dirt-cheap labor. The masterminds behind the new global economy have built corporate profits by exploiting the cheapest possible labor overseas and simultaneously undermining labor in our own country.

What is Fair Trade?

It is built on the conviction that all nations that engage our nation in trade should uphold the rights of labor, including the right to organize, and pay their workers living wages.

How would Fair Trade be implemented?

The most direct route would be to reserve preferred trade status to nations that protect the rights of labor, provide basic health and retirement benefits, and pay living wages to their workforce. All other nations would be subject to a tariff proportionate to the cost of compliance.

The message to China, India and all other nations that now benefit from the imbalance of trade would be clear: Pay your workers at home or pay to protect our workers at the border.

Human rights and the critical issue of carbon emissions also come into the equation but if the goal is rebuilding American industry, then the heart of the matter is labor.

Why is Fair Trade off the table?

There was a time when simply raising the cry of "Protectionism" could defeat any such proposal but after decades of job exportation, Americans are losing their fear of words. Protecting our workers in the current environment is a moral imperative.

Accordingly, Fair Trade is alive and well in the United States Congress. Even Republicans in the House and Senate are afraid to go on record in opposition. The Trade Reform Accountability Development and Employment Act proposed by Senator Sherrod Brown of Ohio and Representative Michael Michaud of Maine would fundamentally reshape America's trade policy, bringing labor to the forefront.

Unfortunately, the silence of the White House enables congressional leadership to keep the measure from coming to the floor for a vote. President Obama presses forward on Free Trade deals with Korea, Columbia and Panama, ensuring the exportation of jobs to even more nations.

Even progressive economists are reluctant to address trade policy, preferring to attack trade imbalance through so-called currency manipulation. The idea is if our trading partners increased the value of their currency it would be more expensive to buy their goods and less expensive for them to buy ours. If the revaluation were large enough and sustained, it would certainly have an effect.

The problem with the currency approach is that it allows the tenets of Free Trade to stand. It does not end the anti-labor measures enforced by austerity regimes under the dictates of the International Monetary Fund. That is why even the prototypical corporate candidate, Republican Mitt Romney, feels free to advocate punitive actions against China based on the charge of currency manipulation. It leaves workers out on the lurch and the rights of labor out of the picture. Moreover, all nations manipulate currency. That is the primary function of the Federal Reserve.

Of course, if we were to insist that other nations respect the rights of labor we would have to do a better job of protecting our own workers. We could no longer allow individual states to effectively crush unions with so-called Right to Work laws. We could no longer allow legislative attacks on collective bargaining without paying a price.

It is as if the entire liberal establishment, from the politicians to the intellectuals to the media, signed on to Bill Clinton's Free Trade mandate back in the eighties and have adhere to that agreement ever since.

It was a deal with the devil, a betrayal of every workingman and woman not only in America but throughout the world, and it demands to be revisited now.

In 2008 candidate Barack Obama said, "I voted against CAFTA, never supported NAFTA, and will not support NAFTA–style trade agreements in the future. While NAFTA gave broad rights to investors, it paid only lip service to the rights of labor and the importance of environmental protection."

Where is that candidate now? He disappeared upon taking the oath of office.

In retrospect, it seems amply clear that candidate Obama made a deal with Wall Street, his leading campaign contributors, before he embarked on his road to the White House. Fair Trade was off limits. It was the one territory he could not visit. It was the one line he could not cross.

An original sponsor of the Employee Free Choice Act (an affirmation of the right to organize and establish a union by majority vote) had President Obama remembered his labor roots in his address at Osawatomie, had he raised the banner of Fair Trade to initiate his campaign for a second term, then that address might have stood alongside Teddy Roosevelt's New Nationalism or Franklin Roosevelt's New Deal inaugural address.

As it stands, it is the perfect symbol of his presidency to date: A promise unfulfilled.

If we were to initiate the age of Fair Trade it would fundamentally change the debate and ultimately alter the structure of the global economy. The world would face a choice. The European people would insist that their governments follow our lead. China and India would fight back but they are as dependent on us as we are on them. A bargain would be struck and a transition would be negotiated.

America would win back her industries and the middle class would re-emerge at the heart of the global economy.

It will happen in any case. It is inevitable. To

continue on the path we are on will lead only to massive civil unrest and the result will be the same. By initiating Fair Trade now we could avoid much of that inevitable pain and disruption.

If only we had a leader with the courage to break his pact with Wall Street in order to keep his promise to the American people.

Jazz 14 December 2011.

THE WAR ON LABOR
RIGHT TO WORK

"When you are approaching poverty, you make one discovery which outweighs some of the others. You discover boredom and mean complications and the beginnings of hunger, but you also discover the great redeeming feature of poverty: the fact that it annihilates the future.   Within certain limits, it is actually true that the less money you have, the less you worry."

George Orwell
Down and Out in London and Paris

As a fan of George Orwell I have grown to wonder if too many of our political geniuses misinterpreted his classic work *1984* as a how-to book on controlling the masses. Had they read his earlier autobiographical work *Down and Out in London and Paris*, they would have understood that Orwell was a man of the people and his sympathy was planted firmly with the poor, the outcast and the working class.

Of all the Orwellian phrases in common use these days one of the most egregious is the Right to Work. Adopted in twenty-three states, right-to-work laws effectively ban labor unions by prohibiting workers from gaining union representation by a majority vote.   The Right to Work is the right of a worker to refuse to pay union dues. Because unions gain power by representing workers as a united front in negotiations with management, right-to-work laws negate that power.

As a result of these union-busting laws, unions have ceased to function and workers earn less. The average worker in a right-to-work state earns anywhere from $1,500 to $5,000 less per year than workers in other states. They receive less in health benefits, less in pension benefits and less protection from unsafe conditions or unfair dismissal.

Studies have been inconclusive on the decline of union representation as a result of right-to-work laws because unions must already have declined in order for such laws to be adopted. The law therefore serves as a substantial roadblock to rebuilding a union movement.

The war on labor does not end with Right to Work. Having decimated labor in the private sector (as of January 2011, according to Bureau of Labor Statistics, the number of union workers in the private sector fell to a 100-plus-year low of 6.9 percent), anti-labor forces have taken aim at the public sector. The tactic of choice against police, firefighters, teachers and other government employees is attacking the right to collective bargaining and binding arbitration.

To fully comprehend this attack, you need to understand that government employees are often prohibited by law from striking to achieve fair treatment in negotiations with their employers. In those cases where it is legal to strike, conscientious employees are loath to do so because of the harm it would do to students and communities. Binding arbitration by an impartial body is an alternative to the strike.

When you take away the right to fair arbitration, you leave workers at the mercy of their employers and you cut the union off at its knees.

These same politicians who yearn for yesteryear

when the middle class was strong and the American dream of upward mobility was still alive, neglect to tell you that those were the days when unions were on the rise.

The peak rate of union workers in this nation was the mid 1950's. After the experience of the Great Depression and the Second World War, Americans understood that if workers were to achieve financial security they needed representation to counter the power of corporations and bankers. Combined with the GI Bill, enabling veterans to gain a college education, the union movement more than any other single phenomenon created the working middle class.

The statistics are staggering. From a high of 35% of workers represented by a union to a low of 11.9 % today, if you wonder why wages have stagnated while corporate profits have exploded, look no further.

Both of the key strategies in the war on labor operate on the same principle: divide and conquer.

The right-to-work laws divide the workforce into those who support the union, who feel a sense of responsibility to fellow workers, who recognize the need for unity in representation against the powerful, against those who will not sacrifice a red penny of their paycheck for the common good.

The assault on collective bargaining is an attempt to divide private workers, who have already lost their union rights, against public workers, who earn more and claim greater benefits because they have retained union representation.

We are all in this fight together. If we wish to push back the most powerful force the world has ever encountered, corporate greed, we must unite against the tide. The right to organize the workplace, the right to unionize, must be fought for and defended.

We are under siege. We are the victims of a

devastating fifty-year war against workers that is relentless and without mercy. The corporations have taken control of our government with unlimited sponsorship of elected officials. They have moved our industries to China, Malaysia, Indonesia and elsewhere, without any concern for the welfare of our nation or its people. They have outsourced our technology service, drafting and infrastructure planning jobs to India. They have reduced their share of tax responsibility to a minimum with offshore accounts and favorable legislation, forcing a beleaguered workforce to pick up the tab. And they have done all this with a sense of entitlement.

We are just beginning to fight back. We are beginning to understand that if we speak out in one voice, the 99 against the one, our politicians will begin to listen. We are beginning to understand that fighting for labor rights overseas will bring the jobs that are rightfully ours back home.

China does not own America.

The low point in this war on labor was in 2010 when the anti-labor forces took control of our legislatures but they overplayed their hand. In 2012 we must take back control and reverse the course of the nation.

The corporations do not own us.

The first part of the labor agenda must be to strike down right-to-work laws in the 23 states that now embrace them. The most efficient means is a federal law affirming the principle of majority rule as fundamental to the rights of labor. Barring that, states that uphold the rights of labor should establish a policy of preference to those states that do the same. Right-to-work states should be held to account. States that fail to acknowledge the basic right to organize the workplace should pay a price.

The second part of the labor agenda should be an

affirmation of the right to collective bargaining and binding arbitration as an alternative to the general strike. Again, federal law is the most efficient means to this end but state alternatives should serve to provide motivation should the federal government fail.

The corporations that have taken control of our government will cry foul. They will accuse us of class warfare to which we will reply: yes, but now we are fighting back.

Jazz 19 February 2012.

ROTTEN APPLE
A Symbol of Labor Exploitation

In 1984 I bought one of the first Apple Macintosh computers to roll off the line in Cupertino, California. At 132 K ROM (hardly enough to power a toaster by today's standards), the Mac came loaded with a serviceable writing program (Mac Write) and an ingenious graphics program (Mac Paint) and the age of personal computing was born in earnest.

In those days Apple was a fiercely independent alternative to IBM, the corporate beast that monopolized the computer industry. Apple was a symbol of American ingenuity and innovation. Apple users were loyal to the company and we believed that Apple was loyal to us. We remained loyal even through substandard products because we believed that Apple had a social consciousness.

I don't know when Apple changed. It doesn't really matter. But when Indiana Governor Mitch Daniels delivered the Republican response to the State of the Union address, trumpeting the late Apple co-founder Steve Jobs as a job creator, I knew something was rotten to the core. Daniels was right about Apple job creation. The trouble is some 95% of those jobs were created in China under deplorable working conditions.

In America the very same politicians whose policies wreaked havoc on the global economy spend most of their time attempting to exploit the devastation by attacking what remains of the rights of labor. Too often the so-called liberal establishment falls silent on the right to organize and the right to collective bargaining (an alternative to a general strike).

In Europe the same voices that claim to represent the left are planting their staffs with the anti-labor forces of austerity.

The recent New York Times article exposing Apple's exploitation of Chinese labor ("How the U.S. Lost Out on iPhone Work" by Charles Duhigg and Keith Bradsher, January 21, 2012) reads more like a rationalization if not an outright defense. On international labor rights the Times is as bankrupt as the Greek treasury. An unashamed proponent of Clintonian Free Trade, the Times argued with an unmistakable tone of admiration that Chinese workers at substandard wages (workers at the leading Apple manufacturer, Foxconn Technology, recently received two wage increases from an equivalent of $135 per month to roughly $300 per month) were so motivated that they could be roused to work at a moment's notice. They frequently work 24 or 36-hour shifts at tedious jobs with little complaint (except for the occasional riot or threatened mass suicide). The story noted that there were plenty more sweatshops making complementary products just down the road.

The Times glossed over the rumored suicide rate and the fact that the company running the largest sweatshop on the planet had to install nets outside its walls to prevent workers from jumping to their deaths.

The Times' Nicholas Kristof and his fellow compassionate complicters will tell you that the workers are better off as exploited labor than they otherwise would be. They could be back on the farm tending rice fields at a meager existence or worse; they might be on the streets of protest in open rebellion.

There is little to distinguish the defense of Apple and labor exploitation from the antebellum defense of slavery. The advocates of slavery also argued with characteristic audacity that the slaves were better off than they would have been on their own accord. They had roofs over their heads, clothing, medical care and meals on the table. They were slaves, subject to beatings, inhuman treatment and whatever torture can be imagined, but at least they had food to eat. Their white masters could rape the women at will and the men could do nothing about it but at least their basic needs were fulfilled. If not for a few rabble rousers, malcontents and radical idealists, the slaves would have been happy to live out their lives, generation after generation, in contented servitude.

We recognize now that such arguments are an affront to human decency but in the land of antebellum slave plantations they were tolerated if not embraced.

It is by no means admirable that workers can be roused from sleep at any time of the day or night to work another twelve-hour shift. It is not laudable that workers can be forced to work in unsafe environments with toxic chemicals and hazardous waste. It is not acceptable that children of twelve are subjected to these conditions. When workers riot and threaten mass suicide it is not a sign of relative wellbeing.

I know that Apple is not alone. Foxconn has contracts with Dell, Hewlett-Packard, Sony, Motorola, Nokia, Toshiba, Samsung, Amazon, Nintendo and IBM.

Apple has responded predictably to the negative publicity of the Times report and the potent monologue of Mike Daisey now playing at the Public Theater in New York ("The Agony and the Ecstasy of Steve Jobs"). It has hired an "independent" watchdog to monitor and report on labor abuse in China and elsewhere. Unfortunately, that organization receives its funding from the industry.

Apple perceives labor abuse as a public relations problem because Apple does not care about workers in China or anywhere else. Apple cares about the bottom line and Apple is afraid that this wave of negative publicity will forever tarnish its image and affect its profit ratio.

I know the futility of calling for a boycott. We are addicted to our intelligent devices and there are no viable alternatives. We cannot for a moment believe that the sweatshops in Indonesia or anywhere else where the economy thrives on cheap labor are any better than those in China.

I am calling for a different response and one that would have an impact on the bottom line. We do not need the latest gadget. We do not need the immediate upgrade to the latest technological innovation. We can wait.

That is what I am suggesting that every conscientious consumer should do. Delay that next purchase. Delay it as long as possible. Make that purchase only when it is necessary.

If enough people take this approach, Apple and all the others will notice. They will make changes. They may not move their plants back home immediately but in time, who knows?

If they were to move back home, you can bet that those 750,000 Chinese jobs would translate to 500,000 robotic devices and a handful of managers and maintenance crews.

So be it. If they continue to operate as they are, they need to know that the fight for labor rights does not end at our shores.

Jazz 16 February 2012.

AUSTERITY BACKLASH
THE MYTH OF EUROPEAN SOCIALISM

The countries that are doing very well in Europe are the Scandinavian countries. *Denmark* is different from *Sweden*, Sweden is different from *Norway* – but they all have strong social protection and they are all growing. The argument that the response to the current crisis has to be a lessening of social protection is really an argument by the 1% to say: "We have to grab a bigger share of the pie."

Joseph Stiglitz

There are few themes the American right likes better than accusing the centrists of the Democratic party of trying to enact European socialism. Led by their corporate candidate for the White House, they point with apparent glee at the economic slide in Europe and proclaim the triumph of conservative economic theory.

Nothing could be further from the truth. Europe's decline was in fact a direct consequence of its adopting American-style free enterprise economics. The initial crisis (along with our own) was caused by drinking the kool-aid of Wall Street's brave new theory: that wealth can be created where none actually exists.

Under the leadership of Europe's new Iron Lady, Angela Merkel of Germany, and France's conservative Nicolas Sarkozy, the continent embraced the assumption that financial markets could govern themselves. When the fraud was exposed in America and the markets imploded worldwide, Europe responded with rightwing ideological zeal.

Europe discarded the lessons of practical economics and marched lockstep down the road to austerity. The result is a prolonged, profound, double-dip recession that threatens at once European unity and the sovereignty of its member nations.

Spain should have been an exception to the austerity mandate but its socialist government fell in line, yielding to the influence of Europe's more powerful nations. Socialist in name only, Jose Luis Rodriguez Zapatero followed the examples of discredited former Prime Minister Tony Blair and former American President Bill Clinton. Claiming the mythical "third way" he discarded his most fundamental principles by lowering taxes on the wealthy, cutting public spending by record amounts, cutting wages for public workers, and freezing pensions.

As any practical economist would attest, Zapatero and indeed most of Europe not only failed to act responsibly; they did the opposite of what was required.

Zapatero was swept from office at the end of 2011 and others will soon follow. The democratic backlash against the austerity mandate has swept through the Netherlands, smashed through Greece and Italy and today (as I write these words) it rolled over Sarkozy's France.

The people have served notice that they will not stand idly while their governments sell out to the interests of the elite. They will not pay for what the financial institutions broke. They will not suffer while the wealthy prosper. They will not watch their pensions disappear, their wages cut, their unions broken, their services stripped bare while the international corporations that conspired in this crisis continue to prosper.

If this sounds familiar to American readers, it should.

Austerity is what the Republican right wants to bring to our nation in the name of freedom.

Socialist Francois Hollande of France has promised to challenge the austerity mandate, fundamentally changing the Euro Zone by strengthening the European Investment Bank, launching Euro bonds to finance the debt while funding infrastructure projects and public works. He proposes a financial transaction fund (a tax on the wealthy) and fiscal reform to allow nations to carry larger deficits. He seems to understand what economists have long understood: that deficits must be allowed to stimulate a stalled economy in a prolonged recession.

We can only hope that Hollande holds true to his principles and, backed by popular support throughout the continent, he is able to hold sway over his more powerful rival for the reigns of the European Union.

The only nations that have largely been spared the ravages of the austerity regime are the Scandinavians of Denmark, Norway and Sweden, who managed to retain their social safety nets and social consciousness.

There is much we can learn from the lessons of Europe but we must first lose our irrational fear of words. The economic principles of socialism are neither the enemy of democracy nor of the American people. In its essence, socialism is less an economic system than an ideal. Whenever the public good is considered in public policy, the principle behind that consideration is socialism.

There is not and never has been a purely socialist economy on a national scale. Simply because a government exerts control over the economic sector does not mean its policies are for the public good. The oligarchies of Russia and China (though both have incorporated significant elements of free enterprise capitalism) use their control largely for the benefit of the elite and ultimately to the detriment of the people at large.

I would argue that any nation that does not employ democracy as its system of government is inherently anti-socialist because it denies the will of the people as an expression of the public interest. Moreover, any nation that denies the fundamental rights of labor is anti-socialist as the vast majority of people work. By this standard the most socialist nations on earth are the Scandinavian nations that have survived the global economic downturn relatively unscathed without exploiting labor.

All social programs, including public pensions, public works, public health care, public education, job training and unemployment benefits, proceed from the socialist ideal.

To imagine an America without its socialist component is to imagine a nation without highways, without dams, without Medicare, without Social Security, without public hospitals or clinics, without public schools or universities, without unemployment benefits, without mass transit systems, on and on. In short, a purely capitalist America would be a very different place and not one that many of us would enjoy.

There is of course no nation on earth that is purely capitalist. Every nation strikes a balance between individual interest and public good, between the wants of the one and the needs of the many, between free enterprise and social responsibility.

Free enterprise provides an economic force that generates wealth but it also tends to encourage greed and corruption. Governments must function to control that force, to mediate inevitable conflict between workers and employers, to counterbalance the powerful against the powerless, to counteract corruption and moderate greed. Social programs by any name are essential to a functioning society.

The American electorate is too easily dazed and

confused by words meant to evoke a guttural response. Socialism is one of those words. In the next election we will hear that word like a daily drumbeat. The word we will rarely hear is austerity. That is a shame because the party seeking the White House, controlling the House and obstructing the Senate is running on an austerity platform.

Listen to the people who have experienced austerity first hand and heed their warning. Austerity is economic suicide and all but the wealthy will suffer. Listen to the people of Europe and understand what is at stake.

Jazz 8 May 2012.

VOLUME V

SUPREME INJUSTICE

CONTENTS

PREFACE

THE CORPORATE COURT

The significance of the judiciary, the third branch of government, can hardly be overstated. Headed by the nine individuals appointed for life by a sitting president, our nation has achieved voting rights, civil rights, marriage equality and curtailed the excesses of government by rulings of the judiciary. The courts have the power to propel the nation forward or hurl it reeling backwards. It can protect the rights of citizens or it can serve the interests of the elite.

The millennial decade began with a distinctly conservative Supreme Court led by the epaulet wearing Chief Justice William Rehnquist. It consistently represented corporate interests and tended to the right on social issues. It was known as a federalist court for its strong defense of states rights although its most famous and infamous decision (Bush v. Gore 2000) was distinctly anti-federalist.

The court's personnel has changed significantly since the reign of Rehnquist gave way to the chiefdom of John Roberts, appointed by the younger Bush. As under Rehnquist the pivotal vote is in the hands of Anthony Kennedy, a Reagan appointee who has shown surprising flexibility despite his conservative philosophy.

The Roberts court retains Reagan appointee and rightwing stalwart Antonin Scalia, the silent regressive Clarence Thomas appointed by the elder Bush, Clinton appointees Ruth Bader Ginsburg and Stephen Breyer, the George W. Bush appointee Samuel Alito, and Barack Obama's appointees Sonia Sotomayor and Elena Kagan.

While no court in history has been entirely predicable the current court as the last court is "as predictable as the salivation of Pavlov's dogs" in one essential way: It favors corporate interests. The Roberts court awarded corporations all the rights of citizens without the corresponding responsibilities. The Roberts court allowed unlimited corporate contributions to political campaigns. The court found that the Environmental Protection Agency had no authority to regulate the emissions of power plants. This court has ruled against the interests of workers at every opportunity.

It is repeated nearly every presidential election cycle and it is generally true: The most important and far reaching consequence of electing a president is that she or he may well appoint the member of the court that tips the balance and affects real change.

These chronicles concern justice in America over the last decade and how the judiciary has altered the course of history.

Jazz.

THE FEDERALIST COURT
Blame the Democrats and Move On

Judge John G. Roberts of the District of Columbia Court of Appeals has been nominated to replace Sandra Day O'Conner as the pivotal member of the Supreme Court. Who is John Roberts? By all accounts, he is a very conservative and brilliant lawyer who will rise to a position of elite power at the age of 50. Most importantly, he is a favored son of the Federalist Society and he will be confirmed.

Did we really think there would be no price to pay for rallying behind a pro-war candidate in the last election? (No, Howard Dean supporters do not get a pass; he was pro-war after the first bomb fell on Baghdad.) Did we really think there would be no price to pay for playing into Karl Rove's right hand by raising the specter of gay marriage? (No, we cannot ask a movement to stand down but we might have expected just a little political moxie.)

What follows now is as predictable as the salivation of Pavlov's dogs. The Democrats will give a show of opposition just as the Bush administration gave a show of consultation with the Senate. The inevitable capitulation will be followed by a rationalization that it could have been much worse. Indeed. Then again, it might have been much better.

So now, we are saddled with an overwhelmingly regressive Supreme Court, a court that will define its mission by harkening back to the original intent of the founders. Women had no voting rights in 1787, no less reproductive rights. Minorities had no rights in 1787 and the landless masses shared their disenfranchised status. The Constitution falls silent on the rights to clean air, clean water and global climate change. The Bill of Rights was belatedly added to the document to appease the poor working class stiffs who won the War for Independence.

What were the intentions of our founders?

There is nothing wrong with a love of history. There is nothing wrong with studying the words and thought processes of the nation's founders.

Attempting to decode their intentions, however, and applying them to a 21st century world is something akin to consulting the ancient art of Tarot to arrive at foreign policy.

As if it were a matter of central importance, strict constructionists (i.e., those who do not "legislate" from the bench) are fond of pointing out that Thomas Jefferson was not present at the Constitutional Convention (he was in Paris serving as ambassador to France). If Jefferson could have known that his absence would have implications more than two centuries later, he would have declined the assignment. Without Jefferson, the republicans (those who believed in and were committed to the principles of democracy) were left with an aging Ben Franklin (with Tom Paine, author of the most progressive constitution in the young nation -- that of Pennsylvania) and future president James Monroe. The opposing aristocrats (i.e. Federalists) were led by Alexander Hamilton, John Adams, a silent George Washington, John Jay and James Madison. The latter would join the party of Jefferson but he was one of three authors (with Hamilton and Jay) of the notorious Federalist Papers.

When the modern day strict constructionists, including John Roberts, look to interpret the intention of the founders, they do not look to the republicans; they look to the Federalists. At the heart of the current and inevitable tipping of the balance of judicial power is the adoption of the Federalist Papers as the definitive subtext to the Constitution.

The Federalists (like the Federalist Society today) were not interested in democracy or securing individual liberties. They were interested in forming a bond between government and the wealthy elite. To that end, they established a national bank. They grudgingly conceded the lower house to a direct electoral process, provided only white men with substantial holdings in land could vote. Members of the upper house were appointed by the state legislatures and the president was selected by the Electoral College. Hamilton proposed that the Senate and the President be selected for life.

What were the intentions of the founders?

The Federalist Papers are no more a political treatise than the *Communist Manifesto*. They are a collection of ideas for establishing and maintaining an economic ideal. In the hearts of the Federalists, that ideal is the protection of wealth, the protection of property, and the perpetuation of the ruling class.

I do not believe this court will reverse *Roe V. Wade*. If they do, they will further divide a polarized nation and we will begin the long process of passing a constitutional amendment. Rather, they will limit a woman's right to choose by increments and the feckless Democrats will hardly register an objection. They will not outlaw gay marriage though they will likely uphold a state's right to discriminate in any manner they choose. They will allow school prayer and religious displays on public property to appease the religious right. They will kill affirmative action and attempt to bury it forever.

The court's primary function will be to strike back government regulation of private business at every turn. Anti-trust law is dead. Environmental law is rendered toothless. Regulation of essential industries – energy, water and food – is barely breathing. Security reigns supreme over individual liberties and the only rights that count are corporate.

I hope I am wrong. I am no happier with the state of our judiciary than the most dedicated judicial activist, yet I cannot escape the sense that we all share responsibility. We abandoned our principles. We sold ourselves short. Ralph Nader was right. At the critical moment (perhaps the most critical time we will ever encounter), we failed to push for a candidate who opposed the war. By allowing the opposition candidate to get by with parsed words and nuanced policies, we failed to give the people a reasonable alternative.

In our hearts, we know the truth. When every political argument ended with: Well, he's not George Bush, we knew it was over. It was over because we did not believe – and even then, we almost carried it.

Those who abandon principle for expediency do not deserve to prevail.

If we had stood on principle, if we had demanded an end to the war, we may still have lost but we could have held our heads high for the struggle ahead. On the other hand, we might have won a landslide.

As it is, wrap it up and move on. The more they push their regressive-oppressive agenda, the stronger the opposition will grow.

We still have a war to fight.

Jazz 20 July 2005.

NO TEARS FOR REHNQUIST
The Legacy of a Chief Justice

"Don't waste your time mourning – organize!"
Joe Hill, the day before his execution.

Forgive me if I have no tears to give for the passing of Supreme Court Chief Justice William Rehnquist. As thousands of my brethren lie dead in New Orleans and beneath the rubble of countless communities along the Gulf, forgive me but I cannot bow my head in mourning for this one more.

William Rehnquist was the legacy of Richard Nixon, a reminder that presidents often far outlive the terms of their presidencies. He was at the vanguard of the modern conservative movement, a movement dedicated to reducing the power and responsibilities of the federal government. In over three decades of jurisprudence, Rehnquist opposed state's rights against federal responsibility only once: Bush v. Gore. That singular fact (alongside the golden epaulets adorning his gown) is all you need to know about the judicial philosophy of William Rehnquist.

State's rights were employed to fight back desegregation in the south. State's rights were used to fight back civil rights and the voting rights of African Americans. State's rights were employed in the battle against organized labor and women's equality. And state's rights were denied in order to make George W.

Bush president.

Now, given the retirement of Sandra Day O'Connor, the legacy of one of the most ill equipped leaders ever to inhabit the White House will be felt for generations to come.

President Bush the elder was fond of speaking of "a thousand points of light" (a concept his son converted to "faith based" charities) but a thousand points of light are not capable of fortifying levees, restoring wetlands, cooling an overheated planet, or amassing the kind of response required in a major disaster.

All issues surrounding the Gulf Coast catastrophe, its prevention and relief, are the essential responsibilities of the federal government. I am not impressed with the unity tour of former presidents Clinton and Bush to raise private funds for the most basic of government functions. This is why we pay taxes and, yes, taxes should be raised. As the financers of our government, the responsibility belongs to all of us and all of us should pay our fair share – beginning with the corporations that profit from war and national tragedies.

We need not wonder what happened to all those billions of dollars we paid for Homeland Security. They went to the wars and the occupations. They went to stealth operations, sponsoring coups in Haiti and Venezuela. They went to the development of a new class of tactical nuclear weapons. They were shuffled around to pick up pork projects in exchange for midnight votes for another round of payoffs to the pharmaceutical industry, the banking and credit industry, and of course the oil industry.

We are facing the national disgrace of an abandoned city, a predominantly poor black city, and an army of lost, desperate souls, yet the White House is already shifting gears, biding its time, waiting for the cameras to turn away from the suffering so that the government can proceed with its program of austerity for the masses and tax relief for the elite.

At its very core, the modern conservative philosophy holds the poor responsible for their own poverty.

At the core, the new conservatives do not believe that the federal government is responsible for rebuilding New Orleans or restoring the afflicted to stable and decent lives.

They will not say so in public but in the private smoke-filled rooms where William Rehnquist held court, where his brethren found him charming and illuminating, it is openly acknowledged and embraced.

So forgive me if I do not bow my head for the passing of the Chief Justice. My heart is already consumed in mourning. Forgive me if I do not honor the tradition of paying homage to the dead. He was only one man, one life against a backdrop of thousands.

As labor leader Joe Hill said: Don't waste your time. Organize!

Jazz 5 September 2005.

THE ACTIVIST COURT
The Neoconservative Agenda

The remaking of the United States Supreme Court has been framed by the most extreme ideologues in modern political history as a battle between strict constructionists in white hats and their counterparts in moral darkness: the judicial activists.

In keeping with the Orwellian nature of the neoconservative culture, whose programmed indifference is delivered in the name of compassion, whose evisceration of individual rights is coaxed in the name of justice, and whose wars are prosecuted in the name of peace, the real judicial activists are the very same champions of neoconservative federalism.

It is ludicrous to suggest that either John Roberts or Samuel Alito do not have an agenda. For all of their professional lives, they have been devoted to a rightwing cause of judicial activism. That their cause is regressive hardly negates its blatant activism. Far from ruling passively on the merits of the law in a given case, both men have pressed the cause of federalism to the detriment of individual rights.

Federalism, with its roots extending backwards to the anti-democratic, pro-aristocracy sector of our founders, is yet another Orwellian term for it is dedicated to undermining, limiting and ultimately reducing federal authority to a military function. The federalists elevate states rights to the detriment of federal authority because it is only the federal authority that can protect civil rights, women's rights, voting rights, worker rights, the right to privacy and the right to dissent.

In the federalist stratosphere of elites, corporate rights reign supreme and the states form a barrier to federal interference. Far from ideological intransigence, when states step out of line (as Florida did in the 2000 election), the federalists close ranks and conspire to restrict them. The true goal of the Federalist Society is the creation of a permanent ruling class with an unfettered corporate elite to sponsor it in perpetuity.

At its very core, the federalists equate democracy with mob rule and anarchy. They will go to the ends of the earth and beyond to prevent the manifestation of a free and democratic society.

It is encouraging that a significant number of Democrats are rising to their obligation as a party of opposition, finally questioning the war and raising serious objections to the nomination of Judge Alito. On the matter of the Supreme Court, however, as they are well aware, the battle is lost. Whether it is Alito or some subsequent nomination that prevails, the federalists will rule the court of John Roberts and, unless time works its wonders of transformation (as it has before in judicial history), Lady Liberty will rue the day for years and generations to come.

That we have lost the court, however, does not mean that we must surrender the war. Rather, we must find new battlegrounds on which to press our own cause: the cause of individual freedom and democracy.

First, we must exploit the battleground our enemies have exploited so well: statewide referendum. Since we can no longer rely on federal authority to secure our rights and liberties, we must do so on a state-by-state basis. Given a lengthy history of deference to state authority, the Roberts court will be reluctant to abandon precedent. When we attack the excesses of corporate power, however, they will quickly shed their reluctance and stand exposed as the judicial activists they are and have always been.

Second, we must begin the long and difficult process of amending a constitution that falls short of its greater purpose: the establishment of an enlightened democracy.

1. <u>The Right to Vote</u>. The inherent right of all citizens to vote in free and fair elections shall not be infringed by any act of government or its authorized agents. In the aftermath of the last two presidential elections, it came as a shock to many of us that the citizens of this nation do not possess a constitutional right to vote. It is past time that deficiency was corrected.

2. <u>The Right to Privacy</u>. The right to privacy in one's person, thoughts and possessions shall not be infringed without compelling interests established in due process of law. It has become something of a judicial conundrum that the right of privacy is only implied in the constitution. Let us make it explicit.

3. <u>Military Conscription</u>. No individual shall be compelled to military service against his or her expressed will. There is general if not bipartisan consensus that military conscription is a crime against humanity. Let us lead all nations in banning forever this barbaric remnant of despotic rule. If there are not sufficient soldiers to fight a war of their own free will, that war should not be fought.

4. <u>Equal Rights Amendment</u>. Men and women shall have equal rights throughout the United States and every place subject to its jurisdiction. This common sense amendment, authored by Alice Paul in 1923, in its revised version of 1972, was ratified by thirty-five of the required thirty-eight states. It is time it had a second run.

These four amendments are only a beginning to the process of achieving enlightened democracy. Others include securing an independent media, distinguishing individual rights from the presumed rights of corporations, and the right of labor to organize on the principle of majority rule.

All is predicated on a favorable outcome in congressional elections.

As Tom Paine said in the first *American Crisis*, "Tyranny, like hell, is not easily conquered; yet we have this consolation with us, that the harder the conflict, the more glorious the triumph."

It will not be easy.

The battle lines have been drawn. We have witnessed an American insurgency, a revolution, and a takeover of all three branches of government by the most repressive elements in our society. We have seen what they have wrought and we have glimpsed the darkness they have promised. We have never had greater reason to fight.

The counter-revolution begins next November.

Jazz 4 November 2005.

CONSTITUTIONAL SUSPENSION
An Abdication of Democracy

It is increasingly difficult to find outrage against the assault on civil liberties epitomized by the USA Patriot Act and the NSA domestic spying scandal. The sad truth about the recent "compromise" to extend the Patriot Act is that it may not matter.

Under the most arrogant interpretation of constitutional war powers in recorded history, congressional mandates have been reduced to an exercise in symbolic posturing for the duration of an eternal war.

If an authorization for use of force against the Taliban and a nebulous group of terrorists under the banner of Al Qaeda can be used to justify a sweeping program of surveillance on American citizens, in direct defiance of the Federal Intelligence Surveillance Act, then any cosmetic modification of the all-encompassing powers of the Patriot Act are frankly irrelevant.

Fundamentally, if this miserable excuse for a congress does not stand up as an equal branch of government to challenge the blatantly illegal NSA spying program, even if it requires impeachment, then the entire debate on reauthorization of the Patriot Act is nothing more than a public display of the castration of the opposition party.

Assuming a relevance that does not in fact exist, the proposed changes that have reportedly satisfied such Democratic luminaries as Senators Diane Feinstein and Hillary Clinton are so miniscule that the New York Times could not delineate them with any degree of clarity.

Under the proposed changes, could the government still conduct "sneak and peak" searches of a citizen's home on the most specious of grounds, under the authority of a secret court, without recourse or even informing the victimized citizen? Yes.

Under the proposed changes, based on the lowest legal standard of relevance, could the government tap your library records, business transactions, internet activities, health records and other personal information? Yes. The only change is that, a year after the fact, the collaborating agents would be free to inform you, leaving you with the impossible burden of proving that the government's actions were both unfounded and irresponsible.

Are there any limits on how long such information can be stored or to what nefarious uses it might be employed? No.

In short, under the new and improved Patriot Act, the individual citizen yields his or her rights and the government is shielded from any reasonable recourse or accountability. Under the most egregious circumstances of abuse, such as those revealed under the Nixon administration and the reign of J. Edgar Hoover, the abused would have to prove beyond doubt that the government acted in bad faith.

Not even the National Security Administration can document "bad faith."

In short, for those of us who still believe in civil liberties, these are trying times.

These are times in which a singular tragic event has been employed to render our bill of rights, the core and foundation of our democracy, null and void.

Ultimately, it does not matter that our president has already nullified our basic rights by executive decree, if our elected officials do not understand the essential nature of universal human rights to the democratic form of government, then it is our solemn and highest duty to replace them with those who do.

It does not matter whether the betrayers of our democracy are Republican or Democrat: There is no place for them in a nation founded on law, a nation that values liberty and justice above privilege and wealth. There is no place for them in the future of our democracy.

If we believe in liberty, if we believe in democracy, if we believe in a society that respects all cultures, all religions, all philosophies and freedom of expression, then we will not endure what our government has thrust upon us in the name of security.

Do not believe that the American experiment in democracy is a straight line from the revolution to the present. Our liberties are the product of an endless struggle against the forces of oppression by an elite class often found in our government. The same arguments that are now given for unrestricted executive spying and the Patriot Act were once delivered by the defenders of the Alien and Sedition Acts.

Historically, we have had to struggle to establish a theoretical republic (rather than an aristocracy) after the revolution. We endured with the newly formed constitution of 1789. We fought back John "Alien & Sedition" Adams and the Federalists with the election of Thomas Jefferson in 1800. We fought for the abolition of slavery circa 1865, the enfranchisement of minorities (circa 1870) and women (circa 1920), the rights of labor to organize (1930s) and freedom from racial discrimination (circa 1965). We fought against the excesses of McCarthy (circa 1954), Nixon (circa 1972) and countless others throughout the pages of history.

The struggle is not over. The pact that the people made in the original revolution was made with a higher authority than government. It was a promise to future generations of vigilance in the pursuit and protection of liberty and justice. The lesson of history is that those who do not value liberty will surely lose it.

Jazz 14 February 2006.

STENCH OF THE PLAME AFFAIR
Obfuscation of Justice

Early in the movie *Philadelphia*, there is a poignant moment when the attorney played by Denzel Washington first confronts potential client Tom Hanks with the request: "Explain it to me like I'm seven years old."

That line has been running through my mind as I've observed the unfolding of a peculiar form of justice in the trial of Lewis "Scooter" Libby.

For those who reside on melting icecaps, without access to media, the Libby perjury-obstruction trial is a surrogate proceeding for a vast cornucopia of crimes committed by the White House in the falsification of the case for war with Iraq.

What is incredibly clear from repeated testimony is that vice president Dick Cheney was ground zero in a determined and concerted effort to defame former ambassador Joe Wilson for having the audacity to challenge the bogus administration claim of an Iraq-Niger yellow cake uranium connection.

That the claim was demonstrably false is undeniable yet the media seems to have converged on the Washington Post's dubious and self-serving assertion that Wilson's challenge was false. The argument seems to center on Wilson's assertion that he was sent to Niger at the vice president's behest. Because Wilson was only indirectly sent at the vice president's behest, the Post vindicates its own soft-pedaling of the story and incredibly blames Wilson for outing his own wife, CIA agent Valerie Plame.

It had nothing whatsoever to do with Post editor Bob Woodward's belated admission that he was one of the recipients of the White House smear campaign. Whatever made them think that a cheerleader for the war would be a suitable "fence" for White House propaganda?

Where I come from, that is called mendacity.

The programmed obfuscation of the truth proceeds with the revelation that presumed "good guy" and Daddy Warbucks look-alike Richard Armitage, assistant secretary of defense to Colin Powell, was among the first to expose the identity of Wilson's wife as an agent. How we arrived at the conclusion that either Armitage or his boss were good guys and therefore incapable of engaging in a White House smear campaign, is mystifying.

Colin Powell was fully capable of presenting a case for war he knew to be "bullshit" to the United Nations Security Counsel on the eve of invasion. It is hardly inconceivable that Armitage, a seasoned intelligence expert, would score a few points with the VP gang by nonchalantly revealing the identity of a covert agent of intense media interest on the understanding that he was (of course) completely unaware of her protected status.

Where I come from, that is called incredible.

The final sticking point in this grand obfuscation scheme is the revelation that Dick Cheney somehow managed to get the president to declassify highly guarded documents without public notice to shield himself and his lair from criminal culpability.

Someone explain it to me as if I'm seven years old. How does the instant and anonymous declassification of secret documents clear any official of the deliberate outing of a CIA operative?

In a White House that is already on record punishing analysts and agents who do not produce twisted, tainted and falsified intelligence to support the mandates of preordained policies, what would be the consequences of knowing that the chief executive could compromise your security on a whim?

If this is the state of American law on protecting its most valued human assets, then every operative, agent and analyst has been served notice they will be called upon to produce whatever "intelligence" the administration desires.

So it seems this whole masquerade is just another opportunity for the White House to bend the law to its own maleficent purposes.

Everyone connected to this case carries the stench of criminal conduct, cover-up, negligence or complicity.

Tell me again, like I'm a seven-year-old, why isn't Dick Cheney on trial as the mastermind of this conspiratorial scourge?

Somebody tell me, like I'm seven years old, why Richard Armitage, Robert Novak and the president, himself, are not called to the witness stand to tell what they know?

What reasons did the vice president give when he persuaded his boss to declassify the critical documents? If he told the truth, then the president is culpable. If he lied, then the hammer falls on the VP.

No one has suggested that Scooter Libby is stupid. He would not lie, intentionally and repeatedly, if there were no crime to cover up.

The tears of defense attorney Theodore Wells aside, Scooter Libby is not an unknowing victim in this scheme. It is neither conjecture nor speculation: CIA agent Valerie Plame was maliciously exposed in a political vendetta campaign. She is the forgotten victim in this sordid affair.

So tell me once more, like I'm seven years old, why are we supposed to admire the grim determination of Chief Prosecutor Patrick Fitzgerald?

JAZZMAN CHRONICLES

Jazz 22 February 2007.

SUPREME BETRAYAL
Democracy Lost

"It would be impossible to understate the dangers that corporate dominance poses to democracy. Corporate democracy is an oxymoron. It cannot exist. It is an unconscionable perversion of democracy."

"As the World Turns: America Left Behind."
Jazzman Chronicles, September 6, 2009

As a progressive libertarian independent the events of the week were enough to send me into a tailspin of despair. No, it was not the Massachusetts senatorial race, which I found rich in irony and something of a mixed blessing. No, it was not the precipitous decline in the stock market, which served to remind us that brokers and bankers are far more afraid of populist rage than they are of any mainstream political party.

No, it was rather the boldest assertion to date that the Supreme Court of Chief Justice John Roberts has one and only one defining characteristic: Corporate bias.

History informs us that there is perhaps no form of government more vulnerable to corporate takeover than a democracy in which there are no controls on the funding of political campaigns. Knowing this, there is no democracy in the western world that allows unlimited corporate funding. Knowing this, our Supreme Court delivered a ruling (Citizens United v. Federal Election Commission) that allows just that with one caveat: corporations cannot contribute directly to political parties or candidates. It is a curious exception in that it seems to confess that the court's reasoning is flawed. If corporations are in effect citizens, entitled to the rights of individuals, on what grounds should they be denied direct engagement?

It is however an exception that has no teeth. Corporations do not need to contribute directly to parties or candidates. They are fully capable of running their own political operations. They can operate their own focus groups. They can use their resources, even those gained from public bailouts, to tip the balance of power and control the policies of government.

We've grown accustomed to hyperbole from pundits and politicians but this time it is real. Democracy can be compromised only so far before it ceases to be democracy. In this case the alternative our Supreme Court has thrust us toward is corporate fascism not unlike Mussolini's Italy, a government that found nothing objectionable in Hitler's Third Reich. It was only business.

In the bold new world the court has laid out for us the electoral process will become a mere formality as it is in Russia or Iran. It will become a ritual to commemorate the democracy we once treasured. In this new world neither the people, the mom and pop corporations nor the unions will hold any sway, though this ruling applies to them as well, for they cannot compete with the power of the almighty dollar that corporate monoliths bring to bear.

Leaders of the Republican Party have embraced this decision and never fail to include the unions in their analysis. Yet the labor unions are a red herring. After half a century of decline, there is no union in the land that can compete with any major corporation. By this ruling union influence is rendered negligible and corporate power reigns supreme.

Among the many questions that remain unanswered are the international implications. The modern corporation is an international leviathan with tentacles extending across borders in every direction. It has no loyalties, no patriotism, no ideology, no principles and no virtue. It is governed by the profit margin, plain and simple. If selling out the workers of America (by exporting jobs and banishing the rights of labor) will boost the profit margin, it is not a decision that will be contested.

The corporate behemoths may allow Barack Obama to continue as president, they may allow the major parties to exist, but with this ruling the nation just got a charter for a new board of directors that will replace all branches of government as the ultimate arbiter of decisions. If any member of congress, Senator or President violates the dictums of the corporate masters, they will be targeted for extinction. In that sense the parties themselves will become irrelevant. All parties will become agents of corporate interest.

For as long as this decision is allowed to stand we are no longer a democracy.

It must not be allowed to stand and yet overturning a Supreme Court decision is a daunting task. Among the courses of action suggested thus far, none shows any real promise of success. Amending the constitution requires two thirds of congress and three quarters of the states. Removing the majority members of the court for treason, however justified, would require an overwhelming push by congress. As long as Republicans remain convinced that corporate dominance is to their advantage it cannot happen.

Perhaps Congressman Barney Frank, who noted that

corporations are creations of law, offered the most interesting approach. Corporations are granted corporate status by the government and the government retains the right to enforce standards and regulations. It is therefore possible that congress can control the power of corporations through corporate law rather than campaign finance law.

There are at least two major obstacles to this approach. First, congress has not been able to pass re-regulation of the financial institutions even after the lack of regulation played a primary role in a near catastrophic collapse. How are we to believe that congress will act in this case even as the minority party throws up a roadblock of united opposition?

The dismal truth is congress is paralyzed. While some may give lip service to the necessity of systemic change, there is no real movement toward striking down the filibuster rule in the United States Senate. As long as the filibuster remains there can be no real change.

Even if we could get beyond systemic paralysis, any effective legislative attempt to undo what the Supreme Court has done would surely be struck down by the same court.

Those of us who believe in democracy must continue to fight but it seems to me we must also recognize reality. In all likelihood we are stuck with this decision until the balance of the court is altered. The way things are going it could be decades and by that time the nature of congress and the White House could be so altered that change may be impossible.

Once lost, the road back to democracy is paved with hardship.

That is the problem with Supreme Court decisions. They have the power to alter the very heart and soul of a nation.

So welcome to the corporate world: We are up

against the wall, rifles pointed at our chests, and our only remaining choice is whether to be blindfolded or to confront our destiny with open eyes.

Jazz 23 January 2010.

ROBERTS' DECLARATION OF INDEPENDENCE
Affordable Care Act Survives

On June 28, 2012 Chief Justice John Roberts took control of his own court by casting the deciding vote to uphold the constitutionality of President Barack Obama's keystone legislative achievement: The Affordable Care Act of 2010.

Until that decision America's highest judicial body was the Roberts Court only in name. Its most influential member was Anthony Kennedy and its most powerful voice was Antonin Scalia. With one stroke of the pen John Roberts became a man of substance, never again to be taken for granted. By dramatically asserting his independence from the conservative wing of the court, he becomes the second most powerful man in the most powerful nation on earth.

I am neither a fan of the Affordable Care Act nor of the Chief Justice. Roberts has presided over some of the most destructive and partisan decisions in the court's modern history. As predictable as Pavlov's dogs, he sided with Scalia and the majority in Citizens United v. Federal Election Commission 2010, declaring corporate contributions to political campaigns protected free speech.

In the current term, Roberts and his conservative wing upheld the principle of Citizens United over the principle of states' rights in American Tradition Partnership v. Bullock, overturning Montana's 99-year-old ban on corporate political contributions and upholding the view that states' rights are secondary to corporate and political interests (see Bush v. Gore 2000). The court also approved a strict limit on Union political contributions (union members must have prior approval as well as opt out provisions), neglecting to note that corporations have no similar requirement (Knox v. SEIU). Imagine the uproar if Exxon had to poll its shareholders and provide an opt-out in the form of a dividend before it could contribute to political campaigns.

The Roberts Court famously ruled against equal pay for women in Ledbetter v. Goodyear Tire & Rubber Co. 2007, necessitating congressional action in the Lilly Ledbetter Fair Pay Act of 2009.

On the environmental front, this court has never met a polluter it did not favor. Witness Exxon v. Baker 2008 imposing severe limits on compensation to the victims of the Exxon Valdez catastrophe. The Roberts Court continued their anti-environment corporate assault with two decisions in 2009: Entergy Corporation v. EPA and Couer Alaska, Inc v. SE Alaska Conservation Council.

A recent review by the Constitutional Accountability Center found that the Roberts Court had upheld all cases the Chamber of Commerce advocated in the current term, an unprecedented record of success, upholding the opinion that this court represents the greatest corporate bias in Supreme Court history.

From the Lilly Ledbetter decision to the ruling that allowed public interest laws to be used for corporate development (Kelo v. City of New London 2005), the Roberts court has laid down no precedent stronger than corporate supremacy.

That corporate bias stands with the ruling on the Affordable Care Act. The Chamber of Commerce supported the individual mandate (a requirement that consumers buy a corporate product) but argued that the entire law should be struck down if the mandate fell. The dissenters in the case (Scalia, Kennedy, Alito, Thomas) adopted the Chamber's argument.

It turns out there was never any chance that the individual mandate would be struck down without eliminating the entire law. That is a shame for that is exactly the decision many of us would have favored.

Failing all other means, the mandate was needed to pay for the program. Had it been overturned while the law survived, the administration would be scrambling today to find other ways to fund it. The most obvious and equitable means to cost efficiency is the elimination of the middleman.

Otherwise known as single payer, it should have been the approach to healthcare reform all along. The only difference is that the advocates of this approach should call it by a name that rings virtuous, familiar and true to the vast majority of Americans: Universal Medicare.

What the Supreme Court has achieved with its ruling is to assure us that universal healthcare remains a very remote dream. It's provision that states can opt out of the Medicaid expansion provision gives us further assurance.

To be sure, most Americans will be better off after the Affordable Care Act is fully enacted than they were before but healthcare in this country remains an unsustainable system because it wastes trillions of dollars on an industry that serves no useful function. Indeed, the function of the insurance industry is detrimental to our health and wellbeing.

Every individual who has ever had to deal with insurance providers knows: they do not have our interest at heart.

Meantime, while we have not witnessed a sea change in our healthcare system, we have seen a potentially radical shift in the balance of power on the Supreme Court.

Chief Justice John Roberts did not stand up to his corporate benefactors but he did stand up to Antonin

Scalia, Anthony Kennedy and the right wing radicals who are striving to take over not only the Republican Party but all branches of the American government as well.

For now, they have failed and that is something to celebrate.

In this one case, Roberts has shown some of the essential qualities of a good justice: independence of thought, a willingness to compromise, an ability to see beyond the immediate case, and a determination not to be ruled by political bias.

What he has not yet demonstrated is the courage to stand in opposition to the corporate bias that has defined his court.

For that we can only hope.

Jazz 3 July 2012.

LEGALIZED CORRUPTION
The Jesters Capture the Court

We have sent to Washington a company of court jesters, supplying them with portraits of knights in shining armor in the shape of a handheld mirror, so that when they gaze at themselves they perceive heroes standing strong for all that is good and right. They have been given a script and they will not wander from it. They defiantly disbelieve everything the president, the economists and even the corporate wing of their own party says. They alone represent truth, justice and the American way. They alone are God's chosen.

Can you imagine a less effective spokesperson for a political party than the honorable Speaker of the House, John Boehner? (If you answered Senate Majority Leader Harry Reid you would get little argument here.) Can you imagine a less appealing populist than Joe McCarthy look alike, Senator Ted Cruz of Texas, Congressman Louie Gohmert of Texas or Representative Michelle Bachmann of Minnesota? Where did this band of misfits come from and how can we rid ourselves of them before they can do any more harm?

In Common Sense, The American Crisis and The Rights of Man, Thomas Paine argued that the ultimate proof that the monarchy is a flawed system of governance is the incredible number of misfits and miscreants who find themselves on the throne. Paine's argument can now be applied to our own democracy.

A representative government was designed to select the best and the brightest to lead us in decision making, to guide us through difficult times and to inspire and improve our lives in the best of times. Instead, we have prostituted the electoral process, offering offices to the highest bidder with little regard for the consequences. To the local counsel we elect individuals with ambition and private interests, with little knowledge of their political leanings, yet from this pool we select candidates for higher office. To congress we elect buffoons who share our biases and prejudicial leanings as if bias can be made acceptable when adorned with public office.

It is popular in some quarters to assign equal portions of blame for our paralyzed and dysfunctional government to both sides of the corporate aisle. In the case of the so-called debt crisis (a typical invented crisis at the convenience of a political party) there is some validity to this unofficial fairness doctrine.

The Democrats have encouraged Republican obstinacy by rewarding it time and time again. In the healthcare debate, Democrats took universal Medicare off the table before negotiations began. In the last trumped up debt crisis, the GOP was rewarded with sequestration, resetting the table and reframing the debate on firm Republican ground. We were told that sequestration was the ultimate package of across the board budget cuts; a process so crude and ill conceived that not even the most rigid debt obsessed fanatic could support it. Not so. Now the sequestered budget has become the standard from which additional cuts must be carved.

Again and again the Democrats have allowed the opposition to skew the debate rightward until we are left with a right versus far right contest. We have backed our country into austerity and our leaders seem more and more determined to press it forward. For this we can thank President Obama and the spineless Democrats. When you have continually backed off every time you have been confronted, when you finally plant the staff and say "This far and no further", it is not surprising that the bully party does not believe you.

However, the combination of stubbornness and ignorance required to defy the debt ceiling and risk national default is distinctly a Republican phenomenon and, therefore, to them goes the lion's share of the blame.

If an individual were to come from a faraway land, without any prior knowledge of our government and its evolution, and he were to observe the deliberations of congress in its present form, he would likely come to the conclusion that something very fundamental was wrong with our democracy. He would not be wrong and yet his understanding would fall well short of the entire truth.

If you were to judge a cake recipe by its finished product and it failed the tests of appearance, taste and smell, you would conclude that the recipe was flawed. But if you learned that rotten eggs were used in the making of the cake you would suspend your judgment. Applying a similar test to our current government, a government so flawed it fails the most basic tests of viability, you would be tempted to conclude that our democracy is at fault. You would not be wrong but your understanding would fall well short of the truth.

Our democracy *is* flawed but it is neither the design nor the principles of representative government that has produced this dysfunctional system. It is the rotten eggs of corruption, sanctified and institutionalized by the Supreme Court, that has produced the failure of government we see today.

When the court in its infinite wisdom ruled in Citizens United that corporations have a first amendment right to unlimited sponsorship of political candidates, for the first time in history, it legalized corruption. In the next term we can be sure that the court will extend its decision to individual contributions, striking down all limitations on campaign financing. We will then have a system in which all candidates for public office must be vetted and approved by wealthy donors and corporate sponsors.

We will then have a system that more resembles an auction than an electoral process: How much can I get for a series of bills outlawing collective bargaining and banning unions from the workplace? How much for opposition to raising the minimum wage? How much for blocking the development of green energy? How much for the renewal of a Free Trade agreement? How much for another war to capture control of Middle East oil?

Some would say we have already reached that point and from all appearances they may be right. It was the corporations that gave us the Tea Party and their trademark obstinacy now threatens the stability of the global economy. It was corporate sponsorship that gave us the bipartisan Free Trade mandate and the third way that is President Bill Clinton's legacy. It was corporate sponsorship that made George W. Bush and his war for oil possible. It was corporate sponsorship that reduced government oversight to a shadow, leading inevitably to the near collapse of the global economy.

Over the short term, corporate sponsors will likely rescue the nation from the lunacy of the Tea Party. The debt limit will be raised but we will continue the policies of austerity that have crippled Europe and stunted our own recovery from the Great Recession. I would admire these Tea Party zealots a lot more if they stood their ground and allowed the nation to default but the damage would be too great and too enduring (some say it would be irreparable) to condone their actions. They will not hold their ground. They cannot. They have fallen in love with their power and legitimacy. They will yield to their sponsors' greater interests.

Through all this debate the greater tragedy has been ignored. We are losing our democracy. When money interests must approve all candidates, is it a democracy at all? When districts can be manipulated to protect money interests from the will of the majority, what kind of a democracy is it? Is it a representative government or corporate fascism with a democratic façade?

We used to make fun of third world nations that claimed to be democracies but were so overrun with institutionalized corruption that their claims were a joke. We have now become the banana republic that we used to deride.

Correcting the flaws and recovering a reasonably representative form of government, one that serves the people first, will not be easy. It will not happen this year or next. It is not likely to happen in the next decade. That is the problem with a corrupt Supreme Court. The damage they do becomes systemic and resistant to all attempts at remedy. We cannot rely on the corrupted to fight the disease. They are the disease.

What we need is a new dynamic on the Supreme Court and a genuine grassroots rebellion of the electorate. What we cannot allow is for the current dysfunction to become the norm.

Throw all the bums out: The Tea Party, the Blue Dog Democrats, the corporate Republicans, the Free Trade Democrats, all of them! Let us begin again to establish democracy in America.

Jazz 14 October 2013.

J'ACCUSE!
Supreme Court Challenge to Democracy

"There is no right in our democracy more basic than the right to participate in electing our political leaders."

Chief Justice John Roberts
McCutcheon v. Federal Election Commission

In January 1898 Emile Zola published an impassioned defense of General Alfred Dreyfus, accusing the French government of anti-Semitic bias in convicting the general of treason. Dreyfus went to Devil's Island and Zola fled to Great Britain to escape prosecution for libel. Both Zola and Dreyfus would ultimately be exonerated and the French government shamed in the annals of history.

The title of Zola's article became the battle cry of the oppressed for generations of dissidents: J'Accuse!

The phrase should not be used lightly. It should be reserved for matters of profound betrayal, extraordinary hypocrisy and high crimes worthy of the charge: Treason!

With *McCutcheon v. Federal Election Commission* (2014) the United States Supreme Court pushed to the very edge of that criterion. In a series of decisions beginning with *Bush v. Gore* (2000) the court has set a pattern of repeated and methodical betrayal of democratic principles.

JAZZMAN CHRONICLES

In its cardinal assault on the fundamental tenets of representative government, the court affirmed a standing assumption that citizens do *not* possess a right to vote. It further refused to consider the most pressing issues of the day: voter disenfranchisement and outright fraud.

In rendering a decision so compromised, convoluted and self-contradictory, the court called on future jurists to discard its precedent value (as if that were possible). The court pleaded ignorance in delivering a commander-in-chief so unprepared and ill-equipped that he was virtually guaranteed to become the disaster that followed. One cannot help but wonder if the court ever reflected on the dire consequences of their decision as President George W. Bush stumbled through Afghanistan, Iraq and the near collapse of the global economy. Decisions have consequences and history will account.

Perhaps the worst decision of the modern era, *Bush v. Gore* was compounded by *Citizens United* (2010), a decision that defined money contributions by corporate entities as synonymous with speech and therefore protected by the first amendment. CU empowered international corporate conglomerates to deliver unlimited money to electoral campaigns and that in turn led to the rise of the Tea Party and the takeover of congress by the most inept legislators in memory. It is not by accident that a clear majority of the American electorate voted for the party not in power.

The recent decision sets the trend for as long as this court remains in power: Money and its interests will be protected at all costs. Money is the voice whose speech will be broadcast on all stations at all times so that the voices of ordinary citizens can never be heard. Money is the ultimate arbiter of power and everyone who seeks office must bow before its almighty grandeur. When money determines who will be elected from the town council to the regal halls of the United States Senate (and ultimately the White House), our elected officials will represent the interests that empowered them.

Plain and simple, when one voice (or the collective voice of the elite) is entitled to speak out as long and as loud as it pleases, all other voices are muted. Plain and simple, the highest court in the land has scheduled the demolition of our democratic institutions and set the course for aristocratic rule.

When our Chief Justice declares "there is no right in our democracy more basic than the right to participate in electing our political leaders," he omits the right to vote. Could it be that his political interests are served by this telling omission?

Despite its adherence to a rigid judicial philosophy, consistency has never been the hallmark of this court. The rightwing majority has a marked tendency to wink as it hands down its judgment. In the case of *McCutcheon v. FEC* the court allowed the limit on individual contributions to individual campaigns to stand though it struck down the total amount a contributor can spend. This too is a revealing exception. It concedes that unlimited contributions to a single campaign could compromise an elected official even while denying that unlimited contributions can corrupt officials in general. Both cannot be true.

It is as if the prevailing justices of the Roberts court know they will be judged harshly in judicial history so they hedge their bets.

It is of little consequence. They have shown their hands. They have declared their intent. They are the enemies of American democracy and there is no immediate remedy. Those in congress who claim that transparency will correct the problem are mistaken. The effects of massive funding injected into the political process will be little mitigated by unmasking the sponsor at the end of a television ad.

JAZZMAN CHRONICLES

The only effective defense of democracy we can hope for is at present remote. It will not happen as long as the court remains as it is. The moneyed interests have taken control of the lower house of congress and they will retain it. They have set their sites on the Senate and they are likely to succeed. If they do so, our cause is lost for the Senate has the power to confirm or reject Supreme Court nominees. If they take the White House (some would say they already have) we will lose access to any remedy for generations.

What we need and what our republic demands is a court that believes in the principles of democracy. If some future court would rule that a citizen has a right to vote that simple decree would open up the lines of defense. If a citizen has a right to vote, the court would have jurisdiction over voter disenfranchisement, election fraud and gerrymandering.

A Supreme Court that actually believes in democracy would consider unlimited financing of political campaigns an affront to common sense and a betrayal of our most sacred principles of government.

Jazz 7 April 2014.

VOLUME VI

EDUCATION

CONTENTS

PREFACE

THE RIGHT TO EDUCATION

I was raised with the fundamental belief that all children in the greatest nation on earth were entitled to a free quality education to the fullest extent of each child's ambition and ability.

The proposition did not seem at all controversial. It only made sense that society would benefit when its most valuable resource was fully developed.

My experience as a student in public education was decidedly mixed. I had excellent teachers and poor teachers, teachers who encouraged independent thought and teachers who refused to bend and punished students who challenged traditional rules. I learned early on that the history taught in our public schools was not always accurate or truthful.

By the time I reached high school our nation was fully engaged in the Vietnam War. American youth was in rebellion, searching for alternative ways of life that were less harmful to the planet and less destructive of our fellow beings. I learned to question everything and found my voice of protest.

My attitude of resistance was not fully appreciated by some of my instructors. But there were always teachers who understood that education was more than indoctrination. There were always teachers who encouraged free thought. We need more of those teachers today and more administrators who understand

and appreciate that need. We need representatives in state, local and federal government who refuse to blame education for all society's woes. We need a government that fully supports education and recognizes the importance of developing every child's curiosity and talent.

Education today is handicapped by the overwhelming burden of formal testing. Fully half of our school year is devoted to test preparation. Every good teacher knows that testing is not teaching. When we are obsessed with test scores we lose a child's curiosity. We lose the ability to inspire new ways of thinking. We punish creativity and ultimately ensure that all those who adhere to our new educational philosophy will be least prepared for an unpredictable world.

Fortunately, there will always be individuals who do not conform. In them our hopes for a brighter future reside. I have full confidence in the next generation. I believe they will overcome the handicap of the rigid educational policies they have confronted.

We will prevail but we must wonder what might have been had we encouraged free thought and creativity. How many more of our students would be better prepared?

I attended college in the seventies on financial aid. I received grants and loans that I could readily pay back. I benefited greatly from my college experience and so did the society that supported me.

It is painful to acknowledge that in today's world I would likely not have been able to pursue higher education. If I somehow found a way I would have been crippled with debt.

It is clear that our government and our nation, despite all the rhetoric, no longer values education. It seems every politician has an idea for reforming education and most of those ideas involve testing, firing teachers, privatizing public schools, punishing schools that do not produce adequate test scores or shaping the curriculum to their own points of view.

We do need education reform but the needed reforms do not involve any political agenda. We need fully funded schools in every district, no matter how poor or disadvantaged. We need quality teachers and that begins with enabling prospective teachers to attend college at a reasonable cost. In fact, higher education should be free of charge to those who are able and committed.

We need a curriculum that is dedicated to discovering the interests and aptitudes of every child and providing the tools to fulfill both. Not every child can or should pursue an academic higher education. Those children should be given a path to skilled labor.

We need schools that embrace the arts for in the end a society will be judged as much by the art it produces as by any advancement in science or technology. Too often the artist is left behind in our current approach to education.

Finally, we need to recognize that every child has a right to an education that fulfills his or her needs and aspirations. It only makes sense.

Jazz.

NO CITIZEN LEFT BEHIND
All Governments Can Govern Well

Much has been said about the inequities of the Bush administration's education reform, popularly known as No Child Left Behind. Critics contend that the approach is designed for failure but how can you object to the simple premise: Every child can learn?

Teachers protest that the standards are unreasonable but if they were so unreasonable, why did Ted Kennedy sign on? So called education experts protest that the program was never fully funded but the legislation does not prohibit teachers from contributing a portion of their salaries to the educational process – perhaps a nice private school or a faith-based tutoring program. Furthermore, where public education cannot measure up, private education (unencumbered by mandatory testing and accountability standards) can readily fill the gap.

Now that we have had a chance to see the program in action, it is time to stop the partisan bickering and accept that it has been a resounding success. Our children can learn and our teachers can achieve higher test scores if given the proper incentives.

Every year our educational system is producing more and more students properly qualified for entry-level positions in service to our country. What more can we ask? Yes, our children can learn and among their lessons are American values: Fear of God, patriotic duty and respect for authority.

Inspired by the unprecedented success of No Child Left Behind, it is high time we expanded the approach to government itself. After all, who can deny the simple premise that all governments can govern well?

We therefore call on our national leaders to drop this nonsense regarding social security and tax reform in favor of a massive new program, with a proven ideological track record, that we can all support without trepidation: No Citizen Left Behind.

The goals of this bold new initiative will be simple. Within five years:

1. All American citizens will earn an average income or better.

2. All citizens will gain access to adequate health care and medical services.

3. All communities must fall below the national average for air and water pollution, crime and unemployment.

4. All communities must climb above the national average on independent measures of living standards and quality of life.

5. The nation as a whole must exceed international standards of developed nations for education, quality of life, clean air and water, medical and health care, civil liberties and human rights.

What government could honestly object to such common sense standards? Remember: Given half a chance, all governments can govern well. If they can do it in Oslo and Copenhagen, surely we can do it here.

Of course, establishing goals would be a futile gesture if there were no means to objectively measure our progress in reaching them. Therefore, all governments will be required to devote no less than one quarter of their resources and time to comprehensive self-evaluation.

To facilitate the accountability process, we will provide an extensive list of acceptable private institutions and corporations capable of making these assessments, such as the American Enterprise Institute, Stanford's Hoover Institution and, of course, Halliburton.

Finally, for any program to take effect, there must be an enforcement plank. In keeping with the well-established principle of "tough love" (remember the boot camps for troubled youth? well, they're still there), governments failing to achieve objective measures of progress on consecutive years will be subject to a stiff regimen of sanctions.

First, floundering state and local governments will be subject to reforms, including mandatory rehearsals and focus group sessions on how to explain and defend the austerity approach to social welfare.

Second, upon a third year of failure, automatic recall elections will take place.

Third, if failure continues, the floundering governments must pay for the relocation of its citizens to successful states and communities.

In the event that the nation should fail to meet its own standards (inconceivable as it may seem), constitutional modification may be required but the consequences should be similar. Americans, faced with a failing nation, will have the right to relocate at government expense to the successful nations of their choice.

In lieu of these consequences, governments may of course choose to abolish themselves – or rather convert themselves to private corporations.

Some may be concerned that an absence of government would abolish democracy itself in favor of anarchy or corporate fascism. Mindful of these concerns, we commissioned several studies by unimpeachably independent sources and they assure us this is not the case.

To the contrary, we are certain that all Americans will embrace this bold new approach to good government.

JAZZMAN CHRONICLES

After all, who can deny the simple premise: All governments can govern well? How can anything so simple be wrong?

Jazz 2 February 2005.

TROJAN HORSE
The Problem with Education

In California there were two propositions on the June ballot that claimed to be protection of property rights against the abusive eminent domain practices of government (in collusion with private developers) sanctioned by the United States Supreme Court in Kelo v. City of New London (2005).

One of these measures (Prop 99) was what it claimed to be. The other (Prop 98) was a Trojan horse. It pretended to be concerned with property rights when its real intent was to end rent control – the kind of rent control that allows working people to live in the communities where they work.

One may agree or disagree with rent control but everyone should agree the packaging was deliberately deceptive.

Education reform in the modern era is similarly a Trojan horse. The latest comprehensive reform package that masquerades under the title No Child Left Behind (NCLB) was not an effort to make education accountable as it pretended to be. Rather, it was a prescription for certain failure whose real purpose was to open the doors of public financing for private education. Like the Bush social security package (which began with an option for private accounts), the ultimate goal is complete privatization.

Education is the ultimate fallback position of politicians left, right and center. When economic policies fail, education is the reason. When the future looks bleak, education is the answer. When budgets are pressed as they inevitably are, education is the first program on the block.

Ironically, since the founding of public education there is not a stronger correlation in the social sciences than that of dollar investment per student to school success by any measure (*Prospects: The Congressionally Mandated Study of Educational Growth and Opportunity, Official Report, US Department of Education*, April 4, 1997). This does not mean of course that funding is the only or even primary factor in school achievement but it does support the common sense notion that a district that provides adequate facilities, books, supplies, technology, support services, optimal class size and competitive pay will very likely enjoy the benefits of a quality educational program. Likewise, a district that invests minimally will likely stumble and fall.

Perhaps more than any other public endeavor, in education you get what you pay for.

Of course, politicians do not wish to acknowledge such simplistic realities. Some never tire in blaming teachers for their tolerant attitudes, negligent moral values and relatively strong unions. Others preach accountability or wonder at a curriculum that includes matters of faith in the discipline of science. Some want longer school days and tougher standards while others demand more teacher training programs.

Some of these proposals have merit but none will make an impact until and unless every school district is fully funded – including programs for special education mandated but not funded by the federal government.

It is almost laughable that the same schools that teach their students that segregation in the public schools ended with the civil rights movement in the 1960s when in fact segregation remains the rule in every major city in America. We were taught that Brown v. Board of Education (1954) ended the idea of "separate but equal" education and yet "separate and unequal" is the accepted and dominant reality today.

As long as local property taxes are the primary source of public education funding it is impossible that the quality of education in the slums of Detroit should be anything resembling equivalent to the quality of education in Marin County, California.

The difference between then and now is not that we integrated the schools; the difference is we forgot that it was supposed to matter.

The greater mystery perhaps is why this experiment in social integration was carried out in the schools and in the schools alone. There was no comparable effort to integrate the communities surrounding schools. There was no demand for equal funding: for every dollar spent in Marin, a dollar must also be spent in East Los Angeles. There was no concerted and sustained effort to lift neighborhoods out of blight, poverty and despair.

We get what we pay for and we have never paid enough so that no child would be left behind. In fact we have never paid enough to ensure that most children would not be left behind. There is no educational or training program on earth that can sever half the bell shaped curve (normal population distribution) yet that is exactly what NCLB requires.

It is a joke, an unspeakably horrible hoax that should be exposed and discarded for the massive fraud that it is.

Public education must be reinvented from the ground up – not because it was systemically flawed but because the poison delivered in the name of reform by those who wished to destroy it all along has hopelessly contaminated it.

There is no educational or training program on earth that can replace the jobs shuttled overseas by an ill-conceived and shortsighted globalization scheme that attempted to build a sustainable economy on the backs of cheap international labor.

Any politician of any party who tells us we can solve our economic problems through education and training is either pitifully uninformed or deliberately deceiving the electorate.

What we need in education is an entirely new approach built on the foundation of reason rather than some fool's notion of patriotic values or academic conformity. We need students who can grow into thinking, participating citizens, people who can recognize a con job when it slams them like a baseball to the forehead, and citizens who can exchange ideas and observations with their peers.

Instead, the education that has evolved from compulsive testing is one that deliberately neglects the essential principles of reasoning: common sense, inference and deduction.

It is as if the government does not want people who can think and question the dictates of their superiors, who question even whether or not their superiors are superior.

If you teach a man to read, you open the gates of knowledge. If you teach a man to reason, you open the gates of truth and wisdom.

Why would our government want to keep those gates locked?

The problem with education is that our government – at least in its current form – is at cross-purposes to educational excellence. The ideal educational system should have no other interest than to maximize an individual's potential.

A great deal should be invested in determining where an individual's interests and natural talents meet. A child's education should be directed by her or his interest first and society's interest second. For many students, it would make infinitely more sense to develop a natural interest in a useful trade, be it carpentry, plumbing or technology, rather than to continually press the student to pass standardized tests in reading, writing, science and math.

No child should ever be considered a failure. It is education that has failed the child.

Finally, to the full extent possible, education should lead every child out of the dark ages of superstition and ignorance. That is why we cannot allow the indoctrination of religion in the schools. That is why we must teach science as science, literature as literature and comparative religions as its own separate and distinct discipline.

We must teach every child that no one – not the president of the United States, not the governor, the principal or even a child's parents – has a monopoly on the truth. Every child, to the full extent possible, must be equipped with a mind of his or her own.

That would be real education reform. But don't expect that kind of reform from today's pandering politicians. They are far more interested in keeping the dog in its pen to be pulled out and paraded every two to four years and blamed for whatever problems society is experiencing.

The next time a politician calls for education reform, raise your hand like an inquisitive child to challenge him:

What useful knowledge and wisdom is acquired by compulsive testing?

What sense does it make to penalize under funded schools and brand them failures?

How do we improve public education by diverting funds to private schools?

Undaunted, the politician will have the usual evasive answers but they will be as empty as the promise behind No Child Left Behind.

Jazz 24 July 2008.

BLAME THE TEACHER SYNDROME
A Misguided Education Policy

When a district in Rhode Island announced its intention to fire all teachers at Central Falls High School in an unmistakable gesture of blame seeking, I knew without knowing it was an impoverished school. When a school board in Kansas City announced it would close 28 schools before the start of the next school year I knew they were the poorest of the poor.

Indeed, just a little research revealed that Central Falls is one of the poorest cities in the state and after the exodus of some 18,000 students to charter schools and more affluent suburban districts, the remaining 17,400 students in the schools scheduled for demolition in Kansas City are "mostly black and impoverished." (NY Times, March 11, 2010)

If we take a hard look at what the government under the dictates of No Child Left Behind (NCLB) considers failing or failed schools they are invariably schools impacted by a community in poverty. Moreover, if we consider the effects of the recent economic implosion (high unemployment, home foreclosures and declining home values) and the disproportionate impact on impoverished communities, it is easy to see why schools are struggling.

Whenever data are generated by any credible source, the correlation between poverty and educational achievement is so strong it is impossible for any unbiased individual to ignore. When schools are ranked according to quality, those on the top of the list are invariably wealthy and predominantly white while those at the bottom are invariably poor with high proportions of minorities.

As anyone who took Statistics 101 can tell you, correlation does not translate to causality but as anyone who advanced to Statistics 102 can tell you: When you are searching for answers to guide public policy, correlation is where you begin. Ignoring the effects of poverty on education is like ignoring the effect of criminals on crime.

It was therefore disheartening when President Obama seemed to sanction the mass firing in Rhode Island for it signaled a continuation of the Republican philosophy of education embodied in NCLB and cleared the way for Democrats and Republicans alike to join in one of oldest political tricks on the books. I call it: Blame the Teacher Syndrome.

In California we have recently witnessed the now familiar solution to budgetary crises: Fire the teachers and break the back of public education. We also learned that the Golden State has attained the singular honor of being last in the nation in per student funding for public education. For years the state held steady at number 47 but now it has sunk below the Katrina ravaged states of Mississippi and Louisiana.

Having reached that lofty status you would think it would be impossible for any politician to stand before the electorate and proclaim that we can no longer expect to solve the problem of education by throwing money at it. Yet that it precisely what they are doing and have done with a great deal of political success. With a straight face they proclaim that we cannot sacrifice our children's future by running up deficits but that is precisely what they have done by supervising the decimation of our public school system.

No Child Left Behind (the enduring legacy of George

W. Bush) was nothing more nor less than a prescription for blaming teachers and opening the door to the privatization of public education. One of the primary means by which they intended to achieve that objective is the charter school alternative. Charter schools are self-governing and exempt from the testing mandates and accountability measures that regular public schools confront. They are increasingly administered by private for-profit corporations.

The latest available data obtained by the National Assessment of Educational Progress found in 2003 that students in charter schools performed poorer than comparable students in regular public schools. The government's solution to the problem was to stop collecting data.

So much for accountability.

Another means of achieving the goal of undermining public education is commonly known as school vouchers. Under this increasingly popular program public funds are siphoned from public education to finance private schools. Once again, the private alternative is not subject to the same mandates and accountability measures as public schools and, again, there is no data to support any advantage in educational achievement.

So the solution to under-funded public schools is to steal already limited financing and award it to private schools with their own faith-based agenda.

So much for the future of our children.

It is somewhat encouraging that President Obama recently announced a strategy for reforming No Child Left Behind. He wants to lessen the importance of standardized testing by expanding success criteria to include such factors as attendance and "learning climate". He wants to replace the overriding goal that all students should achieve proficiency in reading and math with the goal that all students should graduate prepared for college and career (begging the question: How are students not proficient in reading and math prepared for college and career?) He wants to emphasize the achievement gap between rich and poor students and he wants to expand criteria for teacher evaluations.

It is perhaps a beginning, a modest improvement, but like so many of his administration's initiatives it is dramatically inadequate. It does not lessen the testing burden that has done so much to transform our schools into testing factories. It does not address the underlying privatization motive of NCLB. It does not put a halt to public funding of private schools.

Most importantly, at a time when schools across the nation are being pounded with budget cuts, the Obama education policy does not address the systemic problem of chronic under-funding of the public schools.

The Obama policy does not even ask the essential question: Why do impoverished schools produce impoverished results? Why indeed would any quality teacher want to work in an impoverished district that will almost inevitably blame him or her for the failures of public education?

I would have liked to announce with the Obama administration proposals that the age of blaming teachers was at a close but I am afraid it is only entering a new chapter.

Jazz 15 March 2010.

PRESCRIBED FAILURE
NCLB & The Atlanta Schools Cheating Scandal

"Welcome to Lake Wobegon where all the women are strong, all the men are good-looking and all the children are above average."

Garrison Keillor

National media recently reported two major stories regarding education under the weight of No Child Left Behind without drawing the obvious connection between them.

First came the revelation that an estimated 200 administrators and teachers in the Atlanta school district were engaged in cheating to achieve higher scores on standardized testing. Second came a projection by the Department of Education that an astonishing 82% of public schools could fail to meet proficiency targets for the coming year.

The standards of NCLB are constantly moving. To avoid failure a school must record improved test results in reading and math for all its students and in eight subgroups until all students (100%) are considered proficient by 2014. Failure to meet standards by the slightest margin in one subgroup in one academic area is failure overall.

Imagine you're a carpet seller. You make a decent living by selling three to five carpets a week. One day your employer decides he needs to clear out his inventory. He implements a No Carpet Left Behind program that requires you to boost your sales by one carpet a week. You work extra hard and boost your sales to seven carpets but no matter what you do you cannot get beyond that number. You've tapped the market. By the fifth week you're a three-time loser and your job is in jeopardy. You realize your boss wants you to fail and there's no way out.

Failure to honor the dictates of NCLB threatens federal funding. First year failure to meet test results labels your school "in need of improvement". Second year failure allows parents to transfer their children to other schools. Continued failure, regardless of circumstances, could result in school closure and staff replacement. Teachers and principles could find themselves unemployed and tarred by the scandal of failure.

After five years of NCLB failure schools can offer control to a state that wants nothing to do with them or (here is the key!) can be handed over to private contractors.

When the overwhelming majority of struggling schools are in poor districts, why would any teacher or administrator want to work there? Those who are able to find other positions get out as soon as they can. Those left behind face mounting pressure under impossible conditions. Funding cuts and growing class sizes are not considered in the NCLB formula for success. Educators work hard and long to fight back prescribed failure.

Is it any wonder that a school district in hard economic times fought back against the sanctions of failure in the only way they could?

You cannot pass a law that two equals one. Neither can you mandate that every child will be above average but that is exactly what NCLB pretends to do. The designers and supporters of NCLB were never in fact interested in improving the public schools. They could have seen to it that all students have a chance to succeed by being graded according to their ability. They could have funded special needs and trade schools to develop employable skills. They could have expanded preschool programs and guaranteed reasonable class sizes.

They did none of these because their real goal was to crush public education and open the door to privatization of the schools.

The NCLB crowd invaded our schools like preachers among the heathens. Every child can learn, they preached, to which every teacher replied: Of course but every student cannot test above the thirty-third percentile. It is a statistical impossibility. Why? The normal population curve (shaped like a bell) does not bend to rhetoric or political will. It does not care how impassioned the preacher's sermon. No matter what the measurement, there will always be students at the bottom, students at the top and 68% in the middle. Like gravity or pi it is not negotiable. It does not vary.

The NCLB promoters were fundamentally dishonest. Knowing that the law was a prescription for failure, their intent from inception was mass closure of public schools. It would provide NCLB politicians a convenient scapegoat: blame the teachers. Better yet, blame the teachers union. Their design from day one was for a profit-based, corporate sponsored private school system that they could control.

Why else would they not subject private schools to the same testing requirements and standards as public schools in order to qualify for public funds? How did they figure that punishing schools would improve them when punishment as a means of educating was discredited decades ago? They knew from the start that the schools would fail.

Private schools, while receiving services for special needs from public school employees, can boost the bottom line by refusing to accept lower performing students. Indeed, that is exactly how Texas achieved its vaunted educational success while George W. Bush was governor: by eliminating the bottom of the sample. They forced low-achieving students to drop out and failed to report the drop out rate. Like the Atlanta school district, Texas cheated to claim success and as a result their governor became president and Texas education became a model for the nation. How is it that our discerning press never figured that out until after Bush the younger was in the White House?

Have you ever wondered what a corporate textbook would look like? Would there be any mention of Exxon-Valdez or the Deep Water Horizon oil spill? How would they treat the rise of the labor movement? How would they regard global climate change?

I guess we all know the answers to these questions.

Education is far too important to be trusted to profit-motivated corporations yet here we are on the edge of a bold new world: Private schools, private armies, privatization of Medicare and Social Security.

Who would have imagined that the worst president in modern history could have accomplished so much in so little time? Of course, he could not have done it alone. Nothing on the rightwing corporate wish list, including NCLB, could have been accomplished without Democratic cooperation.

Who are we kidding? Secretary of Education Arne Duncan is a slick, fast talking man of knowledge but they all serve the same master.

Jazz 11 July 2011.

VOLUME VII

MEDIA & PROPAGANDA

CONTENTS

PREFACE

THE FOURTH ESTATE

Propaganda is defined as journalism or literature that appeals to both the hearts and minds of the people. When pundits speak dismissively of propaganda they are not referring to the work of such luminaries as Voltaire, Zola, Sartre, Burke or Paine. They rather refer to those who appeal to the heart to mislead and advance an unworthy cause. They are a disgrace to their professions.

In the wake of the terrorist attack of September 11, the Bush administration employed the despicable form of propaganda with great proficiency. They could not have done so without the cooperation of the media. From his bunker in the White House, Dick Cheney turned to the likes of Dan Rather at CBS and Judith Miller at the New York Times to peddle their case for war.

Though built on a foundation of lies, it worked almost to perfection until at last it fell apart. Cheney would leak information concerning weapons of mass destruction to Judy Miller and Miller would publish the story as confirmed fact. The White House would then cite the Times to support its false case. Meanwhile, Dan Rather took the lead in saluting the commander and demanding that others follow in the name of patriotism.

The tragedy of the Iraq War is as much a story of the failure of the fourth estate as it is of a corrupt and ambitious White House. The spectacle of reporters embedded with the military and pretending to be impartial sources cannot easily be erased. The horror of our forces firing missiles at the offices Al Jazeera can never be forgiven.

The failures of mainstream media in recent years are not limited to its reportage of war, however. That our television news programs have become sensationalizing ambulance chasers even on the national scale is commonly accepted. The networks, cable broadcasters and local newspapers freely admit they no longer value objective news reporting. It's all about numbers and the bottom line.

The reason for this phenomenon is clear: With few exceptions, the media is owned by multinational conglomerate corporations whose sole responsibility is to its shareholders. They are the corporate elite and they serve the interests of their own people.

I do not know how we can reverse the trend but I do know this: Without an independent press, democracy cannot function.

The one area of hope is that we no longer need the traditional press to gather news and analysis. We have the web. No one should underestimate the power this represents. The combination of Julian Assange and WikiLeaks shook the power structure to its core. They have tried and failed to control the web thus far. Rest assured, they will keep trying.

Jazz.

DEFENDING DAN? RATHER NOT
The Failure of Mainstream Media

The buzzards are circling, the scent of fresh kill wafts through the newsrooms, trickles down and spreads, engulfing talk radio and sweeping through the Internet. The sharks are poised and the operatives sharpen their daggers. Dan Rather, the logical successor to Walter Cronkite at the vanguard of American journalism, is down and bleeding. Move in for a close up.

Shall we rise in defense of Dan Rather? Sorry, Dan, rather not.

In truth, Dan Rather's star fell from the sky long ago when he killed the story of an insider's expose of the great tobacco industry lie.

Dan Rather, you are no Walter Cronkite.

When he donned the uniform of an embedded journalist (an oxymoron if ever there was one), it only confirmed what we already knew. Corruption is absolute. A once proud and honorable journalist had become a stooge for his corporate sponsors.

For those who insist that Rather was trying to make amends, trying to set the record straight, trying to stand up against the pervasive cowardice of his trade, take a step back and look at what he and his CBS brethren have accomplished: The story of George W's cowardly evasion of military service in Vietnam is dead. Not a whimper will be heard from now until Election Day.

Was he duped? The obvious analogy is the Nigerian yellow cake document used by the Bush administration to paint a picture of the mushroom cloud as a pretense for war in Iraq. It was an obvious forgery, a juvenile piece of work, and one that Colin Powell refused to place on the record before the United Nations Security Council. The bogus Killian memos were so obvious they were exposed within seconds of airing. If Dan Rather was duped, he was done in by his own people for their own reasons.

Dan and CBS News were used by Karl Rove and the dirty tricks machine. Like Colin Powell at the United Nations, it could not be done without their complicity. Rather got his orders (put out the story as written) and he carried them out like a good little soldier.

It is not necessary to defend Dan Rather. He will be defended by people in high places. By the end of this ordeal, he will be the portrait of a victim and all America will cry out for mercy. If the powers have their way, he will rise again to even greater prominence. Soon enough he will be put out to pasture with all the accolades of an American hero.

Walter Cronkite will know better. Dan Rather is not alone in having betrayed his profession and his country in its hours of greatest need. Where is his apology for willingly promoting a war he knew to be immoral, illegal and unfounded? His place is in the Journalism Hall of Shame.

There are things that should not be forgiven.

The unfortunate truth is: Dan Rather is the symbol of journalism in America. He is the epitome of a once proud profession that sold its soul. And the stench of a dying rat will be his just epitaph.

Jazz 22 September 2004.

JUDY MILLER: ANTIHERO
Cheney's Girl at The Times

The ironies of history are plentiful. Richard Nixon opened relations with Red China, Deep Throat was a lap dog for J. Edgar Hoover, Dan Rather was a cheerleader for war, and Judith Miller was a mouthpiece for the lies that led to war. Now, she is a martyr for her profession.

When you play with the devil, sometimes you get burned.

When *Newsweek Magazine* revealed the desecration of the Koran by American interrogators, the White House laid the blood of the innocent at the reporters' door. If there was any justification for that charge (there was in fact precious little), what then can be said of the reporter whose tireless "journalism" gave credibility to the now infamous weapons of mass destruction fraud? What can be said of an esteemed professional who shamelessly espoused the Saddam-Al Qaeda connection? Is there no blood on her hands?

As a reporter for the *New York Times*, Judith Miller was used by the White House to prosecute an illegal war of aggression that may ultimately cost hundreds of thousands of lives. Instead of learning her lessons and coming clean, she maintained her ties and secured her position as the print media point for White House propaganda.

She was leading the charge to war with Iraq, Syria and North Korea before the curious case of Valerie Plame imploded and brought her operation to a close.

Like Dan Rather before her, Judy Miller has left us in

a quandary. We believe in freedom of the press but we also believe that Judy Miller has prostituted her profession to the White House propaganda machine.

Thus far, we have been given confusing accounts of what happened in this strange and baffling story. This much we know: Robert Novak was employed in a cheap, dirty trick, exposing an active undercover CIA agent in retaliation for her husband's objection to the administration's fabricated case for war. This despicable action placed her life and the lives of her associates in danger, blew the cover off covert operations, and thereby threatened the national security.

In a curious spin, Judy Miller's defenders claim that she was not contacted to publish the malicious outing but rather contacted her White House sources to discover the source of the leak. We know that Miller did not go public with the story, so what can we surmise?

First, that Miller was named by someone (presumably by her own contacts) since no one else should have known. In that case, Miller would owe her sources nothing. The principle of protected sources cannot apply to protecting the very individuals who would put you in jail.

Second, she must have learned who the leak was though she chose not to reveal it. Had she done so, she would have been serving the public good as well as fulfilling her journalistic duty. Had she done so, she would no longer be a White House darling but her current quandary would be heroic indeed.

If she did not discover who the source was then there is literally nothing to protect. She would simply be called upon to state for the record that she contacted certain White House officials and learned nothing. Case closed.

Clearly, there is no scenario we can surmise that would paint Judith Miller a hero.

We have heard Miller's colleagues in the media rally

to her defense on the curious grounds that this is somehow retaliation for the Times' antiwar stance and wondered: What planet have they been living on? The Times was at the head of the list in promoting the cause of war and its subsequent mea culpa was something less than sincere.

We have heard them proclaim in tones of utter disbelief: She is going to jail for a story she never published! I admit I have joined that chorus but now I understand that publishing that story was both her responsibility and her redemption. That she chose not to publish is her own mea culpa.

Is she a journalist or a propagandist?

Did the story fail to serve her cause?

Did it threaten her good standing with the White House?

Of course, none of this can explain why Robert Novak is not in Judith Miller's shoes. What sort of deal did he cut? Unfortunately, given the state of American journalism, we can have little confidence that anyone is even trying to get to the core of this story. Moreover, there is the holdover case of the Bolton memos (demanded by the Senate, withheld by the White House). Given the Downing Street memos and the inexplicable refusal of the White House to yield on this matter, these are potentially explosive documents yet neither Miller nor her courageous colleagues seem interested.

There is also the outstanding question of what Miller knows that Matt Cooper of Time Magazine (released by the court when he agreed to cooperate with the blessings of his source) does not. Apparently, their sources are not the same. As Robert Kuttner of the Boston Globe rightly observed: Something stinks to high heaven.

The curious case of Judith Miller of the *New York Times* forces us to reconsider the rights and responsibilities of the media. Unfortunately, it comes down to this: If a journalist is employed in the commission of a federal crime (like plotting an assassination), he or she is not protected by the first amendment.

In this case, it seems amply clear that Robert Novak was the triggerman and no one has the right to protect the man who ordered the hit.

Jazz 6 July 2005.

SURREALISTIC PILLOW
The West Virginia Mining Disaster

"I can handle big news and little news. And if there's no news, I'll go out and bite a dog."

Charles Tatum, Reporter
Billy Wilder's *Ace in the Hole* (1951)

On the same day that some university media organization moved to ban the word "surreal" from our lexicon, I witnessed one of the most surreal events I can recall.

It was the second day of the Sago coalmine disaster and I was trying to remember an old movie about an out-of-control reporter spinning a very human tragedy about a man trapped in a mine into a marketable yarn.

The story began on Monday with the "breaking news" that an explosion in a West Virginia coalmine left thirteen miners trapped below the surface. CNN immediately went into full-court press with 24-7 coverage, featuring interviews with mining officials, former miners, government representatives, corporate spokespersons and distraught relatives assembled in the local church.

Anderson Cooper, CNN's man of the moment, rushed to the scene to take the lead with periodic updates, rumors and expressions of anguish. Cooper was the man who pushed the stoic Aaron Brown off the air, replacing whatever was left of objective journalism on "The Most Trusted Name in News" with a new, action oriented, in your face brand of news reporting. He had made his reputation playing hardball with freshman US Senator Mary Landrieu, Governor Kathleen Blanco and Mayor Ray Nagin in the aftermath of Hurricane Katrina. At the time, it seemed a refreshing resurgence of backbone in a media that was losing credibility with the viewing public. Later, we learned he was only serving the White House strategy of blame shifting. He never took on FEMA or Michael Brown until the White House made it clear that Brownie was the designated fall guy.

As fictional reporter, Charles Tatum, said to his client: "I'm a thousand-dollar-a-day newspaperman. You can have me for nothing."

As the second day of the Sago mining disaster dragged on, it became clear that realistic hope was getting thin. Reports of toxic air quality filtered in and experts delivered cautionary reports. Still, friends and relatives hung on, clinging to faith and praying for the improbable. As the night drew to an end, 41 hours after the initial explosion, the improbable was delivered with the news that twelve of the miners were alive.

America went to sleep on the surrealistic pillow of a miracle. Our luck had not run out. Our prayers would still be answered and our dreams would come true.

It no longer mattered that the Sago mine had been issued 270 safety code citations over the last two years, including a shut down for dangerous buildup of flammable coal dust and inadequate ventilation to dissipate dangerous gases. It no longer mattered that "clean coal" technology is an oxymoron or that enforcement of safety regulations under the Bush administration is a joke. It no longer mattered that men were compelled to take dangerous jobs in unsafe environments because so few options were available to the workforce. It only mattered that twelve of thirteen survived.

The dawn of a new day brought the heartbreaking news that the media got it wrong, that twelve of the thirteen miners were dead and the lone survivor was in critical condition. Media scrambled to explain an incredible lapse in news reporting as a problem of communication.

It was a hard pill to swallow. What began as the new standard of an ambulance-chasing, pounce and run, news event ended with a betrayal of the public trust. The mass reporting of a false miracle at the end of a daily news cycle was plastered in headlines across the nation.

Reporter to Charles Tatum: "We're all in the same boat."

Tatum: "I'm in the boat. You're in the water. Now let's see how you can swim."

CNN's wall-to-wall coverage of the West Virginia mining disaster continued on the third day. The nature of the story had changed but the drama lived on.

There is something very disturbing in the devolution of our media to the sensation-oriented atmosphere of a 1951 movie starring Kirk Douglas. While CNN was fixated on the mining disaster, the west coast was recovering from disastrous floods and fires were still raging across Oklahoma, Texas and New Mexico. A new wave of violence in Iraq was answered by a targeted US air strike, killing a family of women and children. Iran announced intentions to resume nuclear research, Russia threatened Europe's supply of natural gas by cutting off Ukraine, and Jack Abramoff, the biggest fat cat in Washington, copped a plea in a deal that will shake the capitol to its core.

It was not exactly a slow news cycle.

Democracy requires a vibrant, independent, engaged press if it is to survive. In modern times, the only press that matters is the media. If this is an example of the best they can do, our democracy is in trouble.

The Sago coalmine disaster was a riveting drama. It drew us in. It is important. It is not, however, worthy of three days of full-time coverage. To deliver the news in this manner is a disservice to all Americans, including the exploited families of the event itself. The greater tragedy is that it has become the standard of modern journalism. It is a media of constant distraction. It is a media that shocks and engages the senses but does not inform. It is a media that moves seamlessly from one drama to another with little regard for those stories and events that will shape our nation's future.

It is the solemn duty of the media to provide our citizens with the information we need to make intelligent decisions in choosing our representatives and guiding the affairs of state. To the extent that media is obsessed with the sensational, while the most important developments and issues of our times go underreported, the media have failed.

I cannot but think that it would be different if the same corporate interests did not own the media that our government represents.

My heart goes out to the friends and families of the coal miners in West Virginia. They were not well served in this tragedy. They will not be well served by the continued exploitation of their grief.

Jazz 7 January 2006.

PARIS TRUMPS DICK
The Politics of Distraction

"The idea that [the vice president] is 'not an entity within the executive branch' and thus exempt from a presidential order is both ludicrous and chilling."

San Francisco Chronicle Editorial
June 26, 2007

We interrupt this fair and balanced discussion of vice president Dick Cheney's astounding claim of immunity from executive orders on the grounds that he is not in fact a member of the executive branch in order to bring you the pending release of naughty girl Paris Hilton from the LA county jail.

The people want to know.

I confess the vice president's claim is on its face the most absurd assertion to come out of the White House since Franklin Pierce consulted tea leaves before signing the Missouri Compromise on the grounds that an alignment of heavenly bodies in the house of Jupiter promised a peaceful resolution of the slavery problem. Nevertheless, the fact that the vice president felt compelled to make such a claim cries out for an investigation into exactly what he is hiding.

I confess I do not understand America's obsessive-compulsive fascination with celebrity but having seen Ms

Hilton's Whopper commercial, I understand the girl is hot – talentless perhaps but hot. Nevertheless, when important political discourse is interrupted for twenty minutes of waiting for Paris Hilton to emerge from 23 days in the county jail, something is dramatically wrong.

The question that arises is: Does the media have a responsibility to inform its consumers on the burning issues of the day or must it pander to the lowest common denominator of public obsession at every possible opportunity?

Where were you when OJ drove his white Ford Bronco down an LA highway?

America wants to know.

The vice president has usurped the power of the presidency, led the nation into catastrophic war, employed the energy industry to dictate energy policy, exerted *executive* privilege to deny congressional oversight, legitimized torture by *executive* decree, abolished the foundation of western law (habeas corpus), exposed a CIA operative on a political vendetta, implemented a massive illegal spying operation with an end run around the Justice Department, and reduced the chief *executive* to an afterthought, yet America needs to know every footstep of Hollywood's darling naughty girl.

We get it, Mr. Cheney: you can trash the constitution and lead us all through the gates of hell because the people care more about the vagaries of Paris than the treacheries of Washington.

Maybe it is so: We get what we deserve but I do not believe we deserve what the media deliver us in the name of "Breaking News."

Do we watch because it is there or is it there because we watch? If we were not subjected to 24-7 coverage of mining disasters, Hollywood crimes and misdemeanors, misbehaving sports figures, racist misspeaks, celebrity breakups, runaway brides, shark attacks or family tragedies, would we really miss it?

Someone has to begin playing the grownups in this society and titillation stories, gossip and personal tragedies have no place on programs that pass for news and informative discourse.

If Dick Cheney does not wish to be a part of the executive branch, let us oblige him by removing him from office.

As for Paris Hilton, leave the girl alone.

Jazz 27 June 2007.

AS THE PLOT THICKENS
The Strange Case of Julian Assange

As a novelist with a penchant for political mystery and suspense, I am familiar with the standard plot twist of the endangered protagonist: If only she can get the information out into the public, she'll be safe. The men in black can't touch her then and the world will have to grapple with the truth.

As the plot thickens in the strange case of Julian Assange, founder of WikiLeaks and the man behind the latest uncovering of duplicity, hypocrisy and deception in American diplomacy, what is easily the most fascinating story of the year is also becoming the most important.

Say it aint so: The hero of our story cannot be a sex offender wanted in Sweden for something resembling rape. Even sexual misconduct however it is characterized is not permissible for our man of the hour. A good protagonist may be tortured, twisted, suffering extreme bouts of anxiety and depression but he cannot in any way be a sexual offender. Such a distinction would place our story in the waste bin of literature never to be consumed by the general public. We desire this story to be widely read.

This is not how our story goes. Rather, Julian Assange is under attack by the most powerful forces on the planet. Having outfoxed and outmaneuvered the intelligentsia, the wrath of the United States government is being brought to bear. When we learn that the Swedish government was not much interested in the case until an angry White House condemned the latest WikiLeaks release in terms normally reserved for terrorists and enemies of state, we begin to suspect that Secretary of State Hillary Clinton is twisting some Swedish diplomatic arms. When we learn that Sweden is heavily invested in the international arms trade and may have something to hide, we wonder what bodies might be buried in the Swedish wine cellar. When we learn that the prosecutor refused even to talk the case over before posting Assange's name on the Interpol most wanted list, our suspicions grow. When we learn that the Swedish Supreme Court refused to hear an appeal on the warrant, we suspect our doubts concerning the Swedish judicial process are well grounded.

Moreover, when the Ambassador of Ecuador (perhaps inspired by the revelation of America's betrayal of democracy in Honduras) came to the rescue, offering virtual asylum to our beleaguered hero, it was subsequently withdrawn for unstated reasons. The unseen hand of oppression no doubt belongs to the American diplomatic corps and an incensed Hillary Clinton. (How will this affect her still breathing presidential aspirations?)

Amazon announces that it will no longer allow WikiLeaks to use their servers and Pay Pal, a subsidiary of eBay, severs ties in attempt to cut off financing. The squeeze is on and we begin to wonder if it is even possible to reveal the truth in a corporate world.

In this case the cat is out of the bag. Elvis has left the building. But Assange and friends promise even more fun and games, the next episode exposing the highly questionable and perhaps illegal conduct of a certain powerful American bank.

So what have we learned from the latest WikiLeaks revelations?

Respectfully and with due deference to Julian Assange and his hacker friends, we have learned very little of substance. In fact, we have learned more from the reaction than from the documents themselves.

If anyone was surprised that the Saudis and their Sunni allies in the Middle East are more threatened by an empowered Iran than they are by Israel and in fact were cheerleaders for a preemptive strike on Tehran, then they had little interest in foreign policy and likely remain ignorant today.

If anyone is surprised by the extent to which this American administration has gone to protect officials of the Bush administration from charges of war crimes and crimes against humanity, they have not been following along.

The sum total of the WikiLeaks revelations thus far is to confirm an already dark and cynical view of the American government. It adds to our disillusionment and the realization that a change in presidents and a change in ruling parties did not translate to a change in policy.

For me the most damning revelation (if it can be called that) was our government's response to the military coup in Honduras overthrowing democratically elected president Manuel Zelaya in June 2009.

At the time I correctly read the coup as an unjustified reaction to Zelaya's proposals to help his nation's abundant poor. That he wanted to raise the minimum wage was just too much for that nation's elite to bear. I incorrectly interpreted the Obama administration's neutral response as a step in the right direction. Thanks to WikiLeaks we now know that our own diplomats got it right from day one: The coup was unlawful, ungrounded and therefore deserving of an immediate and forceful denunciation. Our official response neither condemning nor approving the coup was calculated to legitimize the coup with a subsequent election while Zelaya was exiled to the Dominican Republic.

The message to Latin America was and is clear: This

administration like its predecessors is no friend to democracy for whenever the elite come calling we will answer. Tragically, the Obama administration continues to pursue a policy of exploitation under the guise of free trade though it has alienated the entire hemisphere.

This was the administration that was supposed to champion transparency yet the venom it has shown toward the man who forced some small measure of it upon them is palpable. There is nothing in these documents that poses a threat to any lives and the only policies they challenge are policies that deserve to be challenged.

What follows is an assault on the free flow of information through the worldwide web. Members of congress and the executive branch are scrambling to find ways to shut WikiLeaks down. Because the web is international and the WikiLeaks people are highly competent their efforts are likely to fail. For individuals and organizations with lesser resources the effort to suppress might well succeed. That is the greatest danger the WikiLeaks phenomenon entails: that freedom of the web might be compromised.

It is critical to bear in mind that WikiLeaks is not the source of its information; it is the conduit. It receives information from people within the halls of power who believe the public has right to know and that that right supercedes all other considerations.

We need a WikiLeaks. We can no longer count on our corporate-owned media to do the right thing when it may undermine their own interests. We need a neutral conduit. In fact, we need a thousand conduits so that none can be singled out for retribution.

Imagine what might have happened had someone leaked the Downing Street memos or something like them, exposing the lies of war before the first bombs fell on Baghdad. If an unjustified war could be averted and hundreds of thousands of lives saved, how sacred then is the right of government secrecy?

I do not know what happened with two women in Sweden but I have a suspicion that the case would never have come to light if not for the other activities of Julian Assange. If guilty, without question he should be held accountable.

In his role as a provider of information that enlightens or empowers the public, Julian Assange deserves all the protection that freedom of the press can provide. Toward that end we should extract a price on Amazon and eBay with a Christmas boycott for doing the government's dirty work.

I sincerely hope that all efforts at suppression and revenge fall short and that our government finally learns that transparency is not only the best defense against security leaks, it is also the best policy.

This is how our story must end: Not with our hero in jail but exonerated and our government shamed into more open, honest and responsible policies. It must leave us yearning for the next installment.

Jazz 6 December 2010.

THE FALL OF RUPERT MURDOCH
Enemies of Democracy

"Rupert Murdoch is no saint; he is to propriety what the Marquis de Sade was to chastity. When it comes to money and power he's carnivorous: all appetite and no taste. Politicians become little clay pigeons to be picked off with flattering headlines, generous air time, a book contract or the old-fashioned black jack that never misses: campaign cash."

Bill Moyers Journal
June 29, 2007

Which of the following does not belong: Benedict Arnold, Boss Tweed, Richard Nixon, J. Edgar Hoover, Karl Rove, Antonin Scalia, Clarence Thomas, Anthony Kennedy and Rupert Murdoch?

Answer: None of the above.

All are notorious for their groundbreaking betrayal of American democracy from its inception to the present day.

Benedict Arnold was a commander in the Continental Army who secretly plotted to hand West Point over to the British. Boss Tweed was the strongman of New York's Tammany Hall in the mid 1800's who was ultimately convicted for bribery and extortion, dying in the Ludlow Street Jail.

Richard Nixon was a crook whose scorn for American democracy went so deep that he never questioned the necessity of committing crimes of espionage against a presidential opponent so weak he failed to carry his own state. Nixon got his due.

J. Edgar Hoover famously wiretapped and eavesdropped on anything that moved, from politicians and journalists to movie stars and musicians. During his five-decade reign of terror, if you didn't have a dossier on file at the FBI you were nobody. Hoover survived Democrats and Republicans alike because he had the goods to destroy anyone who stood in his way. Blackmail and extortion were his calling card yet he has his name on the building that houses the nation's highest law enforcement agency. American justice will never be vindicated until that inscription is taken down.

Karl Rove was the architect of the largest disenfranchisement scheme since the days of Jim Crow. He is the man who made George W. Bush President of the United States by effectively stealing two consecutive elections.

Supreme Court Justices Scalia, Thomas and Kennedy are the only three members of the high court to vote for both Bush v. Gore 2000 and Citizens United v. Federal Election Commission 2010. Bush v. Gore anointed George W. Bush president without benefit of a majority vote and Citizens United opened the doors to unlimited corporate financing of political campaigns.

Now, with the revelations of media mogul Rupert Murdoch's unscrupulous operations in the phone-hacking scandal, Murdoch can take his rightful place alongside the most infamous betrayers of our democracy.

The founders in their wisdom acknowledged the critical nature of a free press, enshrining the principle in the first amendment to the constitution. Not all lived up to that wisdom (as the Alien and Sedition Acts under

President John Adams attest) but, as a whole, the founders recognized that a vibrant and independent press was an essential fourth pillar of a functioning republic.

The founders did not envision a time when the press is supplanted by the media, when information and misinformation is disseminated by radio, television and the worldwide web, and when a handful of international corporations would own and control the flow of information throughout the world.

The founders never envisioned a media mogul as powerful as Rupert Murdoch. He is the CEO of News Corporation, which in turn owns Fox Broadcasting, the Wall Street Journal (Dow Jones), the Times of London, the Daily Mirror, Sky Television, the Sun, the Star and the New York Post. His tentacles extend from Australia and New Zealand to North and South America, from the British Isles across Europe to the Middle East. He is the closest thing to a media czar the world has ever known.

While his political philosophy is notoriously rightwing, he has courted alliances on both sides of the aisle, befriending conservative Prime Ministers Margaret Thatcher, John Major and David Cameron as well as the Labour Party's Tony Blair. While his Fox News has consistently bent to the far right, providing a litmus test for Republican presidential candidates, Murdoch has offered counsel and support to Hillary Clinton, John Kerry and Barack Obama as well as George W. Bush and John McCain.

Considering his relationship with both the Clintons and Tony Blair, it is plausible that Murdoch played some direct or indirect role in turning the left toward center and the center to the right. In what Bill Clinton and Blair referred to as the third way, the Democrats and Labour abandoned progressive economics while still clinging to progressive social issues. Since Murdoch considers himself libertarian, the new left (which is not left at all) is very much consistent with his own views. Most importantly, it gave him free reign to extend his media empire.

In 1995, with Bill Clinton in the White House, the Federal Communications Commission ruled that Murdoch's ownership of Fox Broadcasting was in the best interests of the public.

It pays to cultivate friends in high places.

Pimping a war for oil, consuming and transforming legitimate journalistic enterprises into broadsheets, and shamelessly operating a propaganda empire to advance his own interests were not sufficient to discredit Murdoch but hacking the phones of innocent victims and their relatives for sensationalist stories finally tipped the scale.

The tar from Murdoch's hands has stained everyone he touched, from the current resident at Number 10 Downing Street to the once-venerated Scotland Yards. Former employees and allies are falling like ducks at a carnival shooting gallery.

Anyone who believes Murdoch's "I'm too old to know anything" act before the Media Committee of the House of Commons is as gullible as a grassroots member of the corporate Tea Party. In the bumbling fashion of an old man in the early stages of dementia, Murdoch stated he knew nothing of the operations and techniques of the offending news corps. He claimed this despite his company paying the equivalent of $3.2 million in settlements to hacking victims on condition of non-disclosure.

What's a few million here and there?

It remains to be seen whether this scandal has the legs to bring the mogul down. He still has friends in high places and on both sides of the Atlantic. Republicans in congress are afraid to whisper his name in anything but a positive light. Democrats are Democrats and Obama is Obama. The investigation in America will not be in earnest unless public outcry demands it and even then, Murdoch has the media to fight back.

The excuse will be that we have far more important matters with which to concern ourselves like a debt crisis that Murdoch and his ilk trumped up for media consumption. (The only real crisis lies in our refusal to remove the debt ceiling in a timely manner.)

Regardless of Murdoch's ultimate fate, the odds of real media reform are something less than the odds of real financial reform after the near collapse of the global economy. That would require breaking up the media conglomerates and requiring news organizations to divest themselves of other corporate interests.

The chances of that are nil. So in a sense Rupert Murdoch has already won the war. He has shaped the media of the future. That it is ruthless, amoral and devoid of public interest should not surprise any of us.

It is a corporate media for a corporate world.

Jazz 22 July 2011.

VOLUME VIII

THE AGE OF CATASTROPHE

CONTENTS

PREFACE

CLIMATE CHANGE & OTHER DISASTERS

On August 29, 2005 Hurricane Katrina missed New Orleans. At the last moment it veered to the east toward Biloxi, Mississippi. Bad news for Biloxi but very good news for the Big Easy and because the heart of the storm hit the low populated area between New Orleans and Biloxi it seemed all of us could take a breath and count our blessings.

We awoke in a different world. Katrina may have missed New Orleans but the levees gave way and the lower half of the city was under water. For the next two weeks or more the cable news programs delivered wall-to-wall coverage of a major American city under severe distress and the apparent inability of our elected officials to deal with it.

We are living in the age of catastrophe. From hurricanes, typhoons, earthquakes and tornados to the purely manmade disasters like oil spills, collapsed bridges and mines. We seem to thrive on them. They awaken our sense of humanity. Like an accident on the freeway we have to look.

Scientists have warned us there will be more and more severe storms, tornados, hurricanes and tsunamis. While no single event can be attributed to global climate change, the fact of a warming planet fueled by toxic emissions leads to the logical consequence of the tragedies we have witnessed.

It is not God's wrath. It is nature doing what nature does. The poisons we have delivered to the air and water and ecosystems since the beginning of the industrial age do not imperil the planet. Earth abides. We along with our fellow inhabitants are the ones in danger. What we do to mitigate the harm is how we will be judged by succeeding generations.

Having been warned, it is time past time we prepared. We know what we must do: Reduce carbon emissions by transferring to a green energy economy. Beyond that we must do all we can to reduce the poisoning of the air and water. Beyond that we must be prepared to deal with the consequences of our actions.

We are living in the age of catastrophe. It is time to stop gawking at the human drama of an unfolding tragedy and do something about it.

Jazz.

PRAYERS FOR NEW ORLEANS
The Day Katrina Struck

Hurricane Katrina streaked across the southern Florida peninsula, turned north and marked a path to the heart of New Orleans. At the last possible moment, with catastrophic predictions filling the airwaves, it veered east, striking Gulfport and Biloxi, Mississippi.

At first report, it seemed New Orleans, jewel of the south, was spared the full force of nature's unnatural wrath. St. Bernard's parish and the ninth ward were subsumed under ten feet of water, power was out, and the damage to homes, businesses and structures was substantial but on the night of August 29 we were confident that the very survival of the city of jazz was not in question.

We were concerned for all the victims in the path of the hurricane. The forces that spared New Orleans had brought death and destruction elsewhere but we were confident that our government would provide sufficient aid and assistance, knowing that they could not fail in the hour of greatest need. Our politicians are good at confronting a crisis. It is one of the blessings of democracy that they cannot ignore the people in a televised disaster.

By the time we awaken on the morning of August 30, we were stricken, paralyzed, horrified by what we saw. Our government had utterly failed to answer the call and New Orleans was under siege. The levees had broken. Eighty percent of the city was submerged. We were told that martial law had been declared. There was no order and no relief. The nation and much of the world began to cry and our tears would not end for seven days and nights.

Our thoughts and prayers are with the city of New Orleans for she has won the undying devotion of every man and woman who has known her embrace, however briefly, and she is dying before our unbelieving eyes.

If you are a praying person, pray for the homeless, the destitute and the stubborn defenders of New Orleans. Pray for the birthplace of jazz, for a culture of tolerance that predates the American nation by a hundred years. Pray for Bourbon Street, Jackson Square, the St. Louis Cemetery and the tomb of Marie Laveaux. Pray for a city of a million unfathomable contradictions and mysteries, city of light and darkness, city of hope and despair, city of faith and godlessness, city of passion and unholy calm, city of blues and ragtime, city of jazz. City of jazz.

Of all the cities in America, New Orleans is the most ancient and the most international. It is a blend of French, Caribbean and southern cultures. It is where slavery was practiced ruthlessly and where former slaves were allowed to flourish. It is where every artist and musician must go to reveal the soul. It is where Robert Johnson, Sidney Bechet, Jelly Roll Morton and Louie Armstrong learned their trade.

If you have never been to New Orleans, you may never know what you have missed. We can only pray that she will rise again and that the world's generosity will not end when the cameras are turned away. We have always known that the sea would someday swallow her whole, that the French Quarter would become a pictorial memory, that the shores of Lake Pontchartrain would no longer be distinguishable, that the triumph, the glory, the profound gloom and sorrow of this mystical American treasure would be swept away. We just did not know that it would come so soon.

JAZZMAN CHRONICLES

New Orleans may be a doomed city. Like Venice, Italy, doomed by its geography and the indifference of world governments to global warming, to melting glaciers, to altered ocean currents: We should have seen it coming. We should have recognized the signs years, decades ago, while there was still time to act. Some of us, in fact, did.

Tragically, it seems it may be America's turn to pay the price of global climate change. We have listened to the mainstream experts. They avoid the phrase "global warming" but they cannot but acknowledge that it is the rising temperature of the Gulf that has precipitated this season of severe storms. It will not end with Katrina and Katrina does not begin to compare with the devastation of the Indian Ocean tsunami. What more will we require to transform sympathy into action?

When there was still time, we should have done so much more. America was late in acknowledging the problem, late in accepting the human contribution, and even now, we stand virtually alone in refusing to sign on to the first modest effort to confront inevitable catastrophe (the Kyoto Accord). It is not too late to accept the challenge but I fear it is too late to avert a chain of tragedy.

For now, we can only pray that the damage can be alleviated and that we can recover the living, breathing miracle of creation that is New Orleans for another generation. We can pray that we have not lost forever the sacred womb of a nation and the sweetest, most enchanting of lovers the world will ever know.

Jazz 30 August 2005.

ZERO TOLERANCE
New Orleans Third Day In

"I have zero tolerance for lawlessness."
George W. Bush, September 1, 2005

Take all the looting and price gouging in New Orleans, Mississippi, Alabama and greater Louisiana and it would not amount to a fraction of a percent of the daily profit margin of the oil industry in the ongoing horror of Hurricane Katrina.

Our president rushes to Washington (canceling a photo-op in favor of a fly-over) and immediately releases a portion of the strategic oil reserves as a loan to beleaguered oil refineries, denied their daily crude from the Gulf, and the DOW Industrial average rises seventy points.

Maybe it is not improper for the president to worry about the price of gas but where is the National Guard? Where is Homeland Security? Where are the legions of support personnel that are supposed to stand ready for the crisis of a terrorist attack? Is this an indication of our preparedness?

What is wrong with this picture? New Orleans is drowning in a toxic cesspool and we have no means of communication, no contingencies for mass evacuation, inadequate provisions for food, shelter, drinkable water, medical care, levee repair or security.

The levees have failed, the pumps are inoperable, fires burn out of control, power cannot be restored, the death toll rises, disease and infestation looms, and three days after the event the National Guard is still en route.

Michael Brown, Director of the Federal Emergency Management Agency (FEMA), appearing on all the news outlets, prefaced every interview with the astounding claim that his gut told him the catastrophe would be extreme. Consequently, he pulled all the assets of his agency back out of harm's way but he forgot that he would not be able to get them back in. Mr. Brown may be a good and decent man but this is all too typical of this administration.

On the third day of hell, the president gets tough: "I have zero tolerance for lawlessness."

With all undue respect, Mr. President, you have a great deal of tolerance for a vast array of lawlessness. You tolerate corporate crime: fraud, tax evasion, no-bid contracts and cooking the books. You tolerate political crime: disenfranchisement, election fraud, slander and outing intelligence agents for political revenge. You tolerate international crime: overthrowing democratic governments, torture, attacks on journalists, the Geneva conventions and wars of aggression. You tolerate the pharmaceutical industry's malfeasance, trading thousands of lives for arthritis relief. You tolerate illegal immigration and intolerable labor standards both here and abroad. You tolerate industrial waste, poisoning the air, land and water, and contributing far more than your fair share to the problem that precipitated this "act of god."

In many ways, yours is the most tolerant administration in history. During the west coast energy crisis, your first response was an offer to tolerate suspension of environmental laws and, indeed, in the current crisis, you are perfectly willing to tolerate unconscionable profits by your corporate partners in the oil industry and suspend regulations on clean fuels.

What is exceptionally clear is that the response to this

nightmare three full days after the event is completely inadequate. What is increasingly clear is that for all the vaunted planning and anticipation, the poor and working people of New Orleans were left to fend for themselves from the very beginning.

Civil authorities ordered a mandatory evacuation but no provision was made for the masses of people who had no transportation, no money for gas or hotel rooms, and no relations in Mobile or Atlanta. Where were the military transports, the helicopters, and the caravan of buses before disaster struck?

Where are they now? For god's sake, where are they?

At some point, we must grow tired of the standard excuse (the same excuse for the war): Mistakes were made but now we must move forward. Now we can begin to understand why we will never "win" in Iraq. We have created the problem (or allowed it to develop) and now we expect to be congratulated for establishing order.

At some point, we must accept that these were not mistakes but deliberate calculations of cost versus harm. The poor in the low-lying areas of New Orleans were not worth the cost of evacuation. Indeed, for the last twenty years, the city itself was not a high enough priority to buttress and fortify the levees.

We have grown tired of the excuse that no one could have anticipated such a disaster. It is reminiscent of Condoleezza Rice's pronouncement that no one could foresee planes flying into buildings. In both cases, the disaster was fully anticipated yet virtually nothing was done to avert it.

We are supposed to be reassured that the president is back at the helm. The White House calculates and recalculates priorities while the people of New Orleans languish in intolerable conditions. The heat in the Deep South is oppressive, stifling, punishing, and the water that surrounds them is venomous and smells of death. The people have no drinking water, no food, no power, no medicine, no medical facilities and no means of escape.

What did you expect to happen?

The people are boiling with rage and desperation yet we are supposed to admire the president's get tough, zero tolerance attitude.

Three days into the horror, we see nothing that even begins to compare to the response amassed for the Indian Ocean tsunami and the White House is still making plans, calculating priorities and preparing to establish order in hell.

Here are the White House priorities: (1) the oil industry, (2) the insurance industry, (3) banking and other corporate interests, and (4) the people.

Some complain that other nations have not rushed to our aid. Like me, they might have assumed that the wealthiest nation on earth could take care of its own. In a prior commentary, I expressed full confidence that our government would respond appropriately to the breadth and depth of the unfolding horror. Three days later, it is my sorry admission that I was wrong. It is beyond belief how wrong I was.

Meantime, the people of New Orleans continue to wallow in unending horror and former presidents Clinton and Bush are planning a reunion tour to raise private funds where the government has fallen short.

Is this America?

Jazz 1 September 2005.

THE AGE OF CATASTROPHE
Preparing for Disaster

We will never fully comprehend the complexities of our planet. For centuries, we have labored to overcome and alter the course of nature. We have redirected the path of great rivers, destroyed vital ecological systems, pumped toxic waste into our waterways, oceans and atmosphere, and buried massive stockpiles of deadly chemicals and radioactive waste deep in the bowels of the earth.

We may not fully comprehend the role of human interaction with the forces of nature but we are all born with an innate understanding that if we poison our own living space, there will be a price to pay. When we witness melting glaciers, warming oceans, altered climates and shifting oceanic currents, followed by a chain of catastrophes, we do not require a panel of experts or an executive commission to inform us that something is radically astray.

It is increasingly clear that we have entered an age of unprecedented catastrophe and we are woefully unprepared to cope with it. In the wake of 911, we have invested hundreds of billions in Homeland Security but in the wake of Hurricanes Katrina and Rita, we are hard pressed to know what that means. Apparently, Homeland Security does not include the fundamentals of civil defense: communications, evacuation, emergency shelters, food, water, fuel, generators and medical facilities.

We all understand that our government has been

fixated on terrorism but these essentials are equally applicable to natural disasters and terrorist attacks, so our negligence is all the more inexplicable.

The investigation into what went wrong in New Orleans and the Gulf Coast must go beyond communication snafus and decision-making blunders. We must demand an accounting of where all the money went. If in fact it was siphoned by the military to pay for black ops in Latin America or worse, to pay off Halliburton and Blackwater Security, then heads should role and the president must be held to account.

We must not allow the administration to whitewash or constrain the investigation as they did the 911 Commission. Whether we call it blame seeking or accountability, it is the only means we have of assuring that it does not happen again.

Whether an objective investigation is forthcoming or not, we should not wait for a final report before we move forward with what must be done. Bureaucracies can wait; New Orleans, Biloxi, Lake Charles and Gulf Port cannot. Levees, roads, buildings, infrastructures, homes, hospitals and schools must be rebuilt. Comprehensive civil defense must be provided for every urban center in the nation, beginning with those that are most vulnerable.

Neither should we wait for presidential guidance, which will invariably come in the form of multi-billion dollar payoffs to the preferred list of multi-national corporations. It is Congress that controls appropriations and the executive branch is constitutionally bound to carry out the will of Congress on penalty of impeachment.

It is also Congress that must decide how we will pay for the massive projects of reconstruction and preparedness that must now be undertaken. We have a crisis in this country that runs from the top down. We cannot allow our government to be paralyzed by the void of leadership in the White House.

As I have noted before, it is the Army Corps of Engineers (not Halliburton) that should lead the reconstruction project. I would now extend that recommendation to civil defense.

In order to perform this essential duty (the largest of its kind since the New Deal and the Marshall Plan), the Corps must be relieved of its responsibilities in Iraq and Afghanistan. The president is dead wrong. If we could have it both ways (war abroad and security at home), the flood walls and levees would not have been shoddily constructed, New Orleans would not be an endangered city, and a thousand souls from the city of jazz would not have left their homes on this earth.

Congress shuddered at the projected costs of reconstruction though hardly an objection was raised at an even greater price tag for our unnecessary wars. Let them shudder again for it will be twice that amount and more to do what must be done, yet when it is done, unlike our wars of choice, it will not leave us with a new generation of American enemies; it will leave us with something we can see, touch, use and appreciate; it will leave future generations with gratitude and admiration.

The lessons of Katrina and Rita were many but one lesson was exceptionally clear in both cases: the overriding need for a safe and efficient system of mass evacuation. With Katrina, the failure to evacuate resulted in loss of life and the most painful scenes we have witnessed since the Indian Ocean tsunami. With Rita on the heels of Katrina, the cities of Houston and Galveston made a valiant effort but it could not prevent a systemic breakdown that snarled traffic for a hundred miles. Even without a pending disaster, vehicular transportation in virtually every major city is a crapshoot of congestion five days a week. How did we expect that same system to accommodate a mass evacuation?

JAZZMAN CHRONICLES

The dirty secret of New Orleans may be that if they attempted to evacuate the poor and immobile, the exit ways would have become so constricted that the bridge across Lake Pontchartrain may have been lined with vehicles when it collapsed.

What is required for efficient mass evacuation is a system of mass transit. On the Gulf Coast, a coastal line would connect the major cities from Corpus Christi, Texas, to Tampa, Florida, with each city connecting to inland hubs at San Antonio, Dallas, Shreveport, Jackson, Montgomery and Macon. The inland cities would be connected as well, with each in turn providing shelters, food, water, medical supplies, busses and emergency helicopters.

Similar systems should be undertaken for the Atlantic seaboard from Miami to Portland, Maine, and on the west coast from San Diego to Seattle. Circular systems should provide for interior cities such as Chicago and Detroit and, eventually, separate systems could become interconnected for a national mass transit network.

It is truly a massive and noble endeavor – not unlike the pledge to put a man on the moon in 1969 or a manned mission to Mars today – but it would serve the nation in multiple ways. Aside from effective civil defense, it would provide meaningful and well-paid employment and those it employed would acquire valuable skills. It would do more to relieve our over crowded and deteriorating highways than a dozen over-priced, pork laden highway bills. It would relieve our atmosphere of millions upon millions of tons of carbon dioxide poisoning. Finally, it would ease our dependency on foreign oil and eliminate the perceived necessity of occupying a nation in the Middle East.

It will not be easy and even then, it will only be a beginning, yet if we take that first step, we may finally become the noble and enlightened nation that we all want to believe we are.

Jazz 26 September 2005.

REMEMBERING NEW ORLEANS
Katrina was a Terrorist Attack

Nearly four years after the attack on the World Trade Center, the Pentagon and an unknown third target, there was a second terrorist attack and the conspiracy to cover up the truth was no less determined.

Katrina was a category three hurricane that missed New Orleans yet the devastation was complete. The lowlands of the Ninth Ward, Gentilly and St. Bernard Parrish were buried under a wall of water, hundreds died, hundreds more would never be counted, and tens of thousands were scattered across the land like third world refugees.

It was not the storm that buried New Orleans. It was not the hand of god or the wheel of fortune that sealed her fate. It was negligence, human negligence, intentional negligence at the highest levels of government.

What is the definition of a terrorist attack? If a man or an agency knows what will happen when an inevitable convergence of events occurs and not only fails to act but acts in a manner that will maximize the disaster, is it really any different than flying a passenger plane into a tower of civilians?

The Army Corps of Engineers knew what they were doing when they used inadequate funds to contract inadequate work to rebuild and reinforce the levees that stood between the poor black folk of New Orleans and a watery grave. Renowned for their genius around the world, the Corps ingeniously erected a façade that created an illusion of strength. The Corps knew it would topple when tested and the Corps knew it would be tested.

When a lonely meteorologist warned that Katrina could spell catastrophe the Corps did not sound the alarm. When there was still a chance at mass evacuation, the Corps stood down. The Corps had a job to do but that job was not to protect the poor of New Orleans; it was to guard their reputation as they skimmed funds from the levees, bridges and dams of America so they could build fortresses for international oil companies in Iraq.

The Army Corps of Engineers was hoping that Katrina would hit dead on at full force so that no one would notice or care that the levees were defective. They were counting on the president to attribute the massive destruction to an act of god and the hammer of inevitable fate. They were counting on every expression of empathy to be followed by a qualifier: There was nothing we could do.

They were not counting on day after day of suffering people pleading for help while the government's representatives threw up their hands in ignorance. They were not counting on floating corpses and an endless parade of homeless people wading through toxic waters to the convention center or the Superdome where no help was waiting.

Before Katrina, not even the most venomous critic could have imagined an American leader so heartless, so indifferent, so out of touch with the common man that he failed to notice his people were dying.

We watched the events unfold, the slowness of federal response, the absence of the guard, the insensitivity of our president, the absolute lack of urgency in the face of disaster, and we knew it was a crime against human dignity that would endure the ages. The entire nation and much of the world witnessed in stark, vivid detail what it was to live in America poor and black.

We had a government that could run the river backwards rather than allow an unfortunate woman, white and brain dead, the dignity of a private and natural death but could not raise a hand to deliver food, water and medical supplies to the birthplace of jazz.

Katrina was a terrorist attack that ripped at the cover of class warfare. Like the targets of our bombs in foreign nations, the poor were mostly dark skinned and faceless. They were not a part of the American dream; they were a part of the American cesspool – or so they seemed to our privileged overlords.

The Corps of Engineers was right that New Orleans would be tested; New Orleans would be tested in Houston, Nashville, Austin, Chicago, Los Angeles, New York and Salt Lake City, Utah. The city of jazz would be tested from Portland, Oregon to Portland, Maine, from the Golden Gate to the shining beacon on a hill. New Orleans would be tested in every two-cent town with a television and a diner.

Every militant Islamist was pointing to CNN and saying: See how they treat their own – and they have oil too.

Yes, New Orleans is rich in oil. It possesses an abundant supply just off its marshy coast. It has so much oil that if it were a foreign nation and its Diaspora were refugees as the media proclaimed, New Orleans would be richer than the United Arab Emirates and it would have no need of our assistance.

New Orleans is rich in culture and irony – jazz and the blues. How ironic that its people were shipped to the four corners of the nation as immigrant Hispanics at substandard wages were hired for the clean up. The powers knew the citizens of New Orleans would insist on rebuilding their schools, hospitals and homes while the illegal immigrants would simply do as they were told. New Orleans would become a Disneyland, a new Mecca for corporate greed, a haven for casinos and high-rise hotels. There would be no room for the poor black folk who were the heart of the city of jazz.

New Orleans would never be the same but the powers were fools if they thought it would go down without a fight. They had unleashed an enduring heartache that would translate into words and music, a story that would be told for a thousand years.

Once there was a city whose citizens were a ragtag collection of slaves and semi-slaves, the misfits and miscreants of a nation whose ambition was larger than its conscience. Once there was a city where blacks, whites, and every shade of gray learned to live together in the harmony of jazz. Once there was a city where French and English were mixed in a steamy brew of Cajun and Creole and the dialects of the Louisiana bayou. Once there was a city that gave birth to the finest music and the most diverse culture the world has ever known. Once there was a city where the poor were not poor for they possessed that richness of spirit and culture and music and tolerance that was the envy of all others.

Once there was a city of jazz. No more.

Mourn for the people who lost their lives. Mourn for the people who lost their souls. Mourn for the people who lost their homes. Mourn for the people who will never return. Mourn for the people who will never stop mourning. Mourn for the people who never knew New Orleans before the storm.

Katrina was a terrorist attack, a conspiracy of indifference, the "shock and awe" campaign of a war on the poor.

Mourn for New Orleans, the most genuine and culturally rich city in the world, and take a solemn vow never to forget.

One year from Katrina do not forget that the Ninth Ward is still barren.

JAZZMAN CHRONICLES

Two years from Katrina do not forget that New Orleans was once more than Mardi Gras and the French Quarters.

Three years from Katrina do not forget that the poor people of New Orleans are still poor but they no longer have the comfort of home.

Ten years from Katrina do not forget that New Orleans was buried in water by an act of man, not of god.

Twenty years from Katrina, remember that New Orleans was once a raw, thriving city where art and artists were born.

Thirty years from Katrina remember New Orleans and mourn.

Jazz 6 October 2007.

FORGOTTEN AND FORSAKEN
A Quake Hits Haiti

"To the people of Haiti we say clearly and with conviction: You will not be forsaken; you will not be forgotten."

President Barack Obama, January 14, 2010

"We have been living for one year now under this de facto government which is destroying the country. 95% of the people...who were working government jobs have been fired. Children cannot go to school. Students cannot advance in their studies. We are wondering how far this crisis will be allowed to go. All of this is why we are in the streets...demanding the...return of President Jean Bertrand Aristide...immediately. This is the only issue the people are interested in today. Aristide is the one who can save Haiti from all its woes."

Dread Wilme, Community Leader
Assassinated in the Cite Soleil Massacre, July 6, 2005

There are events in the world that should enlighten us even as they fill our hearts with sorrow, that should help us to place relative value on the myriad problems and issues that concern us day to day. Hurricane Katrina and the devastation of New Orleans was such an event. The

Indian Ocean tsunami was such an event. And the catastrophic quake in Port au Prince is also such an event.

Bearing witness to such disasters even from a distance must pull at our hearts to reveal our naked humanity. If it fails to move us then we are jaded, numb and dehumanized.

Only days before the Haiti quake our news media showed the same level of obsession that we see today over a failed attempt to take down a plane. Only weeks before the same obsession occurred over the private affairs of golf champion Tiger Woods.

Now, as an epic tragedy plays out before our weary eyes, we can begin to put matters in proper perspective.

We should know by now that the devastation in Haiti (like the lower ninth ward in New Orleans) was a deadly combination of a natural disaster and human deficiency. In another country the destruction would not be so profound.

Days of endless coverage have passed without any real recitation of Haiti's tragic history. Days have passed without any mention of Jean Bertrand Aristide, Haiti's beloved former president removed from office in a CIA coup. (He was spirited away in the middle of the night and transported out of the country, a modus operandi repeated in the recent coup in Honduras.) Instead, we are treated to the spectacle of two former American presidents leading the fundraising effort, both of whom bear their share of responsibility for the devastation of Haiti long before the January quake.

The people who presently make up the population of Haiti are the descendents of slaves imported from Africa by the French when that European power still had dreams of conquering the world. Modern day Haiti was founded in 1804 when the slaves rebelled and overthrew their French masters. In an act so profane it defies belief to this day the nation of Haiti was held financially responsible for asserting its independence.

Faced with a military blockade and without allies, Haiti was compelled to pay punishing reparations to the French, an act of extortion that claimed up to 80% of the nation's budget and continued to 1947. That pattern of extortion was repeated through an American occupation from 1915 to 1934 and again in the modern era through the dictates of global "free trade" policies.

Haiti was the first independent nation in Latin America, the first post-colonial black nation in the world, and the only nation whose citizenry was predominantly former slaves. Without the oppression of European and American powers, Haiti should have been a source of pride to all humanity. Instead, it has become the impoverished and dysfunctional nation that was destroyed by an act of nature in 2010.

If the concept of international justice wanted expression it could find no better place in the world than Haiti. Since when does justice demand reparations from the oppressed to the oppressor? Yet when President Jean Bertrand Aristide, confronted with systemic poverty and the austerity demands of the global free trade establishment, demanded that France repay the extorted funds in the amount of $21 billion, he was summarily removed from power.

Aristide came to power after three decades of brutality under the dictators Francois "Papa Doc" and Jean Claude "Baby Doc" Duvalier. Tens of thousands lost their lives in a reign of terror that allowed no dissent. Yet a preacher from the Port au Prince slum of La Saline spoke out and the people rallied.

Aristide was elected by a landslide vote in 1990 and overthrown by a CIA sponsored coup in 1991. President Bill Clinton restored him to power in 1994 and he was re-elected in 2000 but he angered the American president when he pressed for higher wages and refused to enact the policies of global free trade. Clinton responded by blocking a $500 million loan from the International Monetary Fund and George W. Bush followed with the 2004 coup.

In July 2005 a Brazilian brigade of United Nations peacekeepers cleared the way for an upcoming election by leading a brazen and brutal attack on yet another slum of Port au Prince (a hotbed of support for the ousted president). Community activist Dread Wilme was killed along with many of his fellow citizens in what came to be known as the Cite Soleil Massacre. Their crime was protesting in the streets and supporting Jean Bertrand Aristide. Far from repenting and making just reparations, the action or one very similar was repeated in December 2005.

The citizens of Port au Prince were once again pacified and Haiti's current president Rene Preval was elected in 2006.

Today, as the world's powers make a great show of their collective generosity and charity, remember that France has not paid a penny in reparations for their crimes of extortion, brutality and oppression. Neither has America. Neither has the United Nations.

So when President Obama tells the people of Haiti: "You will not be forsaken; you will not be forgotten," the people of Haiti if their voices could be heard might well reply:

You have already forsaken us and you have already forgotten.

Jazz 17 January 2010.

BP = BEYOND POLLUTION
Destroying the Gulf of Mexico

Lobbying Congress for favorable legislation: Millions

Cost of deep-sea drilling: Billions

Destruction of an ecosystem: Priceless

On April 20th an attempt to cap the Deepwater Horizon, a British Petroleum rig in the Gulf of Mexico, resulted in an explosion. Eleven workers were lost and the subsequent failure to shut off the oil flow and contain the rapidly spreading slick has resulted in an ecological catastrophe of epic proportions.

As the oil continues to flow and a slick of over 2,000 square miles collides into the Gulf Coast, comparisons to the Exxon-Valdez destruction of Prince William Sound in Alaska begin to fall short. Right wing media, unable to fathom the breadth and depth of this catastrophe, unwilling to accept that we have brought this on ourselves, no longer able to justify the usual "so what" response to environmental crises, have decided to focus on conspiracy theories. On the level of pure speculation, the Limbaugh crowd has raised the specter of a terrorist attack.

While I am not one to automatically dismiss conspiracy theories, the purpose of these speculations is as clear as the once pristine waters of Prince William Sound. It is a distraction and one that we as caretakers of the environment that nourishes us can ill afford. What has happened in the Gulf of Mexico is the destruction of an ecosystem, damage that will require decades if not centuries to repair, as the result of shortsighted greed. Even the chemicals now being used to disperse the oil slick have long ranging destructive potential. Even if you think it was a terrorist attack, in the age of terrorism shouldn't that be a part of the equation? Shouldn't we consider that possibility before we erect new targets off our shores?

When President Obama declares that British Petroleum is responsible for this disaster and will be held accountable for its costs, he is not telling the whole truth in either case. The government is responsible for approving the Deepwater Horizon and ensuring that all measures were taken to preclude the possibility of disaster. That clearly was not done. It turns out the drilling operation went deeper than authorized but where were the inspectors? It turns out a safety valve to turn off the oil in the event of disaster was not installed though it is required off the shores of other nations. It apparently was considered too expensive.

As for the costs of this catastrophe, British Petroleum with $292 billion in revenues as of 2007 (ranking it the fourth richest company in the world) will pay only a fraction of the long-term damage. For every dollar they provide in relief to the fishing industry and the myriad businesses that depend on them they will spend two dollars fighting it in court. For every dollar they spend in cleanup they will spend another paying a team of publicists and pseudo-scientists to prove that the damage after all is not so bad.

Twenty-one years after the Exxon-Valdez disaster there is still plenty of Exxon oil polluting the shores and waters of Prince William Sound. Some say the initial cleanup effort was designed to hide the oil rather than to extract it. From day one Exxon treated the spill as an image and media problem with economic consequences rather than an ecological disaster. There are still species that have never recovered. The human victims of the spill have had to fight the constant misinformation and delays of the Exxon media and legal teams. No one really knows the long-term consequences of the spill but we do know it was far more extensive than we were led to believe at the time.

We can expect the same with British Petroleum in the aftermath of this new catastrophe. From the beginning BP followed the same script as Exxon after the Valdez spill. Understate the extent of the disaster, capture the media, assure the public with misleading information, put a friendly face on a heartless corporate machine, always have an answer or three answers to dazzle the reporters, and always radiate confidence.

BP has friends in Washington. It allocated sixteen million dollars to lobbying congress in 2009 and another three and a half million in the first quarter of 2010. While generally favoring Republicans on a ratio of three to two, the leading single recipient in 2008 was Barack Obama. When you compare these figures to BP's billions in annual profits you would have to consider it money well spent.

The record when it is finally revealed will show that BP lied about the risks of deepwater drilling. BP lied about the oil leaking in the initial stages of the disaster. BP lied about the extent of the leakage. BP lied about their contingency plans for a worst-case scenario. BP lied about accepting full responsibility for the costs of this catastrophe. And BP will continue to lie and mislead and pump misinformation through the media to an unknowing and disbelieving public.

The potential destruction of this catastrophe goes well beyond commercial fisheries, the loss of wildlife and the damage to the tourist industry. It goes beyond the restaurants and packing plants that depend on the shrimp and fishing operations. It goes beyond the damage to the reef and the coastline. It goes beyond the harm to the already depleted wetlands and the migrating birds that seek refuge there. It goes beyond anything we can imagine. That is the nature of ecosystems. Everything is interconnected. It will be decades or longer before we can even begin to assess the full extent of harm.

If we had the authority to liquidate British Petroleum and use all its assets and resources to mitigate the harm, it would still be inadequate.

And the oil continues to flow.

Beyond the ecological disaster, consider the sheer audacity of believing you could drill through 13,000 feet of rock beneath 5,000 feet of water without unreasonable risk. Was it in fact a controllable risk or an inevitable disaster? Was BP gambling permanent environmental damage against short-term profits? How is it that an international corporation based thousands of miles from the scene of the crime was empowered to take that kind of risk with the Gulf ecosystem?

Now BP is trying to deflect the blame to Transocean Ltd., the world's largest operator of deepwater wells. Certainly some measure of blame can be shared not only with Transocean but possibly Halliburton who had a hand in the operation as well, but as long as BP was taking the lion's share of profits then BP must accept the lion's share of blame.

In a functioning democracy at least some of that blame must fall to the people. To some indefinable extent we are also responsible for allowing greed and the Drill Baby Drill crowd to have its way with our government.

Someone should have stopped them but it was not in their interest.

The latest legislative effort to deal with the Gulf crisis is a proposal to raise the liability cap from $75 million to ten billion. Dollars to a dime it does not happen and even if it does it is an insult for anyone to think that the damage from this catastrophe should be capped at ten billion (a fraction of the cost of our wars).

Have we learned nothing at all? It is clear that after Exxon-Valdez we learned very little indeed.

This time the least we can learn is that Beyond Petroleum is just a slogan.

If this nation does not move toward renewable energies with the urgency and vigor that time and circumstance demand, then we must forfeit our claim as a great nation – no less the greatest nation on earth.

Jazz 6 May 2010.

WINDS OF DESTRUCTION
Joplin MO & Fukushima Japan

I grew up in a town about the size of Joplin, Missouri. I can imagine what it must have been like to be a child in the path of the storm. I can imagine the howling wind and the horror of twisted metal, trees lifted from the ground and buildings demolished, as half your world was wiped away in a matter of minutes.

It must have felt like the end of the world.

I can imagine what is must have been like for thousands across Alabama, Tennessee, Louisiana and Georgia as dozens of killer tornados blazed a path of destruction like General Sherman's march to the sea.

I can imagine what it must be like for hundreds of thousands still living in the nuclear dead zone of Japan, where the soil is infertile, where the land, the air and the water are contaminated forever.

It must feel like the end of the world.

The religious are inclined to say it is the wrath of God. The secular may say it is nature's revenge. The scientific community says it is a confirmation of global climate change. But to that child in Joplin Missouri, Tuscaloosa Alabama or Fukushima Japan it does not matter. The age of catastrophe is upon us.

We are closer to the end of the world than we have ever been before and tomorrow we will be closer than we are today.

In a sense, Japan is a microcosm of America. Without the natural resources required to support its ever-growing economy, it chose nuclear as an alternative to fossil fuels. Given that nation's history it is an ironic choice.

Now it seems they are stuck with it.

Japan's nuclear crisis is a profound tragedy and one that will shadow its people for as long as they shall live. They chose nuclear energy in an age of natural disasters and they must pay the price. They have become a virtual dead zone, an enigma to the rest of the world. Their days are dark and their future is imperiled.

The story of Japan is a tragedy that might have been avoided. They had a choice. They took the nuclear option with the assurances of a scientific consensus that it was the safer option. It has become clear that that consensus was dead wrong and the harm is compounded because it has damaged the credibility of science at a time when that credibility is needed to prevent further catastrophes on an infinitely grander scale.

The tragedy of Japan's nuclear experiment should be a lesson to America and the rest of the world as we confront a similar choice: In an age of catastrophe, when a single tornado can demolish half a city, when dozens of twisters can mark a path of annihilation through the south, when tsunamis and hurricanes can destroy national economies and wipe out hundreds of thousands from the earth, is the nuclear risk worth the gamble?

Until now most scientists have answered in the affirmative but the Japanese disaster has forced them to recalibrate. Science made a bad promise, Japan committed, France doubled down and Germany followed suit. Like Japan, France is now trapped in nuclear dependency as they await their own inevitable disaster.

Germany wants out. In the wake of recent election losses the administration of Angela Merkel has announced it will close all nuclear plants within eleven years. As news spreads through the back channels about how bad the Japanese crisis really is and how vulnerable we all are we can expect the people of Europe to demand that nuclear energy should be phased out throughout the continent. That is the virtue of democracy. When the people express a clear and decisive discontent, the government must respond or release the reins of power.

In America, the government and their corporate sponsors have been far more effective in deceiving the people. We are among the last holdouts on the science of climate change. Despite the mounting evidence and a string of environment disasters that support the theory, we cling to our monster vehicles and refuse to acknowledge a connection between the poisons we spew into the atmosphere and the planet's revenge. We continue to elect representatives who are making plans for more coal, dirtier and more oil, chemical fracturing to mine liquid gas and, of course, more nuclear energy.

What do we know that the world fails to grasp? We have learned nothing from Joplin, Katrina and New Orleans, from the bulging Mississippi River and a catastrophic oil spill, from tornado strikes in California and Massachusetts, from the latest mining disasters, from flammable water and radioactive wastelands.

Will we learn nothing from Japan?

Nuclear energy, like coal and oil and oil sands and oil shale, is a last resort energy source for very good reason: It is there and we can exploit it but its cost is high and in the end it will destroy us.

We are at a critical point in history. Those nations that turn now to cleaner sources of energy, to solar and wind and efficient mass transit, will be the nations that dominate the future.

If at this critical juncture we hide our heads in the sand and wait for the next chain of catastrophes to render us a third rate power, we will have only ourselves to blame.

Jazz 7 June 2011.

SUPERSTORM SANDY
October Surprise 2012

"I have a job in New Jersey that is much bigger than presidential politics... I have to say, the administration, the president, himself, and FEMA Administrator Craig Fugate have been outstanding with us so far. We have a great partnership with them. I want to thank the president personally for his personal attention to this."

New Jersey Governor Chris Christie
October 30, 2012

No one can predict what will happen in the final days of a presidential election. Last time around the October surprise was the impending total collapse of Wall Street and the global financial system, a crisis so acute it forced a Republican president to go against a fundamental tenet of his party's philosophy by advocating a massive financial bailout.

For those whose memories are short, we were on the verge of a catastrophe that went to the very foundation of our economic system. Had it been allowed to unfold (let the markets correct themselves), a worldwide Great Depression would certainly have followed.

Republican John McCain's muddled response, contrasting with Barack Obama's decisive leadership, paved the way to a clear and decisive victory.

In the 2012 election, the crisis came in a different

form. As if to remind us that the effects of climate change cannot be denied by political decree, Mother Nature spawned a Super Storm whose breadth and depth of destruction throughout the northeastern seaboard was unprecedented.

Just when we thought climate change would not make an appearance this election cycle, along comes Hurricane Sandy to provide a grim vision of what our willful ignorance can do. And while we cannot with certainty attribute one extreme weather event to global warming, we would be fools not to acknowledge that this is exactly the kind of event climatologist have predicted.

Every Romney supporter who laughed when their candidate belittled the idea of a president fighting the rise of the ocean might now have second thoughts, particularly if they live on the east coast.

Welcome to the new world where catastrophic weather events become more commonplace, more extreme and less predictable.

As our hearts go out to the millions of Americans affected by this storm, the lives and homes lost, the towns and communities decimated and the hardships that will be faced for years to come, our responsibility as citizens compels us to connect these events to the choices we face in the coming election.

Governor Chris Christie of devastated New Jersey rose above partisan politics when he praised President Obama's quick and decisive response to this catastrophe.

Republican candidate Mitt Romney staged a fake relief event and refused to comment about his previous positions advocating cutbacks in emergency management, handing responsibility to the affected states and privatizing the Federal Emergency Management Agency (FEMA).

We all remember what the last Republican president did to FEMA and how miserably that agency responded to Hurricane Katrina.

Candidate Romney is spending his final days of the campaign talking about big change but what he's really offering is a change back to the policies of George W. Bush. When a president fundamentally does not believe in the role of government, agencies like FEMA, the Securities and Exchange Commission, the Environmental Protection Agency and the Consumer Protection Agency inevitably decline.

To suggest that a state hit by a disaster and still struggling to climb out of the financial hole created by Republican policies, should somehow manage its own emergencies is flagrantly irresponsible. To suggest that a profit-motivated private corporation would do a better job of emergency management is absurd.

We have already witnessed what private insurance companies did in the wake of Katrina, drawing artificial lines between wind and water damage, finding loopholes and any excuse to deny claims or tie them up in court until wary and beleaguered homeowners are forced to sell out at a loss.

In times of crisis the people deserve and indeed demand an effective federal response to save lives, to mitigate damage and to help rebuild. President Obama is fulfilling that basic governmental responsibility because his administration was prepared for it. He has promised to stay the course and we must hold him to that promise.

That is not the kind of federal response we could expect from a Romney administration. Yes, he would appear on television, he would express his sincere condolences, he would make promises but in the end every state, every community, every homeowner and every individual would be left on their own. When the cameras leave and the coverage fades, the promises would be forgotten.

It is times like these that test the spirit of the nation.

It is events like these that touch our hearts and trigger our empathy for our fellow citizens because we know, at another time and place, it could happen to us, to our families and loved ones.

At times like these we are made stronger by our sense of unity and our confidence that our elected leaders will help us to recover and rebuild.

At times like these we know what good government looks like.

It is perhaps unfair that a presidential election should be decided by a single event but when a candidate disavows virtually everything he has campaigned on to hide the fact that his agenda is to maximize the profits of the corporate elite while the rest of the nation pays for it with an age of austerity, then fairness is no longer in the equation.

The polls say the election is a toss-up (at least in the popular vote). I have no reason to doubt their validity. But with four days to Election Day, with the devastation of the Super Storm fresh in our collective consciousness, I believe we will see a clear and decisive victory for the Democrats in the House of Representatives, the United States Senate and in the White House.

Jazz 2 November 2012.

MARCH OF THE LEMMINGS
Voluntary Self-Destruction

The Lemming Condition tells the story of a community of arctic rodents who blindly follow tradition, culture and peer pressure on a suicidal march over a cliff and into the sea.

Alan Arkin's fable is of course fiction, based on a myth perpetuated by a popular Disney documentary on animal behavior. Creatures in nature generally intuit the path to survival and no species eagerly commits mass suicide or self-destruction – no species that is with the possible exception of the human species.

It occurred to me after the spectacle of the recent election in Wisconsin, where common folks, working people with their livelihoods at stake, signed the death warrant for Wisconsin labor by rejecting a recall of their notorious anti-labor governor.

Despite all the money poured into the state from the nation's wealthiest individuals and corporate entities, no one in Wisconsin could have been unaware of the issues at stake: the end of collective bargaining and an open attack on the last bastion of unionism in the public sector. I listened to the rationalizations of progressive and pro-labor spokespersons, that the vote did not affirm the rabid policies of their governor but rather represented an objection to the process. Based on exit polls, they argued that voters did not believe the recall process should be used for anything less than corruption or malfeasance of office.

Frankly, I know something about human nature.

Based on that knowledge, I have drawn the conclusion that Wisconsin voters lied to the pollsters just as they were likely lying to themselves. With real-world consequences at stake, Wisconsin workers, forming the vast majority of the electorate, stepped in line and walked over a cliff into the sea.

They voluntarily yielded their government to corporate rule. They voted to end organized labor in their state. To their fellow workers in the public sector, the teachers, nurses, firefighters and police, their message was clear: Go to hell!

Until the results in Wisconsin, I had great hope that the people of America would finally awaken. The candidates taking office in the last election did not run on anti-labor austerity platforms. They promised jobs and decried shipping them overseas. They said nothing about busting unions, firing public workers, blocking abortion, women's contraception and corporate tax breaks. Their secret agenda was not revealed until they took office and few were more obvious than Governor Scott Walker. He lied to the electorate but the voters did not feel that was sufficient grounds for recall.

Now I am anything but hopeful.

With eyes wide open we are forming a line, beckoning others to follow, as we march over a cliff into the sea. We sign petitions demanding austerity, knowing full well that our friends and family members will suffer the consequences: Homelessness, joblessness, paltry wages, hunger and denied medical care. Public schools and public health clinics will fall on even harder times with overcrowded classrooms and inadequate supplies.

Students in the working class (the middle class will soon be reserved for management) will no longer aspire to higher education. The cost of college will be beyond their means.

Even college graduates and highly skilled workers

will be unable to match the low wages and benefits of foreign competitors. They will eventually fold, joining a burgeoning number of working poor, counting pennies and pleading for help. Unable to pay their debts, homes will be lost and futures discarded.

Old people, facing severe cutbacks in social security and Medicare, will attempt to re-enter the workforce, competing with their children and grandchildren for low-wage jobs.

Police and fire departments will find it harder to respond to anything but the most dire of emergencies.

Denied access to contraception and abortion, more and more women will give birth to unwanted children, many of whom will be condemned to unhappy lives in poverty and need.

Left to exercise unbridled greed, the stock market will run wild until the next curtain falls and this time the crash will reverberate in places no one but the elite can escape. When we pick up the pieces, massive international corporations will own everything but the bill. Workers and government officials alike will exist at the whim of their corporate masters.

On and on, it is a grim vision on the social-economic front but it is nothing compared to what awaits us environmentally.

Clearly, a society that cannot afford the fundamentals of health care, education and public safety, has no interest in protecting the air, the water and the ground beneath our feet. We seem to believe we can vote global climate change out of existence.

Here's the news: The planet doesn't care what you think or what party you belong to or whom you vote for on Election Day or whom you listen to on the radio. The planet is growing warmer whether you believe it or not. The planet is growing warmer because we refuse to stop pumping toxic fumes into the air.

Glaciers are in retreat worldwide, melting into the sea. Oceanic temperatures are rising along with sea levels. Ocean currents are altered, spawning radical storms and radically altered weather patterns. Shorelines are retreating and island nations are under siege, some fighting for their survival.

In keeping with global trade policies, we have transferred virtually all industry to those nations that not only offer cheap labor under inhumane conditions but also lack minimal restrictions on air and water pollution. Several years back China supplanted America as the leading producer of greenhouse gasses. That economic giant gets an estimated 70 percent of its energy from the world's dirtiest fuel: coal.

According to a 2007 World Health Organization report, of an estimated two million deaths caused by polluted air each year, 656,000 were Chinese citizens. Another 95,000 die from polluted drinking water. In both cases, the numbers are surely rising but the Lemmings march on and the western world's appetite for technological gadgets is never satiated.

Never fear: What goes on in China stays in China. Not so.

As we might have learned from the Fukushima disaster, air and water are globally connected. The toxic waste from Japan's near nuclear meltdown (a crisis still unfolding) is just reaching American shores. The radiated plumes reached us long ago with unknown consequences.

One would think that all talk of reviving our nuclear industry would be silenced. Think again. Just like the Deepwater Horizon disaster in the Gulf of Mexico, all parties concerned consider it a public relations problem that is soon overcome. Give it a few months and keep the applications coming. Issue a press release about how deeply concerned you are.

Deepwater drilling continues at an accelerated rate and we have plans for more nuclear plants (this time they assure us they are really, really safe), more coal mines, more fracturing for natural gas buried deep in the earth and more tar sand oil imported from Canada. All carry a heavy price to our environment and the collective health of the planet.

It seems the only restraint we have in energy is that concerning safe and renewable sources: solar, wind and geothermal. Conservation through mass transit and fuel efficiency is also on indefinite hold. We continue to pretend that it is not exactly the kind of investment we need to put our people back to work and position ourselves to lead the global economy. We must continue to subsidize dirty fuel, peel back restrictions, and cut back on everything else.

We cannot afford clean energy. We can only afford to press on with our mindless march to oblivion.

Get in line, fellow lemmings; the cliff is due west and the view before the fall is breathtaking!

Jazz 14 June 2012.

VOLUME IX

IMMIGRATION
&
DISCRIMINATION

CONTENTS

PREFACE

THE WALL & THE WEDGE:
SYMPTOMS OF INEQUALITY

For decades we have lived under the illusion that America has achieved a free and equal society. We ended racial discrimination with the Civil Rights Act in the 1960's. We are now free to accuse government agencies, universities, employers and landlords of discrimination against white people. After all, in a free and equal society, preferential treatment of minorities is clearly reverse discrimination.

When it comes to race it is astounding how little we have progressed compared to the certainty that we have. The ultimate proof of our equality: The election of Barack Obama to the presidency in 2008. How could discrimination remain a problem when the president is black?

As a recent wave of cases documenting police abuse and killing of black people will attest: Racial discrimination is alive and well and living behind a badge of authority. Is it any different than past years and decades? No. The only difference is that now nearly every citizen is armed with a device that can record the event for all to see.

Despite the color of our president's skin, we remain a highly divided society in which equal treatment under the law is a fantasy perpetuated by white people.

Discrimination is not restricted to black people. It is

delivered liberally to other minorities as well as women, gay, lesbian and transgender communities. The very fact that so many (including members of the Supreme Court) believe we have achieved some semblance of equality is proof positive that we are not even close.

While the killing of blacks at the hands of police, giving birth to the Black Lives Matter movement, has dominated the news in recent months, the most explosive issue of discrimination over the last decade is without doubt immigration.

The hypocrisy of white society regarding this issue is almost beyond compare. Americans import cheap labor from Mexico and South America to work in the fields and in our homes and blame them for all our problems.

For years Republicans have used immigration as a wedge issue to place their candidates in office. For years they did nothing to resolve the problem. It was simply not in their interest. What was in their interest was to keep blame seeking and discrimination against Latinos alive to motivate the voting base.

Well, all that is changing. Now they must do everything they can to keep Latinos and blacks and poor people from voting because the minorities are rapidly becoming the majority.

Someday soon your fantasy about discrimination against white people may actually come true.

Jazz.

LIBERTY & JUSTICE FOR ALL
Libertad y Justicia Para Todos

The immigration issue has been cast as an insoluble problem pitting the philosophy of "free trade" against the rights of the exploited. This representation is fundamentally wrong. Free trade is not the root of the immigration problem; it is the solution.

We must initially acknowledge the essential role of the rights of labor in trade agreements. Any nation that does not provide workers with living wages, decent working conditions and basic benefits is subsidizing corporate profits. It is no different than a government providing direct funding to an industry or imposing tariffs on targeted imports. It is therefore a violation of the essential principles of free trade.

What are the consequences of recognizing the rights of labor in the free trade equation? CAFTA, NAFTA and virtually all international trade agreements negotiated under the banner of free trade are rendered invalid and subject to renegotiation.

When trade agreements are contingent on labor rights, there will be a reduction in the influx of migrants across the border. More and more citizens of Mexico and Latin America will opt to remain in their own nations when their respective governments guarantee that their basic needs will be provided.

That is the end game. It will mandate a virtual realignment of the current international order. Given the failure of that order, it is eminently reasonable but it will require time. Our immediate goal must be more direct:

Liberty and justice for all!

The following measures should be taken primarily to alleviate the plight of the immigrant (secondarily, to solve the immigration problem to the extent that it can be "solved"):

First, document the undocumented.

The obvious solution to illegal immigration is to legalize immigration. The reason there are so many undocumented workers in America is not that immigrants enjoy running from the law; it is precisely because the undocumented have no rights. They can be paid cash wages at below minimum without any considerations of labor. They are cheap and disposable workers. If the employer does not wish to pay them at all, there is no legal recourse.

When employers document the undocumented, they will have to pay them decent wages. They will have to offer basic benefits. They will not be able to ignore industry regulations and worker safeguards.

When the employers begin paying migrant workers living wages, others will begin to compete for the same jobs.

Second, define and establish a minimum living wage in every nation of the western hemisphere, from Canada to Chile and Argentina. Require all nations to abide by that minimum standard in order to qualify for preferred trade status. The penalties for violating the rights of labor should be proportionate but severe.

Third, take down the wall! We have a right to know who has entered the nation and we can find it out at the points of arrival. If the landlords, innkeepers and employers are required to document migrants, the problem is solved and the massive waste of building a wall along our southern border can be transferred to more constructive uses: Rebuilding New Orleans with resident labor, providing universal health services, building schools, hiring teachers, constructing mass transit, developing alternative energy, funding space exploration and training minority citizens for better employment.

For a nation deeply in debt to squander its limited resources on a wall that keeps more illegal workers in than it keeps out is both immoral and bad policy. As Princeton's Douglas S. Massey stated in a *New York Times* op-ed (4 April 2006): "The only thing we have to show for two decades of border militarization is a larger undocumented population than we would otherwise have, a rising number of Mexicans dying while trying to cross, and a growing burden on taxpayers for enforcement that is counterproductive."

It is a national disgrace.

Fourth, rebuild organized labor from the ground up. Given the opportunity, workers in all nations have demonstrated the capability to manage operations and contribute to company policies. The new unions should be democratically structured with meaningful representation in management and on boards of directors. They should be dynamic and cooperative organizations that respond to the dual interests of productivity and labor. The migrant labor force must be unionized.

Above all, government policy must be responsive to the rights of labor rather than exclusively to the powerful interests of corporations.

Liberty and justice for all!

Jazz 7 April 2006.

WHAT WOULD CRAZY HORSE DO?
Misconceptions in the Immigration Debate

We are not a nation of immigrants. We might have been. We nearly exterminated the entire population of indigenous peoples but in the end we failed. The natives are still here despite our determined drive to genocide. The tribes are still identifiable despite our determined campaign to scatter and destroy their languages, cultures and religious beliefs.

We are not a nation of immigrants; we are a nation of conquerors. We are a nation that seizes by force what we desire. We are a nation that has never been content to share our discovered treasures. We did not steal the land from Mexico; we stole the land from the Apache, Lakota, Iroquois, Cherokee, Nez Perce, Cheyenne, Arapaho, Seminole, Blackfoot, Ute, Paiute and countless other tribes that still exist. We joined Mexico is stealing the land from those who did not wish to possess it but merely to live on it in harmony.

We are not a nation of immigrants. We are a nation of natives and ungrateful visitors.

We are not a nation of laws. We are a nation that bends laws to power. We are a nation that chooses not to enforce laws when they conflict with our designs or the all-powerful will of the international corporations that control our government. We are a nation that breaks laws at will and violates treaties and international agreements with willful abandon.

We are not a nation of laws. We are a nation of lawyers, accountants and corporate boards of directors.

JAZZMAN CHRONICLES

When the president explains that employers have not been prosecuted for hiring illegal immigrants because the immigrants have mastered the art of document fraud, he is putting forth another myth. Employers have not been prosecuted because they are the president's constituents. They are in fact sponsors of politicians in all border states. Anyone who actually believes that the authorities will begin prosecuting employers because legal immigrants have better identification cards has drunk from the well of magical wonders. There may be selective prosecutions for show and political retribution but that is all. Anyone who believes that employers will stop hiring low-cost undocumented workers should let his psychotropic prescription lapse.

We are not a nation of justice – justice least of all. If we were a nation of justice, we would honor our debts. We would make just reparations to natives and African Americans who were compelled to migrate as slaves. What the nation owes to the Lakota [1] and Cherokee [2] alone amounts to more than what we will ultimately spend to destroy the nations of Afghanistan and Iraq – more even than our national debt, a debt that is deeper than the skies over Bear Butte are wide.

We are not a nation of justice. We are a nation of exploitation. We have conspired with corporate governments throughout the hemisphere to exploit labor and extract resources. We have created a free trade zone without factoring wages into the equation. Though it seems complex, it is not that difficult to understand. It follows the fundamental laws of supply, demand and profit taking. Corporations will seek all means of maximizing profits, including cutting the cost of production. Jobs will move to where the costs are least. Labor will move to where jobs pay living wages. Wherever possible, good paying jobs will be replaced by low paying jobs and no wall or barrier will prevent these laws from being carried out. In the corporate mind, it is a cold calculation: cost versus benefit.

It is easy to see why our politicians ignore the root cause of the immigration problem: global trade policy. Republicans need a new scapegoat to replace the gays and abortion activists that have served them so well. Democrats cannot afford to alienate their corporate sponsors.

What has happened to Mexico (a momentary beneficiary of job migration) is happening now in America. Regardless of immigration reform in whatever form it takes, we will continue to lose well-paid jobs and real wages will continue to decline until we understand that the cause of our misfortune resides with the corporate masters of a global economy and their proxies in government. It will continue until we embrace our fellow workers in all nations in unity and strength.

If we fail to revive organized labor on an international scale, the bleeding will render us powerless. There are no walls that can prevent our demise. We have allowed international corporate conglomerates to divide and exploit us nation by nation because we are too proud, too naïve, and too nationalistic to value unity with individuals outside our borders.

If we do not stand together to lift up the whole (wages and working conditions in every corner of the globe), then like the children's nursery rhyme in the time of the great plague, we will all fall down.

In the long term, we must make sure that the costs of exploiting labor are greater than the benefits. Hugo Chavez in Venezuela and Evo Morales in Bolivia are showing the way.

In the short term, we must repeal NAFTA, CAFTA and all international trade agreements that regard human labor as something less than cattle.

If the pandering, reactionary right prevails in the

current climate, like the Israelis in Palestine, we will construct a monument to intolerance and ignorance on our southern border. If it comes to pass, there will come a day when a new American president stands in the land of the Chiricahua and demands:

Tear down this wall!

Patriots on both sides of the border will comply and all humanity will applaud.

Jazz 19 May 2006.

1. Payment for the Black Hills and all the resources extracted there from in accordance with the Fort Laramie Treaty.

2. Recognized as a sovereign nation by the US Supreme Court in a decision that was ignored by President Andrew Jackson who subsequently carried out the mass relocation recorded in history as The Trail of Tears.

LIBERATION RAMBLE
SOUTH OF THE BORDER

President Jorge W. Bush was downright timid taking sides in the Mexican presidential election, mindful that his endorsement has all too frequently been the kiss of political death to his allies in the global war on terror and the poor.

Why should he campaign honestly and openly for his good friend Felipe Calderon when the same systems and techniques used to secure his presidency were in place below the border?

According to journalist Greg Palast (the man who broke the stories of election fraud and disenfranchisement in Florida and Ohio for the BBC), the FBI obtained Mexican voter rolls through Choicepoint of Georgia – the same company that performed electoral magic for the American president.

Choicepoint should have a new business motto: Make it close and we'll make it count.

As in Florida and Ohio, the exit polls showed Andres Manuel Lopez Obrador, a candidate who appealed to the great masses of Mexican poor, pulling ahead but by the time the tally made its way through the computer counting system, Calderon was proclaiming victory.

Lopez Obrador has filed charges of massive fraud, demanding a vote by vote recount at all polling places where irregularities occurred, fully in accordance with Mexican law, but Calderon wants to turn the page, book closed, and the Federal Election Tribunal seems likely to comply.

JAZZMAN CHRONICLES

The only development that can secure honest democracy south of the border now is a popular uprising of the kind observed in Venezuela after the American-sponsored coup and the Orange Revolution in Ukraine, which rallied the world, including our own government.

An estimated one hundred thousand people gathered on the central plaza in Mexico City Saturday. If they show the courage and dogged determination that the Venezuelans and Ukrainians did, they will claim a resounding victory for democracy and send a message to the citizens of their northern neighbor: If you want democracy, you must fight for it – not just with words and opinions but with action. If you want to take your government back, you must be willing to stand on the streets of protest.

Do not be fooled by American media coverage: Lopez Obrador is no wild-eyed radical. He is at best a moderate progressive – not of the Hugo Chavez or Evo Morales type but more like Lula of Brazil – but even that would be a sea change for Mexico after the failure and broken promise of Vicente Fox.

The importance of the Mexican election is not so much the immigration issue (the obsessive-compulsive distraction of the north) as the economic "free trade" policies that have exacerbated the problem. The majority of the population is poor and the top ten percent own 45% of the nation's wealth. The already acute divide between the haves and have-nots has only grown worse as the National Action Party of Fox and Calderon played lapdogs to the corporate globalization movement.

Sadly, even if Lopez Obrador were to prevail, he would be unlikely to reverse the trend without control of the Mexican legislature, but he would surely ease the suffering and destitution of the masses by reviving the social programs the globalists decry.

Every American who is concerned with immigration

should stand up for Lopez Obrador now for the only hope of reducing the waves of border migration is not a wall or a thousand corpses on the Arizona desert but raising the standards of Mexico's working poor.

What concerns our government is not so much Lopez Obrador himself but the resistance to corporate globalization that has swept across much of Latin America.

What ordinary Americans need to understand is that Obrador is not a threat. He is fighting for us. What we need in our own government are more candidates who care about the poor and the working class, who realize that New Orleans is infinitely more important than Baghdad or Kabul, and who understand that we all need a little help – not just Halliburton, Bechtel, Wal-Mart and Exxon-Mobil.

The ruling class of Mexico attempted to retain power, despite the overwhelming failure and disappointment of the current government, by raising the red flag of fear. Lopez Obrador would bring disaster and send the nation into spiral descent. When that failed, they resorted to less honorable means. As it is in America north, so it is in Mexico.

Lopez Obrador is only asking what Albert Gore should have asked in 2000 and what John Kerry should have demanded in 2004: that every vote be counted.

Under Mexican law, created against a backdrop of systemic fraud and corruption, a winner cannot be declared until the allegations are weighed and adjudicated. The deadline is September 6.

If we believe in democracy, the issue is clear: Viva Lopez Obrador!

Jazz 11 July 2006.

PROFILES IN COURAGE
Illegal Immigrants in America

Something is missing in the debate on illegal immigration. We listen to Lou Dobbs, the self-proclaimed champion of political independence, blaming twelve million unauthorized migrants for the problems of the American middle class. We listen to a Republican presidential candidate plead for just a little compassion – not for the immigrants but for their progeny – and watch him get hammered by the hardcore right.

Everyone condemns employers for employing immigrants over Native Americans – or rather, legal immigrants – but no one is really demanding the kind of enforcement that would end the practice. Corporations are the sponsors of political candidates and, in any case, it would only hurt the small businesses that candidates promote as the heart of our economy.

Even the defenders of immigration fall back on their heels against the assault, protesting that most immigrants are not of the criminal element, that not all abuse the system and that most contribute to the economy on balance.

What is missing from the discussion is basic common sense – not the brand of common sense that demands an impenetrable wall across the southern border but the kind that breaks it down to human terms.

NAFTA and CAFTA, the landmark "free trade" agreements covering North and South America, have not produced the kind of job and wage increases promised by former president Bill Clinton and his bipartisan allies in congress. Free trade proponents south of the border failed to foresee that absent organized labor wages would remain subterranean and jobs would go to the lowest bidder – most notably India and China. Proponents north of the border failed to foresee that given inadequate wages and marginal social services, the incentive to migrate north would become more powerful than ever.

What is missing from the debate is that, given the circumstances, we would do exactly the same as our neighbors to the south. That is, those among us who are physically strong enough, presented with a choice of watching our children go hungry for lack of food, grow ill from inadequate housing, clean water and health care, would raise whatever money we could, hand it to an unscrupulous "coyote" and make the long hard journey across the northern border.

The bravest and strongest among us would risk anything and everything for a chance to build a decent life for our children and families. They would ford rivers, walk barren deserts, evade border patrol and vigilantes, forge documents, live in crowded conditions and pay bribes for the possibility of a better life.

In America, we used to call such individuals heroes. Now we call them criminals.

In Mexico, Guatemala, Panama, Columbia and anywhere else where people have suffered under the mandates of "free trade" agreements, they still call them heroes.

When rightwing politicians, desperate for an issue that deflects the blame from their own sorry policies of corporate protectionism and greed, condemn any expression of sympathy and decry even the most modest of compromises as amnesty, they are practicing the lowest of the political arts: pandering to the reactionary base.

Let us be clear: Any proposal that requires illegal

immigrants to pay a substantial fine, voluntarily submit to deportation or get in the back of the line is neither realistic nor sincere. The compromise that failed to gain passage in congress was merely an attempt to push the issue off the table.

Those who have come to this country, secured jobs in what can only be described as an underground economy, will not give up what they have worked so hard and sacrificed so much for on these terms. These are poor people. They live day to day at the mercy of their employers, who can choose to pay them or have them rounded up by the immigration service. Asking them to pay thousands of dollars in fines is like asking them to take food out of the mouths of their children. Asking them to return to their homelands to get in the back of the line is like asking them to scale Everest without a guide. Having been raised here since early childhood, many have no homes in their countries of origin. They would become the equivalent of migrants in their own lands, rejoining the pool of slave labor and refueling the vicious cycle of survival and escape.

They could not and would not do it and, in their shoes, neither would you or I.

We call them criminals but what is the crime? They have acted with courage, perseverance and sacrifice. They have done what any people would do.

No one is asking for medals of valor but until we begin to address the enormous problems created by unregulated corporate greed on a global scale by demanding fair wages and minimal standards of labor, the least we can do is accept responsibility and offer forgiveness.

It is strange what politicians can do with words. In every working democracy in the world but ours, there is a viable socialist party. In America we despise anything "social" as in socialized medicine – though the vast majority of us would accept nonprofit health care as not only acceptable but appropriate to the healthcare profession.

Now, the very same crowd that invokes the name of Jesus would have us believe that "amnesty" is a dirty word. Far too many recoil at the word as if it was an unforgivable offense and yet amnesty is the only solution to the problem of illegal immigrants within our borders.

Yes, it is a problem – not because it steals our jobs, squanders our resources and cripples our economy – but because it creates a permanent underclass: people without rights, representation or legal recourse.

We need amnesty to bring these workers out of the shadows so they can contribute openly and be treated with the common decency due all human beings. They would be empowered to organize, lifting wages for all of us. They would be empowered to vote, expanding the franchise and strengthening our democracy.

Even Ronald Reagan recognized that amnesty was the only solution. To suggest that we should or could deport millions of illegal immigrants by force of arms is a fairy tale. Beyond the violence and inhumanity that such a mass deportation would bring, the cost would compel us to suspend all other programs while we pursued this singular endeavor.

There are better ways to end the war.

Of course, if we granted amnesty and failed as Reagan did to address the policies that helped to create the problem, we would be revisiting the problem in short order.

Until fair trade with labor rights and living wages replaces "free" trade in the global economy, there will be no lasting solution.

Jazz 19 January 2008.

THE WASICHU'S LAST STAND
Fall of the White Man in American Politics

"The Wasichu wore so many faces, an endless sea, wave after wave, more than the stars, and each one carried the same darkness beneath his pale skin, each afraid and filled with hate. Two thousand years of hatred and slaughter, two thousand years of death and poverty, two thousand years of genocide and white man rule yet still they feared and hated."

From *The Killing Spirit* by Jack Random

Given the gender gap and the extraordinary racial divide demonstrated in the recent election, it does not take a political genius to conclude that today's Republican Party is more dependent on the white man than at any time since the civil rights movement under Lyndon Baines Johnson.

The Lakota had a name for the pale skinned invaders who came to their land, massacred their people, slaughtered the buffalo, spoiled their sacred lands and destroyed their way of life, pushing them and all native peoples to the brink of extinction. They called them the Wasichu.

The Wasichu has been translated to white eyes or pale face or the white man but its meaning goes deeper. It refers to a class of men who believe in conquering, killing, defeating all others and bending them to their will. It refers to men who are motivated by greed and power. It refers to men who would rather exploit the earth, kill its animals and rape its natural wonders rather than learning to live on the land in harmony.

More than anything else, the Wasichu represents the spirit of greed and that spirit has taken complete control of the Republican Party that was soundly rejected in the 2012 election.

The Wasichu has not changed but the nation has.

In 1876, one hundred years after the founding of the United States of America, the most infamous Indian killer in western lore foolishly attacked the largest encampment of Native Americans ever assembled in one place. The seven tribes of Lakota called it the Greasy Grass but it would be known in the annals of the nation's history by the white man's name: Little Bighorn.

Colonel George Armstrong Custer along with every member of his five companies in the notorious Seventh Cavalry was killed on the field of battle.

Watching Republican candidate Mitt Romney deliver his brief but gracious concession speech two hours after the issue was settled, I was reminded of Custer poised on Last Stand Hill, still believing that somehow fate would intervene, that reinforcements would arrive, that something miraculous would arise to deliver victory from certain defeat.

The miracle never happened and both Custer and Romney would suffer a crushing defeat. Custer's Seventh Cavalry would have its revenge years later at the Wounded Knee Massacre. Romney's Grand Old Party, the last bastion of white man rule, will have no such revenge.

History will record the 2012 presidential election as the white man's last stand.

For two and a quarter centuries the most exclusive

white man's club in America was the executive office of the presidency. That exclusivity ended in 2008 with the election of Barack Obama. His re-election in 2012 marked the last election in which any political party can hope to win based almost entirely on the support of white men.

Yes, Mitt Romney could have won this election by gaining two-thirds of the white male vote. The record will show a landslide victory in the Electoral College but the margin of victory in nearly all of the contested states was thin. President Obama won not only by dominating the minority vote but also by peeling off enough of the white woman vote to close the deal.

Had the Republicans not chosen to openly attack women's rights on equal pay, abortion and contraception, their chameleon standard bearer would likely have won.

Four years from now, given the same strategy and the same policies, it will not be so close. The march of changing demography, the browning of America, continues unabated.

Custer is dead and buried and this time the only revenge will come from women and the minorities as they redefine party politics in America.

The GOP will rue the day their corporate sponsors created and financed the Tea Party, that predominantly white working class coalition who took the reins of power by preaching fiscal conservatism but governed by attacking unions and pressing forward with their radical and increasingly unpopular social agenda.

A wholesale rejection of the Tea Party was one of the underlying themes of this election. If not for census year redistricting, the House of Representatives would have gone the way of the Senate. But redistricting cannot hold back the tide of demographics.

The GOP created this beast and the GOP must now perform the delicate operation of eradicating their influence without alienating their members.

The party must now cater to those it vilified only yesterday and the transformation has already begun. Within hours of the election results, spokespersons affiliated with the Republicans made the first overtures to the Latino community and the word Amnesty, verboten for over a decade, was introduced in the debate on immigration. The first test of the party's ability to bring the Tea Party radicals in line will be the Dream Act, a modest reform that will provide a pathway to legalization for young illegal immigrants.

Beyond immigration reform, the GOP must act to stop the erosion of support among women, particularly unmarried women. The party tried and failed to sever its ties to its candidates who spoke openly about the immorality of contraception, God's will when rape or incest results in pregnancy and other radical right positions. The party did little to separate itself from the decree that life begins at conception or the requirement that women who chose abortion must be compelled to undergo an intra-vaginal examination. That must and will change if the party wishes to be viable in future elections. We may even see movement on equal pay for equal work and day care for women in the workforce.

The Democrats will also be forced to the left on social issues. Obama initiated the process with his embrace of gay marriage and his executive decision that effectively enacted the Dream Act as long as he remains president. The process of liberalizing what is supposed to be the liberal party will continue as they attempt to hold on to their current advantage, even as they continue their rightward migration on economic issues.

The forgotten of the electorate in this equation is also the largest: the working people. The mystery factor is the working white man who has notoriously and consistently voted against his own interest for decades.

In recent years working people have witnessed their jobs exported overseas, their homes foreclosed or devalued, their wages diminished and benefits stripped down to a bare minimum largely as a result of Republican policies. Still, they are counted on to get in line and vote GOP at every opportunity.

Some have suggested that white men or indeed the entire electorate is just plain dumb. I don't buy it. Many working class Americans may lack sufficient education and may choose to rely on a propaganda machine (Fox News, Rush Limbaugh) for political information but they are by no means dumb. Just surviving in the modern world requires moxy, know how, the ability to adapt and work with others. They may be misinformed, they may even be bamboozled but they are not dumb.

Others, including myself, have pointed to willful ignorance to explain the phenomenon of voting against one's interest. I stand by that conclusion but there is something else operating here, something underlying willful ignorance, something most everyone knows but very few in the world of mainstream political discourse openly discuss: Today's Democratic Party is not what it used to be.

There was a time when it could fairly be generalized that the Republicans were the party of business and Democrats were the party of labor. Today they are both the parties of big business (more specifically, large multi-national corporations). The difference is the Republicans are more so, clinging to deregulation and tax cuts for the elite even after the collapse of 2009, holding to an absolute support of Free Trade and openly attacking the very right of workers to organize in the workforce.

If the Democrats have done anything to secure the rights of labor I am not aware of it. Moreover, they have actively supported Free Trade, the single most important policy to all working people. They have won the support of organized labor by default.

Working people is the new frontier of American politics. If the Democrats restore their status as the party of labor, if they push hard for labor rights in America and embrace Fair Trade in our relations with other nations, they will become the dominant party for at least a generation to come. If they fail to take hold of labor, they will leave the door wide open to independent or third party challenge.

There are strong pro-labor and Fair Trade advocates within the Democratic Party, most notably Senator Sherrod Brown of Ohio. The Senator won re-election in the most critical battleground state in the nation and did so against the full force of corporate funding and every dirty trick in Karl Rove's handbook.

Today the Democrats have a decided advantage but if they wish to secure the future they would do well to listen to Senator Brown.

The white working man is dazed, confused, and cruising down the highway to political irrelevancy. He desperately needs a bridge to rejoin the fold. Fair trade and a strong push to protect American workers may provide that bridge.

Jazz 13 November 2012.

THE MYTH OF EQUAL RIGHTS
A Liberal Illusion of Equality

The civil rights movement illuminated the hypocrisy of the liberal promise. It made overt, and recorded on television for the world to see, an old daily fact of American life: that a black person who protested his condition, or moved one step out of line, would be arrested, or beaten, or inundated with water hoses, or killed, and the national government of the United States...would not act to save him.

From *Howard Zinn on Race*

The gateway to the South is Nashville, Tennessee. For five years in the mid nineties I was privileged to live in that sprawling city of over a million citizens. While distinctly southern in culture, its status as a center of music and a magnet for talented and diverse musicians gives Nashville a more tolerant and enlightened feel.

In many ways, Nashville is less symbolic of the South than it is representative of America and, like so many cities across the nation, it is home to two distinct and largely separate communities.

As an itinerant public schools employee, most of my tenure I was responsible for serving two schools: Across the street from Vanderbilt University, Eaken Elementary was perhaps the highest achieving elementary school in the city. Across town, newly constructed Cockrill Elementary was among the lowest achieving schools.

As you might have guessed, Eaken was predominantly white and affluent while Cockrill was predominantly black and poor.

I enjoyed my work in Nashville. In 25 years of experience, I have found educators to be largely selfless and dedicated no matter how trying conditions of employment may become. Teachers regularly absorb budget cuts, endure increased class sizes and tolerate demands of administrators and politicians for better results with fewer resources.

At some point in my Nashville sojourn I was startled to read a story in the Banner that the school district was awaiting word from the Justice Department on its application for exemption to the Supreme Court order to integrate the schools (Brown v. Board of Education 1954).

How could it be that after four decades the city of Nashville, perhaps the most enlightened city of the South, was not a step closer to ending segregation in the schools? And yet I saw it with my own eyes. The schools were a mirror of the society they served, a society so segregated that you knew at first glance whether you were in a white neighborhood or a black neighborhood.

I reflected on my upbringing in central California and realized that it was not substantially different in my own hometown. We had three high schools and one of them (mine) enrolled all but one black student. It was pretty much the same for the Latino population.

The revelation was a shock to my vision of the world for like most of white America I had assumed things had changed for the better after the Civil Rights movement, after Watts and the summer of flames, after Selma and Montgomery and Little Rock, Arkansas, after the jails were filled with black activists and the streets were red with blood. After Martin Luther King, Jr., Malcolm X and most of the Black Panthers sacrificed their lives.

After all the protest, struggle and social upheaval, neither the schools nor the society in which they existed had made any noticeable progress. Separate but equal was still the operating principle but its fallacy was more apparent than ever.

I realized then that racial integration and equality were only myths meant to pacify the minorities, appease the liberal intelligencia, and shelter the government from criticism. If we can maintain the myth that things are getting better, then we can maintain the social order without the violent outbursts that marked the sixties.

If we can sustain the myth of equality and progress, then poor whites can blame blacks and Latinos for their misfortunes. If we can sustain the myth, then whites can demand redress of grievances for reverse discrimination and the courts can uphold them.

I can hear the white liberal voice in the back of my mind: But things have changed for the better. We have minorities and women on the highest court in the land and in 2008, a first in the western world, we elected a black man president.

Of course things are better. But are they?

Things are certainly better for the Obama family but by what measure are things better for the black or Latino community at large? Unemployment? According to the Bureau of Labor statistics, blacks had an unemployment rate of sixteen percent in 2010, virtually unchanged since 1975. Hispanics were at 12.5% while whites and Asians were at 8.7 and 7.5 percent respectively – all unchanged in the last 35 years. According to the Census Bureau, in the year 2010 over 27% of blacks and 26.6% of Hispanics lived in poverty.

The numbers on Asians are somewhat misleading as the subgroup of Southeast Asians (Laotians, Hmongs,

Cambodians, Vietnamese) are disproportionately poor. Data are difficult to track down but estimates range from 25% to 43% below the poverty line in these subgroups.

The most forgotten of all minorities are the Native Americans. When we think of them at all we think of casinos and assume that our penchant for gambling has solved their economic woes. That assumption would fall under the label of mythology. According to the Census, 28.4% of Indians on the reservations and 22% overall fell below the poverty line with an estimated 4-6 times the national average living in extreme poverty. An estimated 14% of homes on the reservations are without electricity, 18% are without adequate sewage and 20% are without indoor plumbing. Reservation lands have been used for garbage dumps, nuclear waste and extensive mining. According to an Economic Policy Institute report (November 2010), unemployment is at 15.2% and things have not improved over the last forty years.

That disproportionate numbers of blacks, Latinos and other depressed minorities live in poor neighborhoods, attend poorly funded schools and suffer every form of discrimination from housing to employment cannot reasonably be questioned.

There is a paradox effect that takes place whenever persons from an oppressed community assume positions of power. Because critics expect them to favor their community in decisions and policies, they tend to do the opposite. They go one step beyond to prove that they hold no bias and will not abuse their power.

Anyone who expected the first minority president in history to press forward in the cause of civil rights has been disappointed to the point of frustration. We can make the case that this administration has held back the wave of rightwing oppression that his opponents would surely pursue but we cannot make the case that he has pushed for equal rights. The Justice Department has finally started fighting back against massive Republican disenfranchisement campaigns but even that seems more like self-preservation than positive action.

What can be done?

It is hardly useful to acknowledge the myth of equal rights (or if you prefer non-discrimination) if all we can do is lament. But the first order of the day is to acknowledge reality: Racial discrimination remains pervasive in American society and it is tolerated as much now as it was in the 1950's.

If the president will not act, the liberal establishment must do so by fighting back against outrageous measures enacted at the state level that legalize discrimination by forcing Latinos to prove their citizenship and compelling blacks to document their right to vote.

We must support amnesty for illegal immigrants whose only crime is to place greater importance on the welfare of their families than on the laws of the American government. They followed the law of supply and demand with the blessings of employers anxious to exploit their labor at substandard wages.

We must support jobs and business development programs targeted to centers of poverty and minority communities. We must provide incentives for businesses to hire minorities and we must not apologize for doing so.

We must restore funding to public education beginning in impoverished neighborhoods and stop the funding of private schools from public coffers.

We must rebuild low-income housing programs that enable minorities to integrate affluent and predominantly white neighborhoods. We should train and employ minorities to build these homes and they should be built in a manner that inspires pride in residency and in the greater community.

The liberal establishment must demand that organizations like the ACLU stop defending reverse discrimination claims and start fighting for the rights of minorities.

If we do not start now to dispel the myth and begin again the struggle for equal rights and equal treatment under the law, we will be condemned to repeat the decade of turbulence that shattered the illusions of those who came before us.

Oppressed communities, especially considering that they will soon be a majority in our society, will not wait forever for deliverance of what was promised and what is rightly theirs.

Jazz 28 May 2012.

VOLUME X

ON DEMOCRACY

CONTENTS

PREFACE

RECLAIMING DEMOCRACY

We have begun the era of American empire and it fills our souls with fear. We are afraid not only for the peoples of other nations, who will be targeted for liberation, but also for ourselves.

We are under attack. We have all but been accused of treason for expressing our dissent. The most oppressive and unforgiving government in memory has proclaimed the right to arrest, detain and deny citizenship to anyone accused of supporting the enemy.

We are terrorized because we know in our hearts that we are the enemy. We are the enemy because we oppose them and everything they stand for. We are the enemy because we believe in democracy. We are the enemy because we believe this government has betrayed democracy. We are the enemy because we believe they have stolen our government.

There is but one way to end the nightmare of this budding American empire and that is by reclaiming our democracy. They have stolen an election. They have gone to war without due cause. They have invaded and occupied foreign lands. They have betrayed and compromised our most basic rights. They have bought controlling interest in the media. They have refined propaganda to new heights. But they have not yet taken our right to vote. They have not silenced our voices. They have not stolen our souls.

The road ahead is a hard road. The odds are stacked to the heavens against us. Search as we may we can find no light at the end of this tunnel. But we must and we will march on. We have chosen our path and we will press on not because we are stronger or braver than our fellows but because we have no choice.

There are times in history when common citizens are called upon to rise above their daily struggles, to set aside their petty differences, to sacrifice their pride and comforts in order to confront a common foe. This foe resides not only among us but also within us. It is our faith and good will. It is our willingness to believe that our leaders have good intentions. It is our reluctance to believe that the entire world could be right and we could be wrong. It is our pride. American pride.

No generation – not the generations of the great wars, the Civil War, the Spanish American War, the Korean War, the Vietnam War, not the survivors of the Great Depression, not even the Revolutionary generation itself – has faced a greater challenge. Our time has arrived. We must channel our pride, our patriotism, our greatness of spirit and ingenuity to reclaim what is rightfully ours: Democracy.

These Chronicles are once again about hope. For we flatly refuse to believe that the greatness of the American spirit has been defeated. We refuse to believe that the American dream has been forgotten. We refuse to believe that Americans have lost their love of liberty and their regard for human dignity. Americans do not believe in empire. Americans would rather severe our hands and cut out our hearts than sacrifice our fundamental rights.

This is my hope and the hope of all humanity: That Americans will stop this madness before it envelops the world.

Jazz 2003.

THE LESSONS OF HISTORY

Within days of the September 11th attack, the president, illustrating his prolific knowledge of world history, announced a crusade against terrorism. In the space dividing Afghanistan from Iraq the president's crusade has undergone various transformations: A campaign against rogue nations and sponsors of terrorism, a war against evil, a defense of United Nations relevance, a strike against weapons of mass destruction and, most insidiously, a crusade for democracy.

It is difficult to go beyond the fact that we have attacked, conquered and effectively occupy two foreign nations. It is difficult to go beyond our obligation to rebuild these nations with the same dedication and commitment with which we have destroyed them. But we are told that our actions are guided by our love of liberty and our desire to spread the blessings of democracy throughout the world. Is this but the latest rationalization for American imperialism or is it sincere? While the Bush Doctrine, with its roots firmly planted in the Reagan-Bush administration, speaks glowingly of the democratic ideal, how are we to judge the validity and purity of motive?

If a traveling salesman came to your door offering a package at considerable cost with the promise that it would substantially improve your quality of life, would you take him at his word or would you greet him with skepticism? You would likely require some evidence of good will. You would want to know his history and whether or not his prior customers were satisfied.

With the shape of the world in the 21st century in the balance, should we demand any less from the Bush administration, whose leading policy makers offer a rich history in foreign affairs and military intervention?

None can or would deny the deep connection between the current administration and that of Ronald Reagan and his successor, the elder Bush. All of the major players in today's White House (Secretary of Defense Donald Rumsfeld, Paul Wolfowitz, Vice President Dick Cheney, Richard Perle, Condoleezza Rice, and Secretary of State Colin Powell) are uniformly proud to claim a practical and philosophical foundation in the Reagan-Bush years. There is considerable evidence that Richard Perle wrote the first draft of the Bush Doctrine under Reagan. (It was considered so extreme that, when it was leaked to the press, it was publicly disavowed.)

So if the intent of our foreign policy is to spread democracy by military means then there ought to be some evidence of that intent on the record.

The Reagan years began with an attempt to undo the successful and democratic Sandinista revolution in Nicaragua. (When all the facts come out, as they inevitably will, we will find that the current administration failed at a similar attempt in Venezuela.) So dedicated was the Reagan effort that he deliberately defied a Congressional prohibition by funding the counter-revolutionaries through the sale of arms to Iran (not exactly a bastion of democracy).

Next on the Reagan-Bush agenda (recall that the elder Bush was Director of Central Intelligence) was the suppression of a popular uprising in El Salvador by financing, training and arming the military junta in power. Similar support was accorded the military despots of Guatemala and Chile. In fact, we have so consistently supported military despotism that it would be difficult to argue that it is not our favored form of government.

In 1982 America intervened in a Lebanese civil war with tragic consequences. In 1983 we invaded tiny Grenada ostensibly to protect American citizens (blissfully unaware that they were being threatened) from yet another popular uprising. In 1986 we bombed Libya to send a message to the world though that message was never articulated. In 1989 we invaded Panama to depose a former CIA employee (Noriega) who was no longer useful or cooperative. In 1991 we launched the first Gulf War under the pretext of protecting the monarchy of Kuwait. But when it came time to support the popular uprisings we had called for, our efforts fell short. In fact, we enabled Saddam Hussein by explicitly granting permission to fly armed helicopters to suppress both the Kurds in the north and the Shiites in the south.

In none of these actions have we left a legacy of enlightened democracy. In all cases we have left death and destruction.

So the record offers no support for the Bush administration's crusade for democracy. In fact, it offers no trace of evidence that we even considered democracy a positive force. In fact, it overwhelmingly argues the opposite conclusion: that America will use any pretext to prosecute its true foreign policy objectives – most prominently, to achieve economic and military dominance.

But we Americans are a loyal and forgiving people – particularly when it comes to our leaders and war. Confronted with overwhelming evidence we resolve to give our president every benefit of doubt. The party of opposition consistently demurs, our media present a "balanced" picture, and the electorate follows suit. We are willing to forgive and forget our past indiscretions no matter how many lives and how many billions of dollars they cost. We retain faith that on balance America represents what is good in the world. We are willing to believe that we have changed. We are no longer the America of Vietnam. We are no longer the America that supports despotism, opposes democratic causes, arms terrorists or finances subversion of lawful governments. We are a new and virtuous nation and we take our leaders at their word.

But have we changed? Is there anything in the circumstances of Afghanistan or Iraq (Venezuela, Palestine, Columbia) that allows us to believe that America will be the first nation in recorded history to impose democracy on a foreign land?

Perhaps it is too soon to give up on democracy in Iraq. Not since the invasion of Cuba at the turn of the last century has the rhetoric of liberation been so pronounced. But the signs are nothing if not discouraging.

What has become clear is that we are unwilling to grant majority powers to the Shiite majority. (It begs the question: How do you achieve democracy without majority rule?)

What is becoming clear is that the resistance goes beyond remnants of the Bathe Party. Those policy makers who reaped such joy in belittling the French for siding with their people in opposing this war ought to study the history of the French Resistance.

It is the story of divergent groups, from anarchists to Free Masons, uniting against a common enemy. It is a story of sabotage, propaganda, counterfeiting, subterfuge, civil disobedience, harassment, guerilla warfare and open defiance. It is a story of courage against seemingly insurmountable odds. It is a story of blood and sacrifice by tens of thousands of French patriots who were shot, hanged, tortured and sent to their deaths in Nazi concentration camps. In the end, it is a story of triumph and it ought not to have been defiled by anyone who loves liberty.

As Americans, we ought to remember as well our own occupation of the Philippines, a shameful act of imperialism, costing the lives of over 4,000 American soldiers, 16,000 Filipino soldiers and hundreds of thousands of civilians. When the liberator becomes the oppressor, it does not bode well for either nation.

As for Afghanistan, the spectacle of appointed president Hamid Karzai, appearing before the United States Senate the week before our invasion of Iraq, inspired nothing more than pity. Here was a proud man, well educated, articulate, by all indications well intentioned, and clearly aware that the tide of American interest had turned against him. He pleaded with a sympathetic audience: Do not forget Afghanistan. But all present seemed to understand Afghanistan had already been forgotten.

Nearly two years after the conquest, the situation in that war-torn nation more resembles anarchy than democracy. Outside the capitol, the same warlords whose violent tyranny paved the way for the Taliban reign supreme. There has been a coronation but no election. There is none on the horizon.

If America was sincere about this crusade for democracy, she has had ample opportunity to prove it. That she has utterly and miserably failed reveals all that we need know. The lessons of history, both distant and near, argue that the cry for democracy is as empty as our claims of an imminent threat. Let us not forget that Ronald Reagan once claimed that El Salvador was a direct threat to this nation's security. The lies of war are many but none cuts more deeply than the lie of democracy.

Jazz 2003.

UNIVERSAL SUFFRAGE

Our leaders have testified on the world stage that it is our solemn duty to bring the blessings of democracy to the lands we have conquered. Then let us take them at their word. Let us set about the business of building democracy. Let us begin with an understanding of what democracy is, what it is not, and how, therefore, its development can be facilitated or negated. Let us begin at the cradle: Democracy at home.

One of the cardinal principles of democracy is that of universal suffrage. All who reside in a nation are entitled to citizenship and all citizens are entitled to vote.

While this may seem fundamental, it should not come as a surprise that our founders did not initially embrace this principle. Only the true believers held forth the hope and the dream that future generations might achieve this prerequisite to democracy. More than a century would pass before our constitution reflected that the right to vote belonged not only to white men of property but to all Americans – minorities, women and the poor. It was not until the sixties that so-called "white primaries" were outlawed in the south. It was not until the culmination of the civil rights movement in the seventies that the literacy and language barriers used to block minority voting were struck down.

So while contemporary generations tend to take the right to vote (like satellite television and computer technology) for granted, we would do well to remember that generation upon generation has struggled to achieve that right at a great cost in blood, labor and heartbreak.

In light of the millennial election, we would do well to realize that the struggle is hardly over.

If the essence of democracy is rule by the expressed will of the majority in a free and fair election, how is it that we are now governed by a president that meets neither criterion?

Where were these champions of democracy – Bush, Cheney, Rumsfeld, Powell, and Rice – when our own national election was determined by the political maneuvering of a partisan judiciary? Where was the righteous outrage over the systematic disenfranchisement of African Americans? Over ninety percent of blacks in the south voted for the Democratic candidate yet not a single one registered in the election of our president. In the critical state of Florida, with the eyes of the world watching, Governor Jeb Bush and secretary of state Katherine Harris contracted Database Technologies to compile a list of voters who may or may not have had criminal records.

The list was used to disqualify thousands of predominantly black, predominantly Democrat, registered and fully qualified voters. Before the eyes of the world, our betrayal of the democratic ideal was not only sanctioned by the highest court in the land but glorified in the name of the democratic process.

Shame where is thy blush?

The right to vote is among the most fundamental of all rights in a government that claims a democratic foundation. Therefore, any attempt to deny that right should be regarded as a crime against the state of the highest order. Why then was the great disenfranchisement not the key issue of that disputed election? Why did the party destined to lose the White House place all its chips on hanging chads and butterfly ballots rather than the disenfranchised?

Democrats would have us believe that they wished to

spare the nation a constitutional crisis. We are instructed to regard their collective silence (with the notable exception of Jesse Jackson and the Black Congressional Caucus) as a noble sacrifice. The truth is more insidious.

In the early stages of the crisis, Republicans responded to charges of election fraud by suggesting similar events in several northern states by their partisan counterparts. New York and Chicago have a rich tradition of rigging elections. Who knows what we might have learned had they chosen to open Pandora's box? Maybe they thought they could win on hanging chads. Maybe they were so disillusioned by their own candidate they no longer cared. Maybe those who possess the power of both parties would not allow a challenge to the efficacy of American democracy. Whatever their reasons, the Democrats – as would become their habit – fell profoundly and criminally silent on a question that went to the very heart of democracy: A denial of the principle of universal suffrage.

The truth is we are governed by two parties whose want of power is infinitely greater than their love of democracy. The truth is Republicans and Democrats alike have long accepted disenfranchisement as an accepted means of manipulating elections. The truth is the major parties are content with a monopoly of shared power and will not rock the boat in defense of democracy. The truth is we have not yet achieved what should rightly be regarded as the foundation of democracy.

This is not a trivial matter to be shunted aside in the national interest. It is the foundation of our system of governance. If we believe in democracy, there can be no margin of tolerance for deliberate disenfranchisement. If we believe in democracy, those who perpetrated this crime against the nation, against all of its citizens, must be held to the highest account. That so many of these perpetrators in a conspiracy against democracy have not only been vindicated but rewarded for their treachery is a testament to our failure as a nation. It is a disease of the heart so profound and widespread that it believes itself to be normal and healthy.

When we recognize that the parties in control of our government have legitimized disenfranchisement as an electoral tactic, we begin to see a great many things in new light.

In a society where a disproportionate number of black and Hispanic Americans will face imprisonment at some point in their lives, we must question laws that allow states to strip citizens of the right to vote based on a criminal record.

In a nation that imprisons more of its citizens (at last count, more than two million) than any other nation on earth, we need to revisit the principle that a debt paid is a debt paid. Society has no interest in denying the vote to those who have paid their debt.

We must ask ourselves: Would our government be so inclined to imprison the poor if the imprisoned had a means of striking back at the ballot box?

When such a large proportion of the incarcerated are drug users, how long would we continue the barbaric and wasteful practice of punishing rather than treating the addicted?

If those released from incarceration could vote, how long would such idiotic legislation as California's "three strikes" law remain on the books?

How long would the Texas drug laws enable a rogue cop to lock up ten percent of a town's black population on trumped up charges? (Remember Tulia!)

In the interest of universal suffrage, we cannot neglect the poor, the uneducated and the disadvantaged – many of whom reside in our prisons. Neither can we neglect the problem of low voter turnout.

Some would suggest that low turnout is a blessing for it allows the educated, privileged, and enlightened to decide the course of the nation. It is the same reason the founders used to discard the landless from the electorate and to disguise their own aristocratic leanings. If you embrace aristocracy, then lay it on the table and speak no more of democracy. If you believe in democracy, then you must recognize that there is a problem when people do not vote.

There are many reasons for not voting. First, though it may seem a relatively small matter, we have made it inconvenient. While upholding the tradition of Tuesday elections may possess sentimental value to those so inclined, it is a tradition that belongs with the rotary telephone.

All national elections should be conducted from Friday to Sunday with mandatory time off for those who must work. Presidential elections should require a fifty percent turnout with maximum effort to facilitate the electorate and criminal prosecution of those who obstruct the electorate.

We must also come to terms with the primary reason people do not vote. They do not like the choices with which they are presented. They are informed enough to know that they do not like Democrats or Republicans yet they are unaware of alternatives. This problem, central though it may be, has no simple, ready-made solution. It will require wholesale, systemic change and it will never happen while the major parties are in power. It can only take place when a third party or independent movement claims its rightful share of the power base. It can only happen by means of revolution.

No, we are not advocating a violent overthrow of the government. The time for such an act is long past. Let those who clamor for the right to bear arms carry that burden (for it is the right to armed revolution they are claiming). No, we are advocating a political revolution in the tradition of Jefferson in 1800. It is in fact the most important challenge we face in the quest for true democracy. None can deny that there are millions of Americans effectively disenfranchised by the dominance of the major parties. More enlightened democracies (i.e., parliamentary systems) have provided for minorities through multi-party representation. In America, we have disenfranchised the masses by providing one party under two banners.

It cannot be overstated: The most important thing any American can do to achieve democracy in America is to vote independent. When we see independents, Greens and Libertarians claiming seats in both houses of Congress, we will see changes we cannot even imagine under the current system. We will witness an invigorated electorate, an involved, informed citizenry, and a government more responsive to its people's needs than ever before in history.

The very least we can do in the interest of democracy and in behalf of universal suffrage is to demand that those who defrauded the electoral process in Florida be brought to justice. These were not harmless politicians engaged in political games; they were traitors to the very heart and soul of democracy.

If the governor, the secretary of state, and all others who conspired in this election fraud are rewarded rather than punished for their offenses, it sends a clear signal to those who would commit similar crimes in future elections. This cannot be allowed and should neither be forgotten nor forgiven by anyone who claims to believe in the democratic ideal.

Until this wrong is made right, democracy in America shall remain in great peril and all who have worshiped at her alter will be in perpetual mourning. This much we can accomplish in a relatively short time: Regime change in November 2004.

Jazz 2003.

EQUAL REPRESENTATION

What is democracy? It is very simply: government by the people. It is by necessity majority rule for, while minority representation is desirable, there is no other practical means of achieving democracy on the scale of a nation.

The democratic ideal goes back thousands of years, beyond the ancient Greeks and Romans, but it is fair to say that its expression in the modern world began with the American experiment. It was born in an age of renaissance, an age of reason, an age of science and an age of revolution.

Never in the recorded history of human kind has democracy been imposed by a foreign power. Since we propose to be the first, it is imperative to inquire: Have we achieved democracy in America? For if we have not, then we are pretenders, emperors in sheep's clothing, our every action cries hypocrisy and invites the scorn of all nations.

One of the primary tenets of democracy is the principle of equal representation: One person, one vote. Each citizen should be equally represented in the government. It is a simple concept, simply measured, and the American system clearly fails to achieve it.

At a recent forum of the Institute for Strategic Studies in London, Condoleezza Rice remarked that her ancestors were valued at 3/5ths of a vote. While it is kind of Dr. Rice to remember her ancestry, like so many of this administration's readings of history, her comment was misleading. Those unfamiliar with American history might have assumed that African Americans could vote but that their votes were at tallied at 60%. In fact, her ancestors were worth 3/5ths of a vote not to themselves but to their white, male slave owners. They were worth 60% of a vote to the institution of slavery but contributed less than nothing to democracy. That was how our founders dealt with the principle of equal representation.

Absent from the discourse surrounding the Florida election fraud was any real debate on the merits of the Electoral College. In a nation that values democracy, our continued reliance on an absurd and definitively antidemocratic system of political manipulation is an outrage. The *only* effect the Electoral College can have is to overrule the vote of the people. It effectively disenfranchises tens of thousands of voters in the most populous states and bestows the south with disproportionate political power.

Every election since the Civil Rights movement has been tailored to the southern strategy. Having inherited the legacy of racial segregation, Republicans dominate the south. Therefore, Democrats must cater to the south. That is why the Bush family chose Texas as its power base and it is why every Democrat elected since Kennedy has ostensibly been a southerner. This would not be possible, of course, if the winner-take-all formula of the Electoral College were abolished. The fact is, in the most important of all elections, the southern African American voter has been negated for decades.

Why again have the Democrats not rallied to the cry of the disenfranchised? First, because they know the game and they believe they can win at it. Second, because they do not wish to grant proportionate representation to African Americans or any other minority. If minorities were allowed to truly influence a national election, Democrats would have to give more than lip service to such causes as civil rights, reparations and affirmative action. The gradual but constant move to the right would have to end and they would be forced to choose between their ideological base and corporate sponsorship. It is a choice they are unwilling to face in the name of democracy.

Similarly, the United States Senate, by its very design, exists in open defiance of the principle of equal and proportionate representation. True to its aristocratic origins, it is as it has always been a house of lords, a legislative check on the people by society's most privileged class. The Senate is predominantly white, predominantly male and universally wealthy. While we have witnessed the value of a two-house legislature, the one to balance the other, it is no excuse for a blatant disregard of the democratic ideal. Like the royalties of Britannia, it is a leftover of a former age and it cries out for revision.

There is a tendency to believe that our institutions are cast in stone and cannot be altered but by an edict of god. The notion that a happenstance gathering of 18th century merchants and money traders possessed a wisdom deserving of deference through the ages is in itself antidemocratic. Ironically, the only document the founders produced that they considered unalterable is that which the current administration considers most malleable: The Bill of Rights.

Senators were originally selected by state legislatures and were not elected until the seventeenth amendment in 1913. The founders would have laughed to hear the reverence with which some contemporary pundits uphold the constitution. Though they could agree on little else, to a man they understood that the government they were entrusting to future generations was a work in progress. Those who believed in democracy (many did not) would be shocked to see how little we have progressed by comparison to our technological advances. They would wonder if we have lost our taste for democracy. They would wonder what went wrong.

Within the context of a nation, states are arbitrary distinctions for administrative purposes. They are not entities that deserve consideration over the rights of individuals. As expressed in the Electoral College and the United States Senate, they are a profoundly unequal representation of the will of the people. That the state of Vermont (population 613,000) should be equally represented as the state of California (population 34.5 million) is an affront to all reasoned believers in democracy.

Senators should be elected from fifty contiguous regions of equal population according to the most recent census. Senatorial districts should be determined by an independent agency whose sole responsibility is the equitable application of the principle of equal representation.

Finally, the practice of gerrymandering (redistricting legislative and congressional districts to maximize party gains) is indefensible. It has been used to deny representation to minority communities for centuries. It cannot be defended on moral or ideological grounds. It can only be rationalized on the basis of party politics.

Thus, we are treated to the spectacle of Texas Democrats fleeing their state to avoid a redistricting orchestrated by the White House. Anyone who has even casually observed the political process has seen the absurdities redistricting has wrought, yet it is allowed to persist with the implied blessings of both parties, as if it is democracy in practice, when in fact it is the tyranny of power at its very worse.

The obvious solution to gerrymandering is the establishment of independent election boards to oversee the process. That it has never been conceived or proposed by the major parties is a clear reflection of their commitment to democracy.

Are we committed to democracy? If we are not, then let us make no claims to champion its cause in the new world order. If we are, then let us take the obvious steps to achieving democracy in America:

1. Abolish the Electoral College.
2. Ban winner-take-all primaries.
3. Reform the election of United States Senators.
4. Abolish gerrymandering.

To all politicians who speak glowingly of liberty, who praise the founders for their foresight, and claim democracy as their foundation: Stand and be counted or be revealed as the false patriots and hypocrites you are.

Jazz 2003.

OPEN ACCESS

The nation that was born of thirteen colonies on this continent was deeply flawed and profoundly undemocratic. It was a government of the elite, by the elite and for the elite. The ruling class was by law restricted to white, male and landed gentry. Modeled after the British Parliament, our legislature consisted of a house of commons and a house of lords in which neither were common. The common people who served in the militias and the Continental Army, who won American independence, were denied access to the newly formed democratic government they had established. Two and a quarter centuries later, they still are.

One of the most important and neglected principles of democracy is open access. A truly democratic system must be open not only to its citizenry but to all candidates of merit, regardless of financial status or party allegiance.

It does not require an incisive mind – no less a political scientist – to recognize that our system is anything but open and the prerequisite is hardly merit. The cost of being elected in America ranges from the thousands for a local commissioner's seat to tens of millions for a statewide election to hundreds of millions for a national campaign.

In this light, it is deeply disturbing that rightwing ideologues have chosen to challenge the most modest attempt at limiting campaign contributions in modern history. In so doing they have defined money as free speech. If upheld by the most partisan Supreme Court in memory, such an interpretation would disallow any real limits on campaign finances and politicians will be bought and sold for chattel on the open market. The difficulty is compounded by the fact that the vast majority of our elected officials are addicted to corporate funding just as the junkie is addicted to the drug of choice.

Now that the pressures of the Enron scandal have subsided, there will be little further talk of campaign finance reform. Their hearts were not in it to begin with. Now the status of electoral politics returns to the perfect dilemma – a Catch 22: You cannot get campaign finance reform without honest politicians and you cannot get honest politicians without campaign finance reform.

Even if such reforms were to be instituted, however, the system would remain essentially closed to those outside the dominant parties. As if the monetary requirements of candidacy were not enough, many states have erected additional barriers (ballot requirements, financial requirements, polling standards and filing deadlines) to third party and independent candidate success. If we believe in democracy and the principle of open access (as virtually all European democracies do), then the laws should be stacked in the opposite direction: To guarantee access to all rather than to obstruct it.

Reform must begin by severely restricting the amount of money that can be collected and expended in political campaigns but it must not end there. Barriers to third party and independent candidates must be prohibited, candidates must be required to participate in fair and open debates, and a forum must be provided at the expense of the electorate to give all candidates a fair hearing.

Those of us who are committed to democracy through independence should never check the box on the federal income tax form that contributes to political campaigns for those contributions go almost entirely to the major party candidates. When we receive tax rebates, we should recognize them for what they are: political pandering for the incumbent party. We should make a point of distributing such funds to third party and independent campaigns.

Those who remain in support of the two-party system should begin to examine their reasons. Without appealing to your sense of the common good or your commitment to democracy, unless you are among the financial elite, the major parties do not serve your interests. If you still believe the Democrats are the party of labor, why has there been no substantive improvement in the condition of labor since the advent of the 40-hour work week (currently under attack)? Why has the movement toward globalization and free trade not been accompanied by international labor standards – including minimum wage?

With apologies to our current president, it was our last president who introduced the concept of compassionate conservatism when he instituted a classically Republican reform package highlighted by welfare reform. That the Clinton administration was blessed with a strong economy is a tribute to his fiscal and economic management skills (as well as good fortune) but he was neither friend nor enemy to the working class, the environmental movement, civil rights or civil liberties. That he was better than his successor is unquestioned. That a Republican could have run on his program and policies for the second term should be a revelation.

The overriding question is whether independents must support a Democrat in order to oppose the disaster in the White House. It is a valid question.

The Bush administration has aggressively attacked all that we hold dear at home while pursuing an American empire abroad. It is important to end the Bush reign. It is also important to acknowledge that the Democratic alternative is virtually closed to progressive influence. Access has been denied to the poor, the middle class and the oppressed. As long as we are willing to support them as the lesser evil the doors will continue to be locked; only the chosen, the elite, the wealthy will be allowed access.

In the name of democracy, the day must come when this self-defeating pragmatism ends.

Jazz 2003.

FREE MEDIA

The fourth principle of democracy concerns the fourth branch of government: A free and independent media. In the modern world it is desperately inadequate to guarantee that the press is not owned or censored by the government. None can deny that the media is the most dominant source of influence in today's society. In effect, those that control the media control the substance and direction of government. Therefore, the principles of open access and proportionate representation must be applied to the media as well as the political system.

Consider what has happened to the media in recent decades. The same deregulatory process that enabled a handful of Texas companies to steal billions from the western states in a contrived energy shortage, has given us a media owned and controlled by a few multi-national corporations. Much has been made of recent Federal Communications Commission rulings clearing the way for even further consolidation of print, radio and television media but the problem goes much deeper than antitrust regulation. The overriding problem is conflict of interest and the solution is divestiture.

We have said so before and cannot repeat it too often: corporations with a vested interest in the packaging of information and the promulgation of propaganda should not own the media. A media with direct ties to Microsoft, Coca Cola and Mobil Oil should not be trusted to inform the American public on our affairs in Iraq, Venezuela, Korea, China, Nigeria or any other country where they stand to gain by the proceeds. The media should not be monopolized and should be prohibited from involvement in the political process in any way. That corporation which feels compelled to finance political campaigns should divest itself of all media holdings. By the same token, if a corporation is involved in media it should not be involved in any other interests. Freedom of the press is a sacred trust. It cannot and must not be sacrificed to those whose greater god is the profit margin.

If a free and independent media can be achieved it would likely provide open access and coverage to all worthy candidates. If it does not, it should be compelled to do so in the public interest.

Any of these reforms would constitute a revolution in American politics and yet, without all of them there cannot be true democracy in America.

So how shall we achieve such sweeping reforms for in the end it is the only way to change the course of the nation? The answer is that it must begin within each and every individual who recognizes the fundamental truth concerning our democracy. It must begin (perhaps it has begun) at the grassroots level and it must be persistent. We win every time an independent candidate gains a place on the ballot. We win every time a vote that would have gone to the major parties is cast instead for the independent. We win when our candidate gets more votes than expected. We win when our positions and issues gain entry to the mainstream instead of being ignored or taken for granted. We win when any one of us gains a voice on mainstream media. We win when our small victories grow into larger ones until they become a political force that cannot be denied. We win by remaining true to our cause. We win by standing strong and surviving the onslaught.

If we do not begin now to address the fundamental problems of our democracy we may never have that chance again. As long as we are governed by party-dominated, corrupt politicians, democratic reform will never happen. As long as we are forced to choose between the moderate right (Democrats) and the far right (Republicans), our causes and concerns will be marginalized. It is time for all of us to awaken to the new political reality: There is only one dominant party in America and that is the corporate trust. Democrats may promise change but, at best, they can only deliver deferment. Real change may only be possible when the Libertarian right unites with the independent left to offer a true alternative. Confronted with the increasingly repressive measures of our government, it is a natural and overdue alliance.

At a time when our government preaches the virtues of democracy to a disbelieving world we must step forward with a reminder: Democracy is a process. What is disheartening is not so much that we have failed to achieve the democratic ideal but that we have lost sight of the goal. We have lost the ideal itself. We have abandoned the process. We are told that our system, flawed and imperfect as it may be, is the best democracy on earth. Sadly, it is not. By all standards, the parliamentary systems of Europe are infinitely more representative and more democratic than ours.

The current state of democracy in America is a reality that should bring us humility and shame. More importantly, it should inspire us with greater determination than any generation before: Let us reclaim our legacy and birthright.

Jazz 2003.

FOOLED AGAIN
Major Party Turnabout

Four months before the end of the year 2005, an image in the political crystal ball is coming into focus. Reminiscent of Richard Nixon's Secret Plan to end the war he had so faithfully prosecuted, Republicans are angling to become the anti-occupation party for the midterm elections. The punch-drunk Democrats, thirsting for the winning duplicity and deception of a Karl Rove special, are positioning themselves as the occupation party. The former mantra of the Republicans will become the bray of an ass: Don't cut and run.

In the ultimate irony, those who oppose the occupation yet still embrace the pragmatic principle of politics, will confront the ultimate dilemma: Vote Republican to end the occupation or Democrat to prolong it indefinitely.

In truth, as it so often is in the politics of a two-party system, it is a false dichotomy and a shallow distinction. Neither major party will alter the course in Iraq. Whether we cut back our troop levels and replace them with strategic bombing campaigns, or reinstitute the draft to bolster our numbers, the occupation will drag on and our military installations will remain secure.

We have seized control of Iraqi oil fields and we will not let go.

The war is in fact not distinguishable from the occupation and those who claim to have opposed the war but support the occupation are disingenuous at best. They have advanced to the head of the class of political opportunism, pandering to both sides and blurring the lines of conviction.

As more Americans awaken to a familiar absence of real choice, the time is ripe for a third party or independent movement to challenge major party dominance at the congressional level. We need no surrogate lackeys of the Democratic Party and we only require unqualified opposition to the occupation. There is a field of potential candidates:

Amy Goodman of Democracy Now, actors Tim Robbins and Susan Sarandon for Congress. Activist Ralph Nader, actor Warren Beatty, journalist Christianne Amanpour and Congresswoman Barbara Lee for the United States Senate.

Numerous principled candidates would be willing to step forward in a united assault on major party dominance if only an organized effort was in place. Why have the antiwar organizations yielded the political battlefield? As efforts are concentrated on mass protest, how can we ignore the midterm elections? We have already mounted the largest protests since the Vietnam War and we have learned that protest is important but it is not sufficient.

The Democratic proxy Move On has created a money-raising machine largely on the backs of the antiwar movement yet they are not opposing the occupation. Where is billionaire George Soros (the businessman who helped financed the political opposition to George W. Bush) now? Was there a seed of conviction in his efforts or was it all about party politics?

Twenty-one troops killed in a single weekend: When did we start calling soldiers "troops"? Soldiers have faces, friends and families. CNN accepts accolades for finally naming the dead and giving them identity. There should be a channel devoted to the lives of the fallen: 30-minute documentaries of who they were before they went to war and who they might have been had the war not happened. Is it too much to ask of our patriotic media?

14-21-42-64: The death toll rises. Ring the bells in every church, synagogue, temple or mosque: One for every fallen soldier, every day until the occupation ends.

How many Iraqis have died? Multiply American losses by twenty or thirty and you will have a rough answer. We do not count Iraqi dead.

While the occupation continues, is there another issue?

We are sick of politicians who make a show of opposition only when it does not matter and never when it matters most.

The nomination of John Bolton as ambassador to the United Nations does not matter. The Bolton documents, sealed by the White House, which would reaffirm the lies of war, do matter. Where is the congressional outrage?

The fight against Supreme Court nominee John Roberts is little more than a Las Vegas review: all show, no content. Regardless of how it plays out, we will be saddled with a Federalist court and John Roberts will be affirmed.

When it might have mattered, the Democrats folded in authorizing the war, relented in approving and renewing the Patriot Act, turned their backs on the failed coups in Venezuela and the successful coup in Haiti. When it might have mattered the Democrats yielded on CAFTA, energy deregulation, aid to the pharmaceutical industry (health care reform) and protection of the gun industry. The Democrats neglected voting rights and election reform and once again lost an election because of it.

The Congressional Black Caucus should be commended for their leadership on these issues but they have fought alone far too long.

The Downing Street memos and the Valerie Plame

affair should be a daily drumbeat on Capitol Hill until New York Times reporter Judy Miller is released from prison to give testimony before the eyes of the world.

Again, the party of opposition falls silent.

Support for the war (less than 40% at last polling) is in steady decline. Even political pragmatism demands a strong and vocal opposition on such a compelling and popular position, yet the Democrats decline. There is only one reasonable explanation for this failure: complicity.

The dominant parties in American politics are united in supporting a war against the will of the American people and the death toll continues to rise.

Is there another issue?

When we have withdrawn from Iraq, given up our bases, and ended the occupation, then we can talk about Afghanistan, Haiti, Sudan, Niger and Palestine.

When we have ended the occupation, then we can talk about civil liberties, energy policy, massive investment in mass transit and renewable fuels, fair trade and labor standards, civil rights and the divisive social issues.

Who will be the last to die for a lie?

Until we can answer that question and our soldiers are no longer on the firing line, everything else must wait.

Jazz 6 August 2005.

REQUIEM FOR DEMOCRACY

Looking for a leader
To bring our country home
Reunite the red, white and blue
Before it turns to stone

Neil Young's *Living with War*

What could be more absurd than the Bush administration pushing the United Nations for a resolution of condemnation against Iran? Three years ago the same White House gave solemn assurances that a similar resolution against Iraq would not be used as justification for war. While lying to the Security Council may not constitute an impeachable offense, it eliminates the need for character witnesses the next time you try the same trick.

Fool me once... well, we're not going to get fooled again.

As if competing for the mendacity of the week award, Senator Rick Santorum (What is wrong with Pennsylvania?) lectured his colleagues on ethical conduct, advising them not to accept private jet rides from corporate sponsors two days after accepting the same from his own corporate sponsor.

Not to be outdone, Director of Central Intelligence Porter Goss retired shortly before his name was dragged through the muck in connection with disgraced former congressman Duke Cunningham, defense contractors, poker games and prostitutes at the Watergate Hotel.

With two and a half years to go, after the latest shake down, the White House is a ghost ship inhabited by misfits and failures. Michael Chertoff and John Negroponte in charge of the nation's security? Who is kidding whom? Karl Rove spends all his time preparing his defense in the Valerie Plame-Wilson case, Dick Cheney is drafting position papers on presidential pardons, Josh Bolton supervises the shredding operation and songbird Jack Abramoff is the hottest ticket in town.

Meantime, the biggest bogey of them all, the NSA Spying Scandal (What part of illegal do you not understand?) hides its ugly head awaiting a fair hearing before an impartial congress. As the latest Orwellian revelation settles in (an apparent attempt to accumulate a data base of every American phone call and email ever recorded), memories of Dick Nixon and J. Edgar Hoover float to the fore. (Was Martin Luther King a terrorist associate?) When you accumulate vast amounts of information, someone is bound to use it. What if it falls into the wrong hands? For instance, what if it gets into the hands of people who would out a CIA agent for a political vendetta?

The president's claim that we only spy on terrorists and terrorist affiliates takes its place in a long line of executive deceptions:

No one could have imagined planes used as missiles.

We know exactly where the weapons of mass destruction are.

The next attack may be a mushroom cloud.

Saddam is the second cousin of Osama bin Laden.

We do not torture.

We do not wiretap without a warrant.

Iran is the greatest threat to peace in the world.

It has nothing to do with oil.

The tax cuts benefit the working people.

The economy is strong.

The Katrina catastrophe was the result of state and local malfeasance.

We have to fight them over there so we don't have to fight them here.

Afghanistan is a beacon of democracy.

No president wants to go to war.

The bogeyman himself, NSA chief, administration stooge and Air Force General Michael Hayden, faces senatorial confirmation hearings to succeed DCI Goss, at which we will surely be treated to the cardboard façade of Democratic opposition. Watch Senator Feinstein agonize: He may have committed a blatant felony, he may have overseen the gathering of phone records on over 100 million "Al Qaeda affiliates", but he's such a nice man, a good technocrat and he does not play poker with prostitutes.

Assuming he passes the test, if Hayden succeeds in his new assignment, the once venerated spy agency will go gently into that goodnight – until the next terrorist attack.

Nearly five and a half years into the worst presidency in recorded history, the stock market approaches an all-time high while working class Americans stare into the abyss of poverty and ruin, the runaway debt climbs to an insurmountable peak, the price of gas is a dagger in the working man's back, New Orleans and the Gulf Coast are the latest forgotten war zones, a reactionary congress searches for fresh scapegoats, America has lost its moral grounding, falling headlong into a spiral descent, and the president believes he can restore his leadership by christening another war with tactical nuclear weapons.

Looking backward in agony, the question must be asked: How could so many Americans have been fooled?

Looking forward in trepidation, is there any assurance we will not be fooled again?

Democracy is far more than the periodic ritual of voting. Saddam's Iraq dutifully practiced the ritual like a moon dance at harvest time. True democracy is founded on real freedom and genuine freedom is wholly dependent on the right of privacy. More than anything else, what distinguishes citizens from slaves is that our lives are our own behind closed doors.

There is no freedom of expression if the government is listening. There is no freedom of choice if the government is keeping tabs. Even freedom of thought is irreparably harmed if our thoughts are shadowed by the fear of a government monitor.

Having sacrificed our rights and freedoms with hardly a whimper, we can only take our government's word that we are more secure. Even now, as we reflect on the years since 11 September 2001, there have been horrific wildfires and massive explosions at chemical and industrial plants. If we cannot rely on our government to tell us the truth (as we clearly cannot under George W. Bush), how would we know if there was a terrorist attack?

The government has already cowed the media and the opposition party is a cruel joke. Now we are told that a majority of Americans is willing to sacrifice the right of privacy for the illusive promise of security. If that is truly the case, we have already lost the battle to retain our democracy.

The problems of this nation go well beyond the deficiencies of a little man from Crawford, Texas. The central problem of this nation is a political system that offers a choice between two corporate proxies every four years: tweedle dee and tweedle dum. The problem is a system that relies on the corrupt to police the corrupted. The problem is a system that disallows innovative thought and reduces acceptable policies to those that are corporate sanctioned. The problem is a system that is dominated and controlled by international corporations without a vested interest in either the nation or its inhabitants.

The only realistic solution to the rapidly unfolding decline of the nation is a third American revolution. The first secured independence from the British Empire at the cost of American blood. The second was a critical affirmation of the principles of democracy with the election of Thomas Jefferson in 1800. The third must be a reaffirmation of the same.

Recently, columnist Thomas Friedman took the most unusual tact of advocating a third party movement. The theme of his imaginary party was green power and its lynchpin was a significant federal gas tax.

With due respect, Mr. Friedman is right and wrong. Green power is the correct theme but a gas tax is its death knell. Presumably, Mr. Friedman resides in the only metropolis in America where an automobile is not prerequisite to employment. Presumably, Mr. Friedman need not worry that another rise in the cost of living will push him over the edge. He will not lose his home, his health coverage and the means of supporting his family. He does not live where the working class lives.

There is in fact a host of measures (see "Paradigm Shift: Embracing the Power of Green" in *Dissident Voice* 1 May 2006) that can be taken without a tax that singles out the most vulnerable among us for punishment. It includes fuel efficiency standards, mass transit, industrial hemp, re-regulation of the energy industry, expansion of alternative energy sources, mandatory solar panels and energy efficient design. It requires assembling the brightest minds in the land to draft a comprehensive energy policy that will wean us from destructive fuels and lead us to the forefront of green technology.

Beyond taxing the elite who have all but received a free pass over the last five and a half years, we need only stop the war, putting an end to a monumental waste of human and financial resources, and invest in the future of the nation and the planet.

Beyond preventing or at least alleviating certain environmental catastrophes and defusing the need for war to secure oil, a successful third party drive to significant power just might rekindle the flame of democracy in America.

Is it an impossible dream? No more so than winning independence from the world's most powerful army in 1776. No more so than fighting back the wealthy aristocrats in 1800. It is in plain fact the *American* dream and if we do not fight to secure it, we will surely inherit a nightmare in its place.

Jazz 15 May 2006.

RETURN TO CAUSE
An American Revolution

As a common man with a life outside of politics, I entered the world of political discourse with a cause born of the conviction that the future of American democracy depended on the emergence of an Independent Movement that could break the stranglehold of two parties dominated by the same corporate interests.

Something happened along the way that caused me to defer my primary cause. The nation was attacked, the people were terrified and the government launched a policy of aggressive war designed to capture a lion's share of the world's most precious resource.

Somehow, the cause of political independence – freedom from corporate governance – no longer seemed pressing. Suddenly, stopping the war machine became a moral imperative, overwhelming all other concerns.

The war is not over – not by a long shot. In many ways, the threat of war and more wars is as great now as it was in the mind-numbing daze of late September 2001. The nation's leading warmongers outside the White House are positioning for another presidential run in 2008 and the corporate media is falling in line.

The war is not over but I am beginning to understand that all our pressing issues, from the policies of war and global "free trade" to government incompetence and indifference to the plight of the poor and working class, from the poisoning of the planet to election fraud, are intimately interrelated.

The war in Iraq would not have been possible without

corporate control of government and corporate control of government is made possible by an inherently corrupt two-party system where both are dependent on corporate sponsorship.

It may seem abstract or radical but it is not difficult to understand when you break it down. When we laid siege to Iraq, we did not claim Iraqi oil as a nation; we contracted it to private corporations – corporations that owed no allegiance to any nation or ideology but to capital and only capital.

To the uninformed American, this was a war of pride and prejudice (the pride of patriotism and prejudice against all things Arabic) but to Exxon-Mobil and British Petroleum, it was a corporate takeover. Check the record: The first requirement of the occupying army on the handover of sovereignty and the adoption of a new Iraqi constitution was that all contracts of the occupying authority would be honored.

America and the Iraqi people have lost a great deal in this war but the oil barons and the corporate scavengers are still tallying their profits. Win, lose or prolonged engagement, the CEO's of Halliburton and Bechtel will not fail to cash their checks and Dick Cheney will still collect his dividends.

The corporate overlords have little interest in geopolitical strategies, little interest in the currency of choice, and are markedly disinterested in the democratic form of government. They require an unlimited supply of energy to fuel the industrial machine and massive quantities of capital to dominate technology. Beyond oil, the only strategy that engages the corporate monoliths is the expansion of the "free trade" zone.

The dirty little secret of "free trade" is that it is not "free" trade at all. It is a devious and extremely effective assault on labor that transcends national boundaries. Every trade agreement operating under the banner of "free trade" regards a cheap working force, devoid of labor rights and unburdened by expectations of a living wage, as a marketable commodity.

There could not be a better operational definition of selling the working stiff down the river. With every expansion of the "free trade" zone, job migration accelerates the erosion of wages and labor rights in relatively affluent nations and institutionalizes exploitation in poorer nations.

As the process continues under the illusion of inevitability (a myth perpetuated by both ruling American parties and the corporate media), the eventual outcome is clear: Universal exploitation of labor (i.e., the Wal-Mart model).

And so I return to the cause of independence, knowing that the odds remain long and the last six years have been utterly wasted.

In the recent midterm elections, only one independent candidate managed a winning campaign and that was the Republican Democrat of Connecticut. Ironically, the election of Joe Liebermann illustrates the potential power of independence, as he now becomes the most powerful figure in the United States Senate: a free agent who can tip the balance of power by changing party allegiance at any time.

The only campaign I am aware of that carried the seed of a winning idea was that of Kevin Zeese for Senator in Maryland. A member of the Green Party, Zeese managed to win the support of the Maryland Libertarian and Populist Parties. Despite that substantial accomplishment, his candidacy attracted only one percent of the vote in the general election.

The Zeese campaign illustrates the best and worst of the Independence Movement. On the positive side, he demonstrated that third parties with distinct ideas and philosophies could be united in the cause of independence. On the dark side, by reaching too high he doomed his campaign to the status of tokenism.

In modern American politics, without the backing of a major party machine, trying to leap from citizen activist to the United States Senate is like defying the law of gravity. It is admirable to dream big but, without a viable goal of victory, the dream cannot be sustained.

Dream big but think small.

The policies advanced by Kevin Zeese may well represent a majority of American voters. What might have happened had he targeted a congressional district gerrymandered for Democratic control? With the Republicans reduced to tokenism, Zeese could have taken dead aim at the muddled middle ground of Democratic politics. With the backing of a national organization allied with the antiwar movement, he might have won. Two terms in congress and he would be positioned for a real run at the Senate. Four years as a Senator and he would be poised for a run at the White House.

What is required, then, is a national movement with a national organization whose objectives are twofold: First, to unite third parties with the fastest growing sector of the American electorate: independent voters. Second, to identify vulnerable congressional districts and run candidates who can win. Some candidates will be progressive, others libertarian, but all will be mortal enemies to the corporate political machine.

The revolution begins in earnest with the first victory and with that victory the age of third party tokenism will end.

In our peculiar, two-party system, as few as a dozen congressional seats and one or two senators would radically alter the political landscape. The Independence Movement would be in position to demand election reform, media reform, Internet freedom, and, at a minimum, trade policy and foreign policy review.

Like Joe Liebermann today, the Independence Movement would hold the key to the balance of power in the halls of congress.

Every revolution begins with a first step and the first step is securing the necessary backing to build the infrastructure and brain trust of a national organization. It requires visionaries of acquired wealth, political foresight and a spirit of philanthropy that transcends the combined works of Bill Gates, Warren Buffet and the celebrities of the day. It requires that the leaders of third parties step forward in the cause of unity.

The political climate has rarely been better. Trust in our congressional leaders has never been lower. If the Democrats, tied down by their dependence on the same corporate overlords that created this despair, fail to end the war and affect real change, they will be playing into the hands of Independence.

Let the revolution begin.

Jazz 2 December 2006.

AN ANSWER TO THE TEA PARTY
Rise & Fall of American Democracy

In the beginning it was a simple concept: majority rule. Whether it claims root in ancient Athens or some unknown tribal community, it has survived the millennia as the democratic ideal and remains today a powerful force in the governance of nations.

Modern democracy emerged in the eighteenth century as an alternative to monarchy, aristocracy, dictatorship and other forms of tyranny. The founding of the American nation, with all its flaws and inequities, was civilization's first marriage of the nation state to the democratic ideal.

Rightwing cynics will point out that America is not and has never been a true democracy; it is rather a republic. They are of course literally correct yet fundamentally misguided. Democracy is an ideal that has never been attempted on the scale of nations and until the advent of advanced technology has never in fact been possible. In the eighteenth and nineteenth centuries no nation could afford to wait for a poll of the franchise before making a critical decision.

A modern democracy is therefore representative yet it embraces the ideal and works constantly toward achieving it. Throughout history it has been a constant struggle. The primary battleground of the nineteenth and twentieth centuries was the franchise, which expanded to include the landless, ethnic minorities and women.

For over two hundred years America has marched toward realization of the democratic ideal and every step of the way we have overcome the bitter and violent opposition of those who consider themselves the ruling class. Change has never been easy but Americans have always intuitively fought for their democratic rights as citizens of this nation.

Now all that is at risk. The new millennium was christened with a presidential election in which we would learn that our Supreme Court does not recognize an individual right to vote. The most massive disenfranchisement of black Americans since the Jim Crow era was therefore allowed to stand and a corporate media characterized what happened in Florida as the shenanigans of politicians rather than treason. Two political parties without any standing in our constitution were allowed to negotiate away the people's right to choose their own president. Five members of the Court decided the election based on their own political biases and democracy was in retreat.

Eight years later, as Americans elected their first black president, the most blatantly pro-corporate Supreme Court in history put the last nail in the coffin of campaign finance reform, ruling in Citizens United v. Federal Election Commission that the government can place no restrictions on corporate financing of political campaigns. A Democratic controlled congress could not even muster the votes or the courage to require transparency.

Thus the CEO's of corporations like British Petroleum or J.P. Morgan can contribute as much as they wish to whatever candidates they choose under deceptive titles like the People's Committee to Elect Patriots. In the media immersed environment of today can anyone even imagine that the corporate elite will choose voluntary restraint? They will engage. They are engaging. And the candidates they choose will represent their interests above and beyond any concern for the people or their individual rights.

Our democracy is under siege and the only people who appear outraged are those who attach themselves to the Tea Party movement. The irony of course is that the Tea Party movement is the creation of rightwing front organizations dedicated to the corporate cause.

What is the corporate cause? De-regulation. Corporate tax reduction. Austerity. Privatization of public service. Anti-labor laws. Unrestricted free trade. Evisceration of environmental protection. Strict limits on corporate liability.

If it sounds familiar it should. Until now the corporate cause has been indistinguishable from the Republican Party platform. Meg Whitman is the corporate cause. Sarah Palin is the corporate cause. John Boehner is the corporate cause.

All that is about to change. Until now the Democratic Party has been the soft side of corporate politics but when the floodgates swing open and corporate funding comes rushing in, Democrats will scramble to grab their share. The Bush tax cuts will be renewed. Deregulation will come back on line. Free trade will once again be a bipartisan mandate.

The two parties will become one, separate but indistinguishable, under the banner of corporate good. Get used to it.

Welcome to corporate democracy, American style, where every candidate must sign a loyalty oath to the corporate mandate, where the dominant parties serve the same corporate gods, where the corporate aristocracy gains the power of government, the power to close whole industries and ship jobs overseas where labor is as cheap as dirt. Welcome to the world of corporate think where we learn to recognize the virtues of poverty and unemployment and what's good for Wall Street is good for all.

JAZZMAN CHRONICLES

What choice do we have? How can you fight back when the other side has all the resources? It's the Bad News Bears against the Yankees but it's not a movie. The Yanks will win and the other side will go home with their heads hanging, grateful that they're still attached.

There may be a way out of this mess but it takes a leap of audacity. Not the kind of audacity that Obama promised in the last election, the kind that turned into the audacity of compromise and the stubborn refusal to deliver jobs at the cost of corporate profits.

No, the kind of audacity we need today is the kind that stands up for real democracy at all costs, the kind that refuses to go along with the corporate mandate, the kind that rejects both parties as surrogates of the same corporate interests and the kind that says quite simply:

Let the people decide.

It is a simple concept like democracy itself. I propose a political organization as a counterpoint to the Tea Party. Its candidates will hold to two sacred promises: First, they will accept no corporate contributions. Second, they will vote the people's will.

It should be called the Direct Democracy movement for that is the ground upon which it stands. If elected the Direct Democracy office holder will register voters from his or her constituency, inform them in advance of important votes, present the case for or against, invite them to make their decisions on line and cast his or her vote with the majority.

Let the people decide.

Many will argue that the people are not equipped to make important decisions. They lack information, education and knowledge. If that is the case, it becomes imperative to make the people more informed, educated and knowledgeable. If we made it more important perhaps we would think twice before under-funding and privatizing education. If indeed we are still the wealthiest nation on the planet, it follows that our people should be the best educated. That we are not is an indictment of our values, not our educators.

While we're pondering de Tocqueville's "tyranny of the majority" and the potential harm that true democracy could bring, add these questions to the equation:

If the people decided, would we still be in Iraq? Would we still be hanging on to a failed occupation with 50,000 troops and an unofficial army of contractors hunkering down in a series of impenetrable fortresses designed to last the long haul?

If the people decided, would we have escalated the war in Afghanistan eight years in with no end in sight and no glimpse of anything resembling success on the horizon? Yes, the president says we are on our way out but after Iraq we don't know what that means. How long, how much and how many more must die before we admit that this too was a mistaken war?

If the people decided, would we have handed the financial industry a trillion dollars with virtually no strings attached? Would we have insisted that an accounting be made, that CEO's not be awarded outrageous bonus checks, that loans be made to small businesses and that some significant share of that fortune be delivered to creating jobs and saving homes?

If the people decided, would we be moving forward on mass transit and alternative energy rather than wallowing in the muck of legislative paralysis as we are today?

We can argue these points and we should but I believe the time has come to place our faith in the people and let the chips fall.

We have a choice. We can either seize control of our own government or yield it to those who do not have our interests at heart.

As I write these words a Los Angeles Times report

indicates that corporate funds are rolling into Republican coffers at a record pace. Over $300 million has been targeted to the coming election by fifteen rightwing tax-exempt organizations, undoubtedly fronts for corporate spenders. That kind of money does not grow on trees and does not come without expectations yet it is a pittance in the corporate political war chest.

If we do nothing we will lose our democracy. Winning it back will require radical thinking and dedicated action. What could be more radical or more worthy than democracy itself?

Jazz 31 August 2010.

US & THEM:
ARRESTING DEMOCRACY
Occupy Wall Street

I know the police cause you trouble
They cause trouble everywhere
But when you die and go to heaven
There'll be no policeman there

Hobo's Lullaby by Goebel Reeves

On September 17, 2011, a group of protesters gathered at Zuccotti Park in lower Manhattan under the banner: Occupy Wall Street. Within weeks the Occupy movement and its message of income inequality and corporate dominance of the political process spread across the nation and the globe. By the end of October occupations were reported in some 2,000 cities worldwide.

On or about November 10, a conference call engaging some eighteen American cities initiated a coordinated crackdown on OWS encampments. Police actions from that day forward have been persistent, forceful and often violent. How else do you explain the use of tear gas, pepper spray, batons and rubber pellets to disperse, corral and arrest non-violent protesters?

Evidence has emerged that federal authorities, including Homeland Security, were tapped to advise or coordinate the assault. While a contentious debate has broken out concerning the particulars, who else but a federal agent could have coordinated mayors and police chiefs in disparate communities across the nation?

Moreover, if it is not so, where are the denials? What political advantage can be gained by maintaining neutrality in this fight? Is the president with us or with them? As the late great Howard Zinn said: You can't be neutral on a moving train.

To the students who were pepper sprayed or the activists who were gassed or the protesters who were clubbed, it does not matter who gave the order or who remained silent to maintain deniability.

It probably did not matter who gave the orders to the officers on the street either. The orders were given and the officers carried them out. But it might have mattered how those orders were phrased.

I know something about what it is to be an officer of the law. My father patrolled a beat in our town for twenty years. In the summer of Watts he served as a liaison to the minority community. An honest, fair and impartial cop, he told me what his captain said as he was called to duty at the community college where students were staging a protest of the Vietnam War: "We are supposed to uphold the law and keep the peace. We're not supposed to take sides... but you know what side we're on!"

I learned then that there were two kinds of law officers: cops and pigs. My father was a cop. Those who lead with their clubs, those who pepper spray student protesters, and those who form lines of oppression against peaceful demonstrators and clear the way with tear gas and rubber bullets are pigs.

As a general lot, cops have always tended to be reactionary and intolerant. Confronted with any dissident group, raw instinct draws them to an adversarial posture. When pressed into crowd control they strike a pose and draw a line: Us versus Them.

My father knew better back then and the police on the streets should know better now. The cause of the occupiers is fundamentally different than the antiwar demonstrators. The very same people the occupiers oppose are waging war against police, firefighters, teachers and nurses. Police forces across the nation are being downsized, their salaries and benefits under assault, their right to collective bargaining challenged and their unions under siege.

The rest of the workforce faces job exportation. Public employees face privatization. Charter schools are just an excuse to hire non-union teachers. Private security forces will soon replace police and private contractors will take over fire departments in the name of budgetary restraint.

The occupiers speak for everyone who draws a paycheck. Consider that the next time you are called to clear out an occupied encampment. Consider it a dress rehearsal for the Hoovervilles to come, when thousands upon thousands erect makeshift camps not out of choice but out of necessity.

As for the mayors who gave the stamp of approval for this crackdown, your political careers are over. The occupiers were doing your job. They were performing a public service. They provided food, shelter, clothing and care for the forgotten homeless.

We could see the writing on the wall early on. At first the media was intrigued. They characterized the occupy movement as the Tea Party of the left and tried to frame it as a partisan divide. But the occupiers refused to sell out. It was not a partisan movement. The media then stepped up its criticism: The movement was without leaders and without a clear message. (Ironically, the message was as clear as ending the war. It could easily be summarized as taking back our government from the corporate elite. Us against Them.) Next, they began to focus on health and safety, rats and public urination. (Welcome to life on the streets.) They took their cues from the mayors and ran stories on the detrimental effects on small businesses and the costs of policing the occupations.

It was all smoke screen. It was all prelude to the crackdown that was to come. The corporate media answers to their corporate masters and they tipped their hands.

Mayor Michael Bloomberg, the presidential wannabe with his Wall Street pedigree, took the lead in showing America how to step on the little guys who dared stand up against the real power brokers of the world. How does libertarianism square with suppressing freedom of speech and the right to assemble in protest? As if we didn't already know, the mayor made it clear whom he stands with in his irrepressible quest for the highest office.

It's over Bloomberg. You might have thought the media blockade was a stroke of genius but it didn't work out. We're all reporters now and every act of brutality was recorded for posterity.

Before you pat yourself on the back, you didn't stop the movement. You only pushed it back. You can't kill an idea. The movement will transform, grow and prosper. It is written in the wind. You might as well try to shoot down the sun.

As for the men and women in blue, the next time you are called to action to enforce crowd control on nonviolent protesters, the next time you are ordered to clear encampments in parks and public spaces, remember who cut your health benefits after September 11, remember who cut your wages and broke your unions, remember why your children will not be going to the university, remember how your neighbors lost their jobs, their homes, their pensions and take a step back.

JACK RANDOM

It's us against them and, like it or not, you are with us.

Jazz 8 December 2011.

PERPETUAL PARALYSIS
Democracy be Damned!

For anyone who thought that the Democrats won the last election and, therefore, the government would move in a progressive direction, think again. The Democrats strengthened their hold of the Senate, gained seats in the House and retained the White House but they did nothing to bolster their power in Washington.

The Democrats may have won a clear majority of votes in the 2012 election but the Republicans held on to a double veto of all legislative action. First, having won the critical census-year election of 2010, they devised a system by which a decisive minority could secure a decisive majority in the House of Representatives. Second, when Senate majority leader Harry Reid settled on a handshake deal rather than meaningful filibuster reform, he effectively yielded the majority power of the upper chamber of congress.

The result is exactly what the Grand Old Party desired: a government in perpetual paralysis. The filibuster is subject to review with the next congress but Republican control of the House, barring a dramatic change in the heart of the electorate, will remain intact until the next census in 2020.

Thus, while a newly re-elected President Obama summoned the ghosts of progressives past in his inaugural address, his agenda is dead on arrival. He can use the power of the presidential pulpit, he can appeal to the voters, he can rally his supporters to the cause, but anything that happens in Washington must have the

Republican seal of approval.

The fact is Republican members of the House have nothing to fear from this or any other president. Their seats are safe. Because you cannot gerrymander a state, they may not be able to take the Senate without some appeal to the minorities, but they can hold on to the House in perpetuity and that is sufficient.

The power of government has been nullified for the foreseeable future.

Immigration reform will be sifted down to the Dream Act and working permits for highly skilled workers. There may be concessions to the families of dreamers but any path to citizenship or real acceptance of the millions of immigrants working, raising families and contributing to our society, will be blocked by unrealistic qualifications. Amnesty remains an unspeakable word. On the whole, things will stay as they are and any suggestion of comprehensive reform will be a mirage.

We have already witnessed a similar process of nullification on gun control. Despite the strong support of the people, what began as a demand for comprehensive reform, an assault weapons ban, limitations on ammunition clips, registration of bullets and universal background checks for the purchase of deadly weapons, has now boiled down to closing the gun show loophole and even that is in question.

There will be no major legislative accomplishments in the second term of Barack Obama. Fair Trade and the rights of organized labor will not be on the table. Unless there is another crash and even then, effective regulation of Wall Street will not be considered. We will have no repeal of the USA Patriot Act. We will not close Guantanamo Bay. The only civil liberty we will move to protect is the second amendment right to bear arms.

The only advances in civil rights for women, gay, lesbian and transgender individuals will be accomplished by the states or in the courts and those advances will be answered by repressive measures in other states and by other courts.

There will be no concerted effort to fight back global climate change or to rebuild our aging infrastructure. We are stuck on the path of economic austerity (otherwise known as debt reduction) despite its failure to produce positive results anywhere in the world.

It is a Republican agenda, one designed to protect the elite and the status quo, and yet the Democrats won the election.

What kind of democracy are we?

Brace yourself. It could get worse. The party that won two presidential elections through massive disenfranchisement of minority voters (aided by the most partisan decision in Supreme Court history) has a plan to recapture the White House by jerry-rigging the antiquated Electoral College system. Republican controlled state governments are in the process of enacting laws that would award electors not in proportion to the popular vote but by congressional district. Since Democratic voters are generally concentrated in cities, such re-apportionment of electors would maximize the probability that a Republican could win the presidency with a minority of the popular vote.

If they were to succeed we would face the distinct possibility that two of the three seats of power in the national government would belong to the party with minority support. That would leave the Senate and the Senate is designed for minority control. When the most populous states (California and New York) receive the same representation as Wyoming and Idaho, we could easily foresee a Republican party in complete control of all branches of government without the support of the majority of voters.

Where is the outcry?

We lost a critical opportunity to repeal the Electoral College after the debacle of 2000 clearly demonstrated that the system failed even at its primary function: to ensure a peaceful and equitable transference of power.

A media owned and therefore controlled by the international corporations that now threaten to strangle our democratic process convinced us that the system was in fact working. Talking heads from all quarters pretended that disenfranchisement on a scale unseen since the days of Jim Crow was nothing more than the shenanigans of the political class. Karl Rove was anointed a political genius.

It was not a wholesale attack on the heart of our democratic system of government. It was rather a system working out its own problems and arriving at a fair and responsible conclusion. Both parties participated in the charade. Both parties turned their backs on the overriding principle of a free and fair election. Both parties betrayed the electorate and allowed the Supreme Court to decide the election for us.

We should have abolished the Electoral College then. We failed. Or rather our two-party system failed us. We should have prosecuted the perpetrators of the disenfranchisement campaign in Florida, including Governor Jeb Bush. We failed. Or rather government failed to represent our interests.

As a consequence of our failure to correct the systemic errors that made the presidency of George W. Bush possible, the parties felt free to continue their practices of rigging the system, democracy be damned, as if it was a part of the plan.

We are saddled now with a two-party monopoly where one party is unabashedly dedicated to the proposition that the wealthiest among the wealthy should rule the world and another party dedicated to the proposition that the masses must be pacified to make the world safe for the elite.

Is there a difference? Yes. But it is becoming increasingly clear that the difference between parties may not make a difference.

There are a great many people in this country who are stockpiling weapons in the belief that they are the last line of defense for our democratic government. It is ironic that they are almost uniformly Republican.

How will they feel if and when their own party takes complete control of government without the benefit of winning at the ballot box? Is it only despotism if the despot is on the other team?

Abraham Lincoln led the nation into civil war so that a government for the people, by the people and of the people would not perish from the earth. I wonder what Lincoln would think today when the party he once served is conspiring to do what the Confederacy could not do by force of arms.

Am I being too dramatic? Is it acceptable that a political party could take over the government without anything resembling the support of the majority? Is that the way a republic is supposed to work?

Are we just supposed to sit back and accept that this is how our founders intended the system to work? Are we supposed to let the system work itself out?

I don't believe that. I believe in democracy. I believe in democracy even when I am in the minority. I believe in the cardinal principle: One person, one vote, majority rules.

If you lose the principle of majority rules, you've lost your democracy. If you lose that principle without a fight, you're telling the world you really don't care – except when it becomes a cause of war.

We are Americans. Democracy is our birthright and our greatest gift to modern civilization. We are entitled to leaders, regardless of party or philosophy, who believe in the democratic form of government.

That is the American way.

Jazz 7 April 2014.

A special thanks to my wife, Julie, for her patience, understanding, encouragement and assistance in editing these writings. All my love.

ABOUT THE AUTHOR

Jack Random is Ray Miller. He has lived both an ordinary and extraordinary life. His roots firmly planted in the fertile central valley of California, he has marched the streets in protest, haunted jazz town bars, read poetry in cafes and town squares, strutted his hour upon the stage, crisscrossed the country by air, rail, highway and thumb, mourned at Wounded Knee, gazed into the eyes of the crow at Grand Canyon, and paid tribute at the grave of Geronimo. He has labored in the fields of plenty, toiled on the assembly line, pursued higher education, and attempted to enlighten children in the public schools. He has been a pilgrim and a seeker of truth. He is married to the love of his life. All the while he has chronicled his thoughts and revelations in words: plays, poetry, novels, stories and essays.

He is the author of *Wasichu: The Killing Spirit, Number Nine: The Adventures of Jake Jones and Ruby Daulton* (Crow Dog Press), *Ghost Dance Insurrection* (Dry Bones Press) and the *Jazzman Chronicles* (Crow Dog Press).

www.ingramcontent.com/pod-product-compliance
Lightning Source LLC
Chambersburg PA
CBHW050641270326
41927CB00012B/2826